Silvester O'Flyn

D1461420

The Good News of
Mark's Year

CATHEDRAL BOOKS
Distributed to the trade by
THE COLUMBA PRESS

CATHEDRAL BOOKS
4 Sackville Place, Dublin 1.

Distributed to the trade by
THE COLUMBA PRESS
93 The Rise, Mount Merrion, Blackrock, Co Dublin, Ireland

First edition 1990
Cover designed by Niamh O'Gorman
Origination by The Columba Press
Printed in Ireland by
Mount Salus Press, Dublin.

ISBN 1 85607 001 8

Nihil Obstat:
Patrick Muldoon DD
Censor Deputatus

Imprimatur:
✠ Séamus Hegarty
Bishop of Raphoe

Scripture texts are from the Jerusalem Bible which is copyright Darton, Longman & Todd Ltd and Doubleday & Co Inc, and is used by permission.

Contents

Introduction

Mark was the pioneer evangelist, the first to capture in written story the encounter of God and mankind which took place in the person and ministry of Jesus Christ. He initiated a new form of sacred literature which he called the Good News, or Gospel, of Jesus Christ, the Son of God. The Sunday Gospels for Cycle B of the Roman Lectionary are, for the most part, taken from Mark.

Our cover-piece for Mark's year is a picture of hands taking up the cross. Mark portrays Jesus as shunning publicity and adulation, for he is the Messiah who has come to serve. And the true path of discipleship is in following Jesus by humble submission to the Father and in loving service for our brothers and sisters. Taking up the cross is an expression of dying to selfishness so as to live in Christian service.

During the Year of Mark, the Lectionary sometimes borrows from John, where his gospel offers a more profound reflection on a theme. For instance, we have five Sunday gospels from John 6 which expand on Jesus as the shepherd who leads his flock in the word of life and feeds them on the bread of life.

As in the companion volumes on Cycles A and C, I offer two reflections for each Sunday. The first is usually a commentary on the text. The second affords the opportunity to develop some point of Christian teaching or to explore some way of praying out of the gospel text.

The book on Luke's Year was dedicated to my parents, who were the first theologians to tell me the story of God.

The volume on Matthew's Year was offered in gratitude to my Capuchin brothers who have put up with me for over thirty years.

I dedicate this book to the members of Cursillo in the dioceses of Raphoe and Derry. I have been constantly renewed by their prayerfulness and enthusiasm. Their kind words and friendship have strengthened me more than they can ever know. May they, in turn, grow in faith, hope and love through these weekly reflections on the Good News of Jesus Christ, the Son of God.

Silvester O'Flynn

First Sunday of Advent

Advent will take us back in time to the people before Christ who were awaiting the Saviour. But the season also looks forward to the Second Coming of Christ at the end of our time. The first week of Advent stresses our vigilance in preparation for the Second Coming.

Mark 13:33-37
Jesus said to his disciples: 'Be on your guard, stay awake, because you never know when the time will come. It is like a man travelling abroad: he has gone from home, and left his servants in charge, each with his own task; and he has told the doorkeeper to stay awake. So stay awake, because you do not know when the master of the house is coming, evening, midnight, cockcrow, dawn; if he comes unexpectedly, he must not find you asleep. And what I say to you I say to all: Stay awake!'

Good News
Christ is coming back to meet us and lead us to the fulness of his glory. Our lives have a destiny and purpose: and we have every reason to be on our guard and spiritually awake.

First Reflection
Watch and Pray
Once upon a time, God, the infinite, eternal and all powerful One, came down to meet us on the dusty roads of human life. In the flesh of Jesus Christ, God walked with us through our light and darkness, our joys and sorrows, our solitude and relationships. Scripture writers called it the 'fulness of time'. Things would never be the same again.

In Jesus Christ, God spoke to us in the human language that we can understand. His life warmly portrays God's love and concern for us. And yet the story is not complete. The journey stretches on until we fully share in Christ's glorification. That will be at the completion of life's journey. For the moment we are a people on the way.

Advent opens the Church's year by picking up the theme of our journey towards Christ who is coming back to meet us. We are not like wandering nomads who have no sure purpose or definite direction. We have the pilgrim's destiny with God. We travel forward on a road of unknown length until Christ will come again.

The focus of the first Sunday of Advent is on the Second Coming of Christ. The parable of the doorkeeper speaks of the master who will come back to the servants. The message for the servants is twofold: 'Be on your guard and stay awake'... watch and pray.

One task of the doorkeeper's employment is to keep out unwanted visitors and intruders. Here the parable is a moral warning not to open up our doors to the ways of sin. Each passing day we are to watch with the vigilant eye of the sentry to prevent any intrusions of the enemy.

The unexamined life is a city with no sentries on its walls. Anybody who is serious about living a spiritual life is advised to undertake a daily reflection on our situation. This means more than counting up the number of our faults. It involves an honesty about what motivates us in the things we do.

We are sometimes surprised when we recognise that some exemplary deeds are done out of very subtle, selfish motivation. We may be doing the right things only to be praised or at least recognised as virtuous, to impress others, or as part of a self-seeking bargain with God. In daily reflection we guard against the intrusions of self-ishness in our motivation.

The second task to the doorkeeper is to open up promptly to all who have the right to enter. Applied to the spiritual life, this means a spirit of prayerfulness or sensitivity to God. The sensitive soul is awake with all the longing of the lover for the approaching footsteps of the beloved. But what is he like, this God-who-comes? In today's first reading Isaiah uses three very appealing names for God ... our Father, our Redeemer and the potter.

God is the Father who has created us with the potential to share in the divine life. God is the Redeemer who continues to pay the price of liberating us from slavery to incomplete forms of life. He offers us life to the full. And God is the potter who is ever crafting our lives anew. The present clay may be messy and, in our view, without meaningful form or beauty. But the divine craftsman can mould and fashion an amazing masterpiece in the twinkling of an eye.

The God who is coming back the road to meet us wants to lift us up as his children, wants to liberate us and fashion us anew.

Do not think of the Second Coming as so distant and unknown as to be irrelevant to the hurly-burly of today's living. If we are spiritually vigilant and alert then the future will draw us forward towards God. Our hope will energise us by supporting us when we are weak and encouraging us to persevere.

Our lives are on a journey towards God who is reaching back to us this day and every day. So, be on your guard lest the ways of sin enslave your thoughts. And watch in prayer, vigilant and alert to the daily visitations of the Spirit to your soul.

The Master of our souls is coming,

Watch and pray.

Second Reflection
Winter of the Spirit

Each liturgical season carries its own message and grace into our various experiences of life.

In our northern hemisphere Advent is the mid-winter liturgy which cries out for the coming of God into the dark, cold and fruit-less days of the soul's experience ... the winter of the spirit. The grace of Advent dares to hope even where it seems that there are no grounds for hope.

The Christian season of Advent-Christmas developed out of the old pagan festival of mid-winter's day, when the return of the unconquered sun was celebrated ... *natalis solis invicti*. The return of light, heat and growth, which is written into the cycle of nature's cal-endar, was a happy choice for the celebration of the coming of the Saviour.

Advent is the season which relates our winter of the spirit to the concept of God who came, will come again and is ever presently coming towards us.

The opening gospel of Advent is the parable of the doorkeeper. It is the story of watching through the dark hours of night. It sug-gests absence and presence, certainty and doubt. The master is absent but his authority is still present for the servants who continue to go faithfully about their tasks. They live in the certainty that the master will return, but as to when it will be, they do not know.

In this scientifically advanced age we can virtually deny the harsh reality of winter. At the touch of a switch we can escape from the dark and eliminate the cold. We have lost touch with the experience of earlier times when darkness restricted the hours of labour, giving servants a welcome time of rest and drawing the family together for longer hours. This ability to deny the harsh side of winter leaves us ill-disposed to accept the winter of the spirit which comes to us in darkness of faith, coldness of religious emotion and utter inability to find the energy for good works.

Advent asks us to accept that winter is part of the Creator's providence. God made winter, therefore it is good. It is not all ugliness and severity. There is a beauty and a wisdom to be found there.

I think of the stunning colours of sunrise on a frosty morning. The crackle and leaping of a log fire which draws the family together. The clear night-sky when the stars invite us to leave our petty squabbles and to think on the scale of infinite distance. The soft falling of the snow-blanket which covers the earth like the mystery of silent life.

I admire the providential wisdom of the frost which cares for the earth by breaking down the substance of compost in order to enrich next year's growth. The benefits of early darkness which enables the compulsive outdoor type (like me) to undertake the necessary deskwork.

Winter is beautiful and good and beneficial ... if only we have the eyes to see. The lessons of winter's providence prepare us to sustain the fires of faith when we are experiencing our winter of the spirit. The constant plea of Advent prayer is for the coming of God. It is not that God is ever absent. But to our experience he seems so distant that we can call it absence. Just as when the sun is so distant that we do not experience enough heat to warm up our blood. Yet if the sun were really absent for a moment, all about us would immediately disintegrate. The spiritual wealth of Advent reveals to us the nearness of God even when our experience is more suggestive of his distance.

In the darkness of the time when someone rebels against God and absolutely refuses to pray, is God absent?

The grace of Advent enables the wintering soul to meet the God who is ever coming towards us: and to see that God is always present.

Advent brings the grace to hope even when all the signs are against hope. The symbolic image of hope is an anchor, which expresses the immovable hold of faith against every wave and current.

Advent is full of the desire for God. And the divine beauty and goodness can shine out even in the ugliest of surroundings.

Advent strengthens us to wait on God in patience. His wisdom, providence and care have not deserted us: they will be revealed in God's own time ... which is surely the best time of all.

Stay awake, spiritually alert in the darkness of night
and the coldness of winter ... for the Lord is near.
Maranatha, come, Lord Jesus, come,
let your face smile on your servant,
and let your sunlight hurry back into our lives.

Second Sunday of Advent

The second Sunday of Advent introduces us to John the Baptist, whose task is to prepare a way for the Lord. Today's liturgy invites us to begin our spiritual preparation for Christmas.

Mark 1:1-8
The beginning of the Good News about Jesus Christ, the Son of God.

It is written in the book of the prophet Isaiah: 'Look, I am going to send my messenger before you; he will prepare your way. A voice cries in the wilderness: Prepare a way for the Lord, make his paths straight,' and so it was that John the Baptist appeared in the wilderness, proclaiming a baptism of repentance for the forgiveness of sins. All Judaea and all the people of Jerusalem made their way to him, and as they were baptised by him in the river Jordan they confessed their sins. John wore a garment of camelskin, and he lived on locusts and wild honey.

In the course of his preaching he said, 'Someone is following me, someone who is more powerful than I am, and I am not fit to kneel down and undo the strap of his sandals. I have baptised you with water, but he will baptise you with the Holy Spirit.'

Good News
The Good News is about Jesus Christ, the Son of God, who came into our world and released the life-giving waters of the Holy Spirit to flow within us.

First Reflection
Introducing the Good News
Today we are beginning the holy gospel according to Mark. He will be our guide to the memory of Jesus Christ for most of the Sundays of the coming year. Hence we can call it the year of Mark.

Mark seems to have been the earliest of the four evangelists. He pioneered the work of setting to paper a comprehensive composition of the Christian community's story of how God met mankind in the life of Jesus Christ.

Mark begins with a glorious statement of his intention to tell 'the Good News about Jesus Christ, the Son of God.' Our older translations used the term Gospel for the Good News. Gospel is the shortened form of god-spel which in Old English meant good news.

This is an attempt to translate the Greek word which Mark used, *evangelion*. We have to imagine a world without TV, radio or newspapers. The town-crier or the herald of the king would proclaim the great events to the people. When the event to be announced was one calling for joy and celebration it was called an *evangelion*. It might be news of a victory in battle or perhaps a birth in the royal family

The Christian writers, Paul and Mark especially, took over this word *evangelion* and invested it with a divine depth of meaning. As the herald of the great king, Mark begins his story of Jesus Christ with the proclamation that this was an *evangelion*. His use of the word has remained until our own day whenever we refer to the Gospel or to the Good News.

After his initial proclamation Mark prefaces his story by relating how John the Baptist went before Jesus, as a messenger preparing the way and as a voice calling from the wilderness. Mark picks up the popular expectation that the prophet of olden times, Elijah, would come back to prepare the people for the Messiah. John appears in the primitive, non-conformist style of Elijah who had been described as 'a man wearing a hair cloak and a leather loincloth.' (2 Kgs 1:8)

Mark differs from the evangelists Matthew and Luke in that he does not have the Baptist preaching a coming judgment as the urgent motive for repentance. In Mark's gospel repentance wears a happy face.

Today's liturgy links this gospel with a great message of consolation in the first reading. 'Console my people ... Jerusalem's time of services is ended ... her sin is atoned for.' Isaiah continues: 'Sion, here is your God.' And that is the Good News which Mark sees the Baptist preparing for ... the coming of God.

The Good News of the Baptist is twofold: it concerns the acknowledgment by people of their sins; and it offers the hope that someone is coming, someone powerful, someone who will release the life-giving waters of God's Spirit upon the earth. Later on the preaching of Jesus will carry on this twofold message: repent and believe.

11

It may seem strange to suggest that the Good News is firstly about sin. But while everybody admits that there is a great deal wrong with our world, we have largely forgotten the name of the disease. When a doctor diagnoses what is wrong with a patient then the anxiety of all unknown possibilities is removed. The name of society's disease is sin. John the Baptist enabled people to accept this diagnosis and led them to the waters of renewal. Here the energy to repent comes, not so much from the fear of judgment, but from the approaching footfalls of the Messiah.

The work of John was not to be an end in itself. He came in the style of Elijah to prepare the way for the Messiah. And so, John's function was to hand over to the One with God's power and worthiness, the One invested with the Holy Spirit.

This Advent, repentance comes as a message of consolation and wears a happy face. It is Good News when we acknowledge truthfully our personal responsibility for sin and when we place our hope in the divine power of the Holy Spirit, which Jesus released for our forgiveness and healing.

The Good News began in the diagnosis of our pain ... sin; and in recognising the healing power that God sends us ... the Holy Spirit.

Second Reflection
A Cry from the Wilderness
In Ireland this Sunday is dedicated to temperance. Appropriately John the Baptist challenges our preparation for Christmas. We have reached the stage when one must state the obvious about keeping Christ in Christmas. These are weeks when people are bombarded with consumeristic pressure, the hectic round of parties, the frantic search for presents (as if my present can ever be an adequate substitute for my presence). Even Sundays are absorbed into the shopping spree.

You can read in the newspapers how well-known personalities will spend Christmas. How few, if any, will delve into the significance of the coming of a Saviour. For many it will be a nostalgic trip across the fields to childhood. Christmas is quickly reduced to sentimentality once we fail to keep Christ at the centre of it.

It is sad when Christmas reverts to being no more than the pagan festival which breaks up the darkness of winter: if we did not have Christmas we would have to invent some excuse for a break. I have great sympathy with true paganism which attempts to relate to the invisible spirit within all forms of life. The trouble with paganism is its inability to celebrate goodness and beauty. Pagan celebrations all too easily turn into orgies of undisciplined behaviour, ugliness and violence.

Modern paganism celebrates in orgies of eating and drinking: orgies of spending beyond all sensible family budgetting: orgies of TV addiction which, like a vampire, sucks the vitality out of people and makes them passive zombies. It is a wise decision to dedicate this Sunday to temperance.

John the Baptist strides into our liturgy and he callenges our preparation for Christmas. He is clad in the traditional garb of the prophet, hairy and unkept. There is a primitive wildness about him, never tamed to society's standards. A man from outside the system, from beyond the edges of civilisation, he is uncompromising and challenging. He has never been to a supermarket or department store for he depends upon primitive providence for his locusts, wild honey, berries and roots, and the untreated animal skins are adequate for his clothing. He will never be a guest on the popular TV chat show for his very presence would tear apart the hyprocrisy of the system. He dared to speak of sin.

But what a stunning affect it had on people! 'All Judea and all the people of Jerusalem made their way to him.' As they listened to him each one got in touch with his/her primitive self which had long been hidden under the expectations and etiquette of civilisation.

This voice that cried out from the wild called up their own untamed forces, showed up their inner contradictions (like Paul's 'I fail to carry out the things I want to do, and I find myself doing the very things I hate') and made sense of the shadows which accompany every light.

It is from the dark, untamed areas within us that the monsters of life come up ... like the temper which goes beyond control, the sexual hungers which express our incompleteness, brutal aggression, the crippling fear of failure, the dark terror of loneliness, the choking parasite of envy. In the preaching of the Baptist people found the courage to be honest: so they confessed their sins. And that was good news.

13

THE GOOD NEWS OF MARK'S YEAR

We must stand out today with John the Baptist at the edge of civilisation lest we be totally sucked into the currents of a modern, pagan Christmas.

Paganism knows not of the Saviour. It cannot cope with our primitive wildness. So it drags people down into orgies which grow out of these untamed energies.

The good news of Christianity begins with the Baptist's call to recognise these unredeemed areas within us and to admit our need of a Saviour. We will appreciate the cure only when we admit the disease.

Who, then, will be able to celebrate Christmas?

Only those who, in Advent, admit their primitive, untamed areas ... their sinfulness.

They will appreciate God's gift of a Saviour.

Third Sunday of Advent

The third Sunday of Advent expands on the theme of joy. Advent joy is born out of the belief that the Lord is very near. He stands among us. The gospel again features John the Baptist. Today we read from the gospel of John of the function of the Baptist to be a witness to the light, a voice preparing the way.

John 1:6-8,19-28
A man came, sent by God.
His name was John.
He came as a witness, as a witness to speak for the light,
so that everyone might believe through him.
He was not the light,
only a witness to speak for the light.

This is how John appeared as a witness. When the Jews sent priests and Levites from Jerusalem to ask him, 'Who are you?' he not only declared, but he declared quite openly, 'I am not the Christ.' 'Well then,' they asked, 'are you Elijah?' 'I am not,' he said. 'Are you the Prophet?' He answered, 'No.'

So they said to him, 'Who are you? We must take back an answer to those who sent us. What have you to say about yourself?' So John said, 'I am, as Isaiah prophesied: a voice that cries in the wilderness: Make a straight way for the Lord.'

Now these men had been sent by the Pharisees, and they put this further question to him, 'Why are you baptising if you are not the Christ, and not Elijah, and not the prophet?' John replied, 'I baptise with water; but there stands among you — unknown to you — the one who is coming after me; and I am not fit to undo his sandal-strap.' This happened at Bethany, on the far side of the Jordan, where John was baptising.

Good News
John the Baptist witnesses to a profound reason for joy: the light of God is among us.

First Reflection
Function of the Baptist

Since Mark is the shortest of the gospels, the lectionary for Mark's year borrows some supplementary passages from the gospel of John. Last Sunday we heard Mark's passage about the Baptist and today we are introduced to him through the evangelist John.

John tells us nothing of the primitive appearance or fearsome message of the Baptist. He leads us straightaway into the theological controversy about his identity, his role and his right to hold a public ceremony of initiation.

Whenever John writes of the Baptist it is noticeable how he clearly places him in a subordinate role to Christ. Some commentators hold that, among the people to whom this gospel was originally addressed, was a community of the followers of John the Baptist, who had not accepted Christ. Hence the constant emphasis in this gospel on the secondary role of the Baptist.

We must catch the significance of the thrice repeated answer of the Baptist, 'I am not'. This is in contrast to the seven great 'I am' statements which the evangelist accords to Jesus. The Baptist disclaims all important names: 'I am not the Christ ... nor Elijah ... nor the Prophet.'

The word which is used four times to describe the Baptist is witness. His role is to point a way from himself towards the Other, the One more worthy by far. He is not worthy even to be his slave, opening the strap of his sandal. In this gospel the greatness of the Baptist is manifested in the utterly unselfish way that he hands over to Jesus. He says that it is his joy to be the friend of the bridegroom and to hand over the bride to him. 'He must grow greater, I must grow smaller.' (Jn 3:30)

John the Baptist is the witness ... Jesus the reality, standing among them though as yet unknown. John is the voice ... Jesus is the Word. 'Take away the word and what is a voice?' asks St Augustine. 'When it conveys no meaning, it is just an empty sound. A wordless voice strikes the ear, but it does not make the heart grow.'

John is the lamp ... Jesus is the light. The lamp awaits the light.

Like John the Baptist, we are asked by God not to be anything beyond ourselves. I am not ... and need not pretend to be ... the Christ, nor the great Elijah, nor the Prophet. The Great One stands in our midst, lives in our souls, though still largely unknown and unrecognised.

Our task is to offer ourselves, like John, to be his witness, his voice and his lamp. We are to recognise in faith his presence within us. We can hear the message repeated elsewhere in today's liturgy. From Isaiah we catch the opening line: 'The spirit of the Lord has been given to me.' And Paul, in the second reading, says, 'Never try to suppress the Spirit or treat the gift of God with contempt.'

It is the Spirit of God who will give the word to the voice we can offer: and give God's light to our lamp.

John the Baptist challenges us to let go of false claims and every vestige of pride. His way is the road to humility which hands over totally to Christ. The way to greatness is the road which starts from knowing our nothingness. Then we can let God be God. Then we let Jesus be to us what his name means ... Saviour.

'He must grow greater and I must grow smaller.'

Second Reflection
Witnesses to Christ

The Jewish authorities, the bigwigs in Jerusalem, were concerned over John the Baptist. What was he saying? What was he doing? Who did he think he was? The big question at the back of their minds was about the Messiah, the Christ. Had the messianic age begun? And so, they came to John and asked him, 'Who are you?' 'A voice', replied John. 'A voice in the emptiness. A voice to prepare the way. A voice waiting for the word.'

Twelve centuries later the same question was put to Francis of Assisi. He had just begun his religious adventure, breaking away from the monied world of his father. He was travelling alone (something he never did once he had discovered the gift of brothers) through the woods, singing the praises of God in French, when robbers attacked him. They found a totally poor victim. 'Who are you?' they asked. The question of identity. In a moment of inspiration Francis replied, 'I am the herald of the Great King'.

John the Baptist and Francis were happy to identify themselves in terms of their relationship with Jesus Christ. All who have been baptised are identified as Christians, bearing the name of Christ, the Anointed One, the promised Messiah.

17

He stands among us ... he is within us ... but he remains unknown unless we see ourselves as his herald and give him a voice by our lives. All who receive the candle of light and are clad in the white garment at baptism are called to be his witnesses.

Let us transpose the Jerusalem concern to our own day. What do the Jews of today think of our claims about Jesus Christ and the gospel?

I think that any Jew would have the right to look at my life and that of my Christian community and ask whether the signs of the Messiah are among us.

He stands among us ... unknown ... unless we witness to him. As I prepare for the Sacrament of Reconciliation during Advent I put to myself that question asked of John the Baptist and of Francis, 'Who are you?'

Am I a voice that prepares the way for Christ in others?

Am I a witness to Christ in my family, my work, my social life? In my language, my political attitudes, my prejudices?

Am I ashamed of my Christian identity when challenged?

Am I proud to let it be known that I wish to live by the gospel values?

Do I have that sense of God which made Francis sing out the praises of God?

Then as I look at the quality of life in my Christian neighbourhood, can I show the inquisitors from Jerusalem that here we have all the signs of the presence of the Messiah:

a community which brings light to darkened lives;

joyful sounds of God to ears which were deaf to goodness;

hope to all who are imprisoned or enslaved in any addiction;

healing to sickness of soul and body;

life to the depressed and moribund;

and the good news of justice to the poor.

There, according to Jesus, are the signs of the presence and victory of the Messiah. Are they to be seen in my life and in my community?

He stands among us ...

unknown,

unless we witness to him.

Fourth Sunday of Advent

The liturgy of Advent today centres on Mary, the blessed virgin, chosen by God as the means of his coming to us. In today's first reading King David learns that it is not his task to build a temple for God but to let God establish a house for him. Mary was uniquely prepared by God to bring the flesh the temple of God's presence among us.

The Annunciation story has three important points:
the divinity of the child, which necessitates a virginal conception;
the name, identity and future glorification of the child;
the free involvement of Mary and her response in full obedience.

Luke 1:26-38

The angel Gabriel was sent by God to a town in Galilee called Nazareth, to a virgin betrothed to a man named Joseph, of the House of David; and the virgin's name was Mary. He went in and said to her:

'Rejoice, so highly favoured! The Lord is with you.'

She was deeply disturbed by these words and asked herself what this greeting could mean, but the angel said to her, 'Mary, do not be afraid; you have won God's favour. Listen! You are to conceive and bear a son, and you must name him Jesus. He will be great and will be called Son of the Most High. The Lord God will give him the throne of his ancestor David; he will rule over the House of Jacob for ever and his reign will have no end.'

Mary said to the angel, 'But how can this come about, since I am a virgin?' 'The Holy Spirit will come upon you,' the angel answered, 'and the power of the Most High will cover you with its shadow. And so the child will be holy and will be called Son of God. Know this too: your kinswoman Elizabeth has, in her old age, herself conceived a son, and she whom people called barren is now in her sixth month, for nothing is impossible to God.'

'I am the handmaid of the Lord,' said Mary, 'let what you have said be done to me.' And the angel left her.

Good News

God, who had blessed Mary in a full and unique manner, now enlists her cooperation in sending us a divine Saviour, Jesus.

First Reflection

Blessed Virgin Mary

'But how can this come about,' asked Mary, 'since I am a virgin?' The virginal conception in Mary is an important belief, not only for reasons of biological statement, but because it is a necessary consequence to the divinity of the child. Here God's power is at work in an utterly unique way. 'The Holy Spirit will come upon you and the power of the Most High will cover you with its shadow.' The bright cloud had been an expression of God's presence ever since the days of the Exodus.

David, in today's first reading, was dissuaded from building a temple for God. For the house of God's presence must be of God's making. 'The Lord will make you a House.' The Annunciation is firstly the news of God's work.

Mary is not simply a virgin at the time of conception: she is the Blessed Virgin. She is the uniquely blessed person, prepared by God from the first moment of her conception, to bring about the messianic encounter of God with mankind.

The angel addresses her as 'full of grace', meaning uniquely blessed or favoured with God's giving to an exceptional degree. By addressing her in this manner the angel is giving her a new name, 'Full of grace'. A new name, in biblical practice, means a new role to play.

Many people today are confused about the virginity of Mary. Some choose not to believe it but their reasoning is clouded by blind emotion or bad theology or a combination of both. A great student of Mary, René Laurentin, writes: 'Those who wanted to eliminate the virginity of Mary have generally, at the same time, and to the same degree, lost sight of the divinity of Jesus.'

In many instances their argument is a justification of their own preconceived ideas. Virginity is not prized highly in today's sex-mad society. Pop psychology has persuaded people that sexual relationships are the supreme attainment of life: and that sexual energy, whether freely expressed, deliberately suppressed or unconsciously repressed, is our most powerful driving force. Totally disregarding what the gospels say of Mary, they have blindly concluded that her virginal conception was a myth dreamt up by the sublimated energy of crusty celibates.

Luke and Matthew went out of their way to write unequivocally of the virginity of Mary and the non-involvement of Joseph in her pregnancy. Both writers, and remember that Luke was a doctor, must have known that it would raise medical questions. But the gospels are more concerned with proclaiming the gracious mystery of God's encounter with our world than with answering the scientific questions of what exactly happened. The same situation would later arise in writing of the resurrection: again no attempt is made to explain how it happened.

The virginal conception is a story of divine power because the child is someone who already exists. Joseph could not have fathered a person who already exists. St Augustine marvellously summarised the theological arguments thus: 'If a God had to be born, he could only be born of a virgin and if a virgin had to give birth, she could only give birth to a God.'

The doctrine of Mary's virginity is not something relevant only to the past. It is full of significance and inspiration for believers today. Her virginity may be thought of as a sort of emptiness and poverty: 'an emptiness that is waiting and a poverty that is an unimpeded openness to God.' (Maria Boulding). God's choice of Mary, his lowly handmaid, expresses the constant gospel theme of the special love of God for the poor.

The divine power which overshadowed Mary indicated the new sharing in divine life which entered the world in Jesus. He would later speak of our new birth as God's children. 'To all who did accept him he gave power to become children of God, to all who believe in him, who was born not out of human stock or urge of the flesh or will of man but of God himself.' (Jn 1:12-13) At the annunciation this new life began to break into the world. It would be released for all believers in the power of the Spirit after the resurrection of Jesus. Pentecost was anticipated at the action of the Holy Spirit in Mary's life.

Another strand of thought to be drawn out of Mary's virginity is the superiority of *agape* (utterly unselfish, disinterested love) over *eros* (the love which brings sexual completion and satisfaction). Mary's virginity is a model for all who voluntarily forgo sexual satisfaction out of love for God, or 'for the sake of the kingdom of heaven'. (Mt 19:12 ... and for Matthew there can be no higher motive than the kingdom).

Mary's virginal conception is a sign of God's power at work. It is a mysterious sign of her unique blessedness. She is not just the virgin Mary but the Blessed Virgin Mary.

P.S. Did Mary remain a virgin after the conception of Jesus? There is a very old tradition that Mary had made a perpetual commitment to virginity, with Joseph's understanding, even before the annunciation. It seems highly probable that Mary and Joseph would have been so overwhelmed by the divine action in her womb that they would not have entered marital relationships afterwards.

Second Reflection
Pondering with Mary

Luke is a writer of actions and reactions. He proclaims the actions of God and observes the reactions of the people who witness them. He is deeply sensitive to the inner responses of people.

If we want to reflect with Luke, the secret is to pay close attention to his verbs which express the divine actions and the human reactions.

Mary is the recipient of an angelic visitation. Hardly an everyday occurence! She hears herself called by a new name, 'Full of grace'. She is told that the Lord is with her. Her initial reaction? 'She was deeply disturbed by these words.' Disturbed. But not in the sense that one is torn apart by sorrow, disappointment, inadequacy, fretting or anxiety. Disturbed, as one is awestruck when a totally new vista of life has opened up. Disturbed, like a green field that is ploughed up all brown to receive a new planting.

How can human limitations cope with a divine revelation? How can our eyes endure a light of supernatural intensity? In one startling moment everything changes. Everything I have ever known or hoped for or thought about: the standards I measured with, the values I respected.

In God's light everything is seen with new eyes. The familiar pattern of thought and behaviour is deeply disturbed. The old world is suddenly ended. And the new ... where will it lead?

'Mary asked herself what this greeting could mean.'

The verb Luke uses here will come up again to show her pondering on the shepherds' astonishing words ... pondering, weighing up, measuring life by this new light of God. And that is precisely what contemplation means, measuring life in the light of heavenly revelation. Mary, who received the greatest divine light, is surely the greatest contemplative.

'Mary, do not be afraid; you have won God's favour.'

The angel reassures Mary. There is no room here for human fear. Human fear concentrates on our own ability, with its limitations, weakness and inadequacy. And it paralyses energy. But this matter is of God's doing, by God's favour. And Mary accepts what God is doing. She is not paralysed. She is enlivened and ready to proceed. Sufficiently composed to address the angel.

'But how can this come about, since I am a virgin?'

She is even aware of her sexual identity. There is strength in her statement, 'I am a virgin'. Here is no weakminded adolescent. She is sure of herself and strong. Calmly she listens to the angel's explanation of the divine plan. She hears of the bright cloud of divine Spirit overshadowing the temple of her virginal body. She is to provide the sacred housing for a child of holiness and divinity.

Then she hears the words which solve all problems ... 'for nothing is impossible to God.' Now she is ready to respond.

St Bernard has left us a sermon in which he builds up the dramatic scenario of a world waiting on Mary's reply. Adam is waiting ... Abraham ... all of our race. What if by her delay, he should pass by?

In the new light of God her old world was disturbed so that her new identity might emerge: 'I am the handmaid of the Lord.' And her free cooperation with God is unconditional: 'Let what you have said be done to me.'

Mary, our mother, help us to follow your way in responding to God. Help us to be sensitive to God's initiative just as you were. Help us to accept the disturbance of life that follows on meeting with God. Help us to measure everything in the light of God's mind. Help us to offer our very emptiness as an invitation to God to work in us. Help us to receive the word of God and give it flesh in our every thought, word and action.

Christmas Day

Luke's Christmas story is the proclamation of the birth of the Saviour of the world, Jesus Christ the one, true Lord. The divine event is fleshed out through the involvement of particular people, at a specified time in world history and in a certain place. These details are beautifully woven into story, though not as a diary of the events of one night, but as a biblically rich setting for the mystery of the divine coming.

Luke 2:15-20

Now when the angels had gone from them into heaven, the shepherds said to one another, 'Let us go to Bethlehem and see this thing that has happened which the Lord has made known to us.' So they hurried away and found Mary and Joseph, and the baby lying in the manger.

When they saw the child they repeated what they had been told about him, and everyone who heard it was astonished at what the shepherds had to say.

As for Mary, she treasured all these things and pondered them in her heart.

And the shepherds went back glorifying and praising God for all they had heard and seen; it was exactly as they had been told.

Good News

The soul that has prepared during Advent now rejoices to hear the heavenly news that God has sent us a Saviour, Jesus Christ the Lord.

First Reflection
A Saviour, Christ the Lord

'I bring you news of great joy, a joy to be shared by the whole people. A Saviour has been born to you; he is Christ, the Lord.'

Three significant names were announced by the angel: three names which constituted news of great joy, a joy to be shared by the whole world ... Saviour, Christ and Lord.

The first name is Saviour. It means the same as the name Jesus given by the angel at the annunciation. Jesus means the one who would save his people from their sins. It is a name which is empty unless there are sinful people who need to be saved, drowning people who need to be rescued. As a doctor's presence is best appreciated where there is someone sick or injured, so the Saviour's coming is good news for those who know they are sinners.

Advent prepared us for Christmas by drawing us beyond the edges of civilised society to face our primitive wildness and to experience the winter of the spirit. It challenged us to be unsophisticated and honest: to strip bare the pretences of life: to pull back the facades of sham: to know ourselves: honestly. And in this honesty to know our need of a divine Saviour.

The name Saviour expresses the coming down of God to fallen sinners. Luke's story extends the lesson. For it was to shepherds that the heavenly message was given. Forget all your religiously romantic ideas about shepherds. Shepherds were too dishonest and too smelly to be allowed into synagogue or temple services. They were among the outcasts. But this Saviour would make a point of being with sinners. And he would scandalise the church-goers by eating and drinking (oh my!) with the outcasts.

The Saviour came down to the poor and the homeless. Mary and Joseph were glad to use a borrowed shelter. And not even that part of the house reserved for the humans (for there was no room for them there), but the animals' shelter. The Saviour's maternity unit was smelly, dirty and unhygienic: just like the world he was entering: just like the souls he was coming for.

The second name told to the shepherds was Christ. He was known as Jesus in his family, to his schoolmates, neighbours and relations. The name Christ expressed his function. The Christ means the chrismed one, the anointed one. In the Old Testament people were anointed for three great services, as prophets, priests and kings.

The prophet was called to be a teacher of God's will. The priest was a mediator who offered sacrifice to God for the people; as mediator he brought the people to God and God to the people. The king was anointed to serve the people with good government and leadership.

Now for the first time, all three anointings were to be found fulfilled in the one person, the anointed one, the Christ. As prophet he would be the bringer of God's light to a darkened world.

As priest he would shepherd the straying souls back to God and lay down his life for them.

As king he would set up the reign of God in souls.

The third name announced by the angel was Lord. Luke took a special delight in that name for he was writing for the Roman world where they were claiming that the Emperor was divine. Luke's message to them is that there is only one Lord, Jesus Christ.

Three names rich in significance.

Saviour ... coming down to us ... into sinfulness and poverty. Christ ... ministering to us as the prophet of light, as the shepherd of souls and as the bringer of God's kingdom. Lord ... raised up, returning to divine glory, and raising up our human nature which he had assumed. He humbled himself to assume our human nature so that, through him, we might share in the divine nature.

Christmas is far more than a sentimental playing out of past history. It is the living celebration of God's gift of Saviour, Christ and Lord. Luke tells us that those who first heard this news were astonished. Mary treasured all these things and pondered them in her heart. The shepherds went back glorifying and praising God.

Let us make time for astonishment ... and for treasuring the memory. And let us return to God in glory and praise.

Second Reflection
A Child shall lead them

The shepherds heard wonderful news that night. News that the world was waiting for. News of a saviour, of the anointed one, of the Lord coming to us.

I imagine these shepherds must have been pinching themselves to see if they were dreaming all this. Was it some collective hallucination? Perhaps that bottle of wine they'd had before settling down for the night. The angel offered them assurance. They were given a sign. Surely we would expect a sign from God to be something stupendous. A revolving sun, or dancing moon or breath-taking miracles. But God's ways are often the reverse of our planning.

The sign was a child. Swaddled in binding cloths, like any child of the time, so that his bones might grow straight and strong. Lying in a manger, not even a proper cot, but in a feeding trough borrowed from the animals.

A sign is something that must point beyond itself. This little sign-baby is someone totally helpless, dependent and innocent. Man's original mistake had been to reach beyond himself for power and moral independence. 'Ye shall be like gods,' whispered the tempter, 'having the knowledge of good and evil.'

We have continued to fall for this same temptation to make up our own convenient code of morality ... to justify violence and selfishness, our neglect of the needy, our pampering of the senses.

But see how God reverses the order. Man reached for the sky and fell. But God came down to earth to raise us up. Came down as a helpless, dependent baby, swaddled by his mother for the strengthening of his frail bones.

The child is a sign from God. We go back to Isaiah's dream of an innocent world at peace.

The wolf shall lie down with the lamb
and the leopard lie down with the kid
and the calf and the young lion and the fatling together
and a little child shall lead them. (Is 11:6)

The Church of the Nativity at Bethlehem has one very remarkable feature, its tiny door. Apparently at one time bandits would ride into the church on horseback, grab the precious vessels and lights and ride off again. The problem was solved by blocking up the great door and letting only a tiny entrance, big enough for a child. An adult has to bend down to enter. Only the child can feely enter at Bethlehem.

The sign of the child points to the necessity for all to be like little children. That is the only way to enter into the kingdom of heaven. Those who try to make gods of themselves or of their appetites cannot enter the kingdom. They must come off their high horses and bend low.

Christmas is the time to rediscover our lost innocence and to admit our dependence upon God.

As a priest I am overwhelmed each year by the workings of God's grace which draws the sinner back to confession for Christmas. Many who were untouched by the penitential services of Advent will be moved by the child of Christmas to rediscover their own lost innocence. As Christmas Eve progresses sometimes it takes the liquid spirit of Christmas to soften the heart and loosen the tongue. *In vino veritas.* All part of the workings of grace. The child in our memory leads us back to God.

This sign-child lay in a manger. No proper bed. No fancy cot made with loving hands by the carpenter husband. Borrowed from the animals ... as his grave too would be borrowed. Though Lord of the universe he had nowhere of his own to lay his head at birth, in life or at death.

The manger itself was part of the sign. For this child would be the one to feed the world with divine energy in the Eucharist. And he was born at Bethlehem which means the house of bread.

Saint Francis, on a memorable night at Grecchio, drew the people together to look into the crib, to see the child and to see the manger. The crib has been popular ever since.

But at Christmas it is even more important to look into our own hearts to see the child of God in our own living.

We have to be small and humble to enter at Bethlehem.

We have to be like children to let the child lead us

... to innocence and peace.

Feast of the Holy Family

The focus of Christmas Day was on the child. Today we consider the family environment which supported the child in his growth towards maturity and wisdom. Luke leads us from the crib at Bethlehem to the temple in Jerusalem, the home of the wide Jewish family. Eventually they came to Nazarth, a town never mentioned in the Old Testament, the hidden environment for the growing years of Jesus.

Luke 2:22-40 (Longer Version)

When the day came for them to be purified as laid down by the Law of Moses, his parents took Jesus up to Jerusalem to present him to the Lord — observing what stands written in the Law of the Lord: Every first-born male must be consecrated to the Lord — and also to offer in sacrifice, in accordance with what is said in the Law of the Lord, a pair of turtledoves or two young pigeons.

Now in Jerusalem there was a man named Simeon. He was an upright and devout man; he looked forward to Israel's comforting and the Holy Spirit rested on him. It had been revealed to him by the Holy Spirit that he would not see death until he had set eyes on the Christ of the Lord. Prompted by the Spirit he came to the Temple; and when the parents brought in the child Jesus to do for him what the Law required, he took him into his arms and blessed God; and he said:

'Now, master, you can let your servant go in peace, just as you promised; because my eyes have seen the salvation which you have prepared for all the nations to see, a light to enlighten the pagans and the glory of your people Israel.'

As the child's father and mother stood there wondering at the things that were being said about him, Simeon blessed them and said to Mary his mother, 'You see this child: he is destined for the fall and for the rising of many in Israel, destined to be a sign that is rejected — and a sword will pierce your own soul too — so that the secret thoughts of many may be laid bare.'

There was a prophetess also, Anna the daughter of Phanuel, of the tribe of Asher. She was well on in years. Her days of girlhood over, she had been married for seven years before becoming a widow.

She was now eighty-four years old and never left the Temple, serving God night and day with fasting and prayer. She came by just at that moment and began to praise God; and she spoke of the child to all who looked forward to the deliverance of Jerusalem.

When they had done everything the Law of the Lord required, they went back to Galilee, to their own town of Nazareth. Meanwhile the child grew to maturity, and he was filled with wisdom; and God's favour was with him.

Good News
The first Christian family is a model of religious observance, in prayerfulness and fidelity to God through light and darkness, joy and sorrow, breaking and growing.

First Reflection
The Christian Family
At the beginning and the end of this passage about the Holy Family, Luke mentions that Mary and Joseph were observing the Law of the Lord. Clearly, here was a family where God was number one and everything was evaluated in the light of faith. They belonged to the larger family of the Jewish religion and their faith was supported by religious customs and ritual.

After eight days every male child was circumcised in observance of the ancient covenant between God and Abraham, the father of believers. In the case of a firstborn male a sacrificial offering was rendered to God as the source of all life. Then after forty days they had the ritual purification of the mother which restored her to participation in religious services.

Through the observance of these religious traditions the faith of the people was supported and the sacredness of life was kept in the forefront. The place of God in the family was deeply respected.

In our present time when there is a great push towards the secularisation of society, the Law of the Lord is disregarded by many in the debates on family morality. Secularism is a pattern of thought and behaviour which seeks to set humanity on a pedestal apart from God. Echoes of the first temptation can be heard: 'Ye shall be like gods having the knowledge of good and evil' ... having the right to decide for themselves what is right and wrong.

Where traditional Christian morality is cast aside there is an alarming increase in the number of unmarried pregnancies, with all the consequent pains and pressures of the single-parent family.

Secularism lacks the vision of God's faithful love and cannot find the grace or courage to say 'forever'. It leads to cohabitation without the permanency of marriage or to civil marriages which are often little more than contracts until further notice. Secularism fails to appreciate the sacredness of sexual intercourse as an act which is open to cooperation with God in the wonder of creating a new human being who will have an eternal future.

The fact that there may be unhappy marriages and bad families does not alter the claim that a good family provides the most natural environment for the growth of a child towards full human maturity.

Luke's portrait of the Holy Family highlights their observance of the Law of the Lord. Jesus himself would later clarify the essence of this law: love of God and love of one's neighbour. Out of these two precepts flow the qualities of the Christian family.

The love of God will be clearly seen as the number one value in a Christian home. There will be time and place for prayer, for discussion on the deep mysteries of life and death, and for the sort of reading which will deepen one's understanding of the faith and inspire virtuous action. As we like to pin up pictures of our heroes, so in the Christian home one will notice the pictures or statues which express religious devotion. Those who share the same faith will be moved towards its expression in liturgy. There is something lacking in a family where prayer is always a private affair and they never have any togetherness in liturgical participation.

The love of God inspires our love for one another in God's family. Charity must begin at home. Home is where we are wanted: where the love is so deep that the storms on the surface never threaten the relationship: where we sometimes let off steam and show our worst features but remain totally confident that we will be forgiven.

The Christian family reaches out beyond its doors to the immediate neighbours. Christian neighbours show sensitivity to the old, the lonely, the sick. They rally round in times of crisis, they anticipate needs and they stay in compassion with the broken-hearted.

31

It was not all sunlight and easy going for the Holy Family. They were to know emigration, searching for work, misunderstanding, and rejection. It would all be part of that sword of sorrow piercing Mary's soul. But God was over all and that was enough for Mary's peace.

At Bethlehem the child was swaddled in binding cloths so that his bones might grow straight and strong. In the years at Nazareth he was surrounded by an atmosphere of faith and religious observance which helped him to mature in character and to grow in wisdom.

Luke notes that God's favour was with him. For the face of God always smiles warmly over the family which observes the Law of the Lord.

Second Reflection
Simeon and Anna

Christmas to a great extent centres on the children. On the feast of the Holy Family we are reminded of the presence of the old people. In Luke's story, Simeon and Anna are people advanced in years and wisdom. Luke always likes to pair off a story about a man with a corresponding one about a woman.

The old must not be forgotten at Christmas. Times of festivity can be excessively lonely for people who have lost their life-partner, whose peers have departed, whose children have gone their separate ways. Coming home is a most important part of Christmas, for the presence of the family means far more than the presents which are sent, no matter how expensive. Grandchildren cheer up the old home far better than tinsel and holly.

How terrible it is to meet the old who will not be visited by any of their relatives at Christmas. And there are the sad cases of elderly people abandoned in institutions, discarded like things of no further use, regarded as embarrassing or awkward because their faculties are diminished.

My son, support your father in his old age,
do not grieve him during his life.
Even if his life should fail, show him sympathy,
do not despise him in your health and strength;
for kindness to a father shall not be forgotten
but will serve as reparation for your sins.
(Eccl 3:12-14)

During Advent we set out to explore the gifts of winter: to see how a spirituality of winter has much to offer us in balancing our lives.

The old have reached life's season of winter. They have lived through spring's growing years, summer's time of high achievement and autumn's mellowing easing of pressure. Winter is when the circle of time is returning to the Beginning.

Simeon and Anna are models of the beauty and giftedness of advanced years. They have aged gracefully, for their lives are led by the Spirit and their happiness is to be in the temple of God's presence. They are close to the point of returning to their Beginning, and they are at peace.

The crisis faced in old age, according to the psychologist Erikson, is between going towards despair or towards integration. Despair is seen in the elderly who are neglected and lonely, or who cannot be happy with the present but pine tearfully for the past. They have no contentment and no sense of blessing. For them all has fallen apart ... personal achievements, family relationships, even faith. There is no hope now, only despair.

Integration is the opposite of being torn apart. Everything comes together as one. The opposites of life are harmonious and balanced. What enables one to hold the opposites together in balance is the gift of wisdom.

Simeon had wisdom: wisdom nourished by the Spirit in his long years of experience. He spoke of falling and rising, of the light of salvation and the darkness of rejection. His wisdom could hold the opposites together. This wise man brought to Mary a second annunciation: that the mission of her Son would be in a world of misunderstanding and sorrow: and that the road of her own pilgrimage of faith would take her through suffering.

The fruit of integration is complete peace of soul in oneness with God. One is finally ready to let go totally into God's arms when the circle of life is completed. Simeon's prayer is the perfect expression of the integrated soul: 'Now, Master, you can let your servant go in peace, just as you promised.'

If Simeon was gifted in his wisdom and prophecy, Anna was gifted in her sense of God's temple of presence and in her constant prayer of praise. Luke notes for us that she was daughter of Phanuel, a name which means the face of God. As children inherit the features of their parents, those who constantly live before the presence of God increasingly reflect the beauty of God. You will see the Anna of today in every church in those pensioners whose lives are now totally given over to God's presence and to constant praise of God. On their faces of light, the beauty of old age is a wonder to behold.

Simeon and Anna, the old members of the family, have aged gracefully. They are no longer torn apart by the untamed energies of youth. They no longer play out the pretences and social games of summer. They have let go of everything into God's hands. They are but one step away from heaven. And already they reflect the face of God.

Second Sunday After Christmas

Today we read the prologue to John's gospel. He takes us beyond the historical happening at Bethlehem into the theological meaning of Christmas. He reaches back to beyond-time. And the incarnation continues to have relevance today for all who accept Jesus.

John 1:1-5,9-14 (Shorter version)
In the beginning was the Word:
the Word was with God
and the Word was God.
He was with God in the beginning.
Through him all things came to be,
not one thing had its being but through him.
All that came to be had life in him
and that life was the light of men,
a light that shines in the dark,
a light that darkness could not overpower.
The Word was the true light
that enlightens all men;
and he was coming into the world.
He was in the world
that had its being through him,
and the world did not know him.
He came to his own domain
and his own people did not accept him.
But to all who did accept him
he gave power to become children of God,
to all who believe in the name of him
who was born not out of human stock
or urge of the flesh or will of man
but of God himself.
The Word was made flesh,
he lived among us,
and we saw his glory,
the glory that is his as the only Son of the Father,
full of grace and truth.

Good News

God is revealed to us in the language of a human life that we can understand. Jesus is the Word of God who came as a child in human flesh so as to raise us up to become children of God.

First Reflection
Down and Up

The evangelist John seemed to take it for granted that his readers were already familiar with the story of Jesus Christ as given by other writers. He wrote for a people who already believed in Jesus as the Saviour who liberated people from the slavery of sin. And they were familiar with the doctrine that Jesus set up the kingdom of God on earth, planting it as a seed growing to perfection.

John considered that it was time to stand back from the familiar story and ask some deeper questions: What did it mean for the history of the human race when God stepped into our world in the flesh of Jesus of Nazareth? Who was this Jesus?

Luke and Matthew had presented Jesus as the descendent and fulfilment of all past hopes and models. In him was the new exodus and the new covenant. He was the fulfilment of all that was suggested in Solomon the wise, David the king, Moses the law-giver and Abraham the father of believers. St Paul had written of Jesus as the Second Adam, bringing about a new level of creation. John stepped back further than these earlier writers. He presents Jesus as from beyond-time.

'In the beginning was the Word.'

The Word uttered by the Father: flowing from the mind of the Father: the perfect expression of the Father: the Word out of which everything that came to be emerged.

'Through him all things came to be,
Not one thing had its being but through him.'

John's gospel is the story of two great movements, down and up. The Word of the Father came down into our world so as to lift us up to a new level of life in his return to glory.

'The Word was made flesh.' A statement of stunning implications for the human race.

In the limited, frail, earth-rooted, death-bound flesh of the child of Mary, John claims, the unlimited, eternal Word of God dwelt. Dwelt among us. Our limited life of the flesh will never be the same again. For he came down to lift us up. From natural to supernatural life.

He entered the weakness of human existence, becoming subject to hunger, tiredness and pain; being restricted in movement, limited in pace and struggling to communicate.

He thus offered himself to his own people. He did not force himself on their freedom. He offered his example and the witness of his signs. Thus he invited people to come to him and to follow his way. But he was rejected and sent to the cross. However, those who accepted him found that his death was but the door to glory. For it was through death that he returned to the Father.

'We saw his glory,' writes John, 'the glory that is his as the only Son of the Father.' And his return to the Father was the condition for sending the Spirit so that all who believe in him might be raised with him to the glory of divine life.

'But to all who did accept him
he gave power to become children of God.'

Down and up. He came down into our humanity so as to raise us up to share in his divinity. He appeared in our flesh so as to clothe us in glory.

It is the centre of human history: the beginning of the new creation.

And it is right that we should celebrate it at the centre of each day by reciting the Angelus..

'The Word was made flesh ... and dwelt among us.'

Second Reflection
The Word was made Flesh
Words abound and surround us.

For many of us, the sense of hearing and seeing, which account for 95% of the mind's intake, are virtually given over to words. Little registers in our awareness unless it is packed in written or spoken words. Our minds are too steeped in words to notice anything else and we let others do the thinking for us.

Shakespeare's characters in 'As You Like It' discovered that an enforced sojourn in the forest revealed to them 'tongues in trees, books in the running brooks, sermons in stones and good in everything.' But too often our word-saturated minds fail to absorb anything which is not dressed out in words.

One page of your newspaper today will carry anything from 500 to 8,000 words. How many words will your eyes scan today?

How many words will your ears hear today? Even when we get away from people words will chase us over the radio waves. And nowadays there is the fiendish walkman determined to search out the last refuges of silence.

Words form the bridge of communication as one person reaches out to another. See the frustration of the two year-old child who is searching for the secret of these shaped sounds which form the code of our messages. And later these shaped sounds can be put on paper in mysterious lines and strokes.

We use words to transmit messages and to share information ... about the weather, health, sport, cooking, politics ... even about God. Limited words trying to express the unlimited God!

Sometimes words carry a weight beyond their dictionary value as we invest them with innuendo and allusion, or use them to trigger memory and imagination into a richer train of thought.

Words enlighten and obscure us, lead and mislead us, educate and drown us. They invite us to good and seduce us to evil. Words of affirmation build up our living: but deflating words can reduce us to nothingness.

Words by the thousand surround us in an endless onslaught on eyes and ears. So accustomed are we to words that we can feel threatened by their absence. Nature abhors a vacuum and so, to break the silence, the vacant mind will pour out endless words of little value. Shakespeare whose own treasury of words exceeded anybody's compared empty words to leaves ... 'where they most abound, much fruit or sense beneath is rarely found.'

The less clear our ideas, the more words we must use in pursuit of clarity. But it was sufficient for the perfect mind of God to utter one Word. Anything that ever was, is or will be originates in the timeless utterance of the Creator's mind. In the beginning ... now ... at any future time. Christ yesterday, today and the same for ever.

The Word was made flesh.

God has spoken to us in a language that we can understand, the language of a human life.

The Word of God that is given to us is the word of life: 'He was with God in the beginning. Through him all things came to be.'

And the Word is 'the true light that enlightens all men.' It offers wisdom and true knowledge. It is a word that calls out to us in the quiet depths of the soul: invites us to share in God's life: to begin to live the life of the Blessed Trinity already here on earth.

But this word of life and light is daily submerged under the torrent of trivial words ... empty words ... words of no direction ... words of no life. T.S. Eliot wrote that we have 'Knowledge of words and ignorance of the Word.' And he asked:

'Where is the Life we have lost in living?

Where is the wisdom we have lost in knowledge?

Where is the knowledge we have lost in information?'

We must protect the Word that God has spoken to us by distancing ourselves from the empty and dead words: in discovering silence. Like Mary, pondering on the things that were said.

Treasuring them.

The Epiphany of the Lord

The Epiphany means the manifestation of the divinity of Jesus. In the Orthodox Church it has always been a more important celebration than the birth of Jesus. The full celebration includes the coming of the magi to adore the infant king, the baptism of Jesus when the voice from heaven pronounced his divine sonship, and the miracle at Cana which was the first sign given by Jesus of his inner glory. Our celebration concentrates on the first event, the coming of the magi to adore the king.

Matthew 2:1-12

After Jesus had been born at Bethlehem in Judaea during the reign of King Herod, some wise men came to Jerusalem from the east. 'Where is the infant king of the Jews?' they asked. 'We saw his star as it rose and have come to do him homage.'

When King Herod heard this he was perturbed, and so was the whole of Jerusalem. He called together all the chief priests and the scribes of the people, and enquired of them where the Christ was to be born. 'At Bethlehem in Judaea,' they told him, 'for this is what the prophet wrote:

And you, Bethlehem, in the land of Judah,
you are by no means least among the leaders of Judah,
for out of you will come a leader
who will shepherd my people Israel.'

Then Herod summoned the wise men to see him privately. He asked them the exact date on which the star had appeared, and sent them on to Bethlehem. 'Go and find out all about the child,' he said, 'and when you have found him, let me know, so that I too may go and do him homage.'

Having listened to what the king had to say they set out. And there in front of them was the star they had seen rising; it went forward and halted over the place where the child was.

The sight of the star filled them with delight, and going into the house they saw the child with his mother Mary, and falling to their knees they did him homage. Then, opening their treasures, they offered him gifts of gold and frankincense and myrrh.

But they were warned in a dream not to go back to Herod, and returned to their own country by a different way.

Good News

A distant star shines through the darkness of night. This light from beyond rests over a house: and all who enter there find Jesus and pay homage to God.

First Reflection
The Coming of All Nations

As this is the only occasion in the present liturgical year when we have a reading from Matthew it will be helpful to recap on his writing and purpose.

Matthew wrote his gospel at a time when the Gentiles were flocking into the church but the relationship between traditional Jews and the new Christian sect was close to breaking point. Matthew writes as a Christian and as a Jew. He reaches out to his fellow Jews to reconsider the claims for Jesus Christ: to recognise how he was the fulfilment of the traditional texts, figures and hopes: and to see how he advanced from the old Mosaic covenant into the new covenant between God and humanity.

The story of the magi forms part of the introductory section of Matthew in which he is hinting at some of the themes which will be developed later in the gospel.

The wise men from the east represent the Gentiles, the non-Jewish nations, who were entering the church by believing in Jesus Christ. The Gentiles had previously lacked the gift of divine revelation, which had been the privilege of the Jews. However, God had given signs for all people to read, even apart from revelation. As St Paul claimed: 'Ever since God created the world his everlasting power and deity – however invisible – have been there for the mind to see in the things he has made.' (Rom 1:20)

The movements of the stars were regarded as very significant and it was commonly believed that a new star appeared at the birth of an important leader.

So, in Matthew's story, these wise men from the east who followed the star represent the Gentiles who followed their lights from natural revelation. But this light proved insufficient. So they had to beg guidance from the Jewish texts of revelation before they could finish their journey. Matthew thereby shows how the Gentiles were now availing of the Jewish heritage whereas the Jews themselves did not move forward.

These Gentiles came to the place where the child was, fell on their knees and paid homage. They brought gifts which expressed Christ's kingdom (gold), his priestly role (frankincense) and his redeeming death (myrrh).

As the Gentiles moved forward, what about the Jews? They stayed where they were in Jerusalem. In Matthew's writing he reaches out to them to reconsider the claims for Jesus. The story he weaves is very rich in allusions to Jewish history and to the hopes of their religion. Matthew presents Jesus as the fulfilment of their greatest leaders of the past, alluding especially to Moses, David and Solomon.

He shows that Jesus is the new Moses. All Jerusalem is perturbed at the birth of the infant king. Here are echoes of the birth of Moses which occurred when the Pharaoh ordered the killing of all the male infant children, as a result of which all Egypt trembled. Moses escaped the massacre and grew to lead his people out of slavery. Through him God entered a covenant with the people and gave them the law of the commandments. Matthew presents Jesus in terms of the new Moses, the new liberator, the new law-giver who would eventually announce, 'This is the new covenant in my blood, which is to be poured out for many, for the forgiveness of sins.'

Jesus is also presented in terms of David who was the ideal king. He was the shepherd chosen by God to be anointed king. He unified the tribes and conquered the hill where they built Jerusalem as their capital and centre. Matthew stresses that it was in Bethlehem, the town of David, that Jesus was born.

Solomon was the king who personified wisdom. The high point of his reign was when his wisdom was recognised by the Queen of Sheeba. She brought him gifts of gold, various spices and precious stones. The magi echo her visit. After her visit 'she went home, she and her servants to her own country' (1 Kgs 10:13), as they did at their turn. And there was a legend popularised by Jewish teachers that the Queen had found her way to Solomon by following a star. The point being made by Matthew is that Jesus is the new Moses and law-giver, the new David and shepherd-king, and the new Solomon in his wisdom.

Matthew has constructed a brilliant and fascinating story in this introduction to the story of Jesus. The magi anticipate the coming of the Gentiles into the house of faith. As the story reaches back in time, Matthew sums up the hopes of Jewish history and he claims that it was all fulfilled in Jesus.

The Jewish secret is now available to all nations. In today's second reading we see how Paul rejoices at this: 'the pagans now share the same inheritance, they are parts of the same body, and the same promise has been made to them, in Christ Jesus, through the gospel.' (Eph 3:5-6)

The wise men from the east were the first travellers on this road of faith. As believers we are privileged to follow their star.

'All nations shall fall prostrate before you, O Lord.'
(Responsorial Psalm)

Second Reflection
The Men of Wisdom

There are three groups of people in Matthew's story: Herod and the political set in Jerusalem; the scribes, priests and religious leaders; and the wise men who came from the east.

This story of the magi shows the different responses of people to the news of the infant king. It was true what Simeon had said to Mary in the temple, that this child was destined for the fall and rising of many in Israel. He would be God's light, in which people would be their own judges.

The first group were the political people in the capital. Herod was perturbed at the news 'and so was the whole of Jerusalem.' These are the power-people whose only religion is their own advancement. But the tyrant is always desperately insecure. Herod is threatened by a tiny infant. The tyrants of history from Pharaoh to Herod, from Cromwell to Hitler, from Stalin to Ceaucescu have thought nothing of huge massacres in the interest of their own survival.

Was Herod genuinely interested in paying homage to the infant king? No way. Herod was interested in only one god ...himself. He shows us how selfishness can take over our lives so that we become blind to the light of God that comes to us.

In the second group of people were the scribes and religious leaders of the Jews. They were consulted about these rumours. So they looked into their books and came up with the answer 'Bethlehem'.

But did they go there, did they take the road to Bethlehem? Not they. They stayed in Jerusalem, content with their books and debates.

They represent those who have all the philosophies, all the theories, all the arguments for and against ... but they will never take a single step of commitment. They live in the world of theory and never step out on the road of reality. History is repeated in that many who fail in this way still belong to the priestly circles and religious families. They bury their commitment in learned theses, abstract speculation and dry debate. But will they ever step out and share the light of God with a world which is drifting in darkness towards despair?

The wise men stepped out on the road and followed the star. We must note that a star is such a little light: it is a very distant light: and it is only in darkness that we can see it. For the wise men the star in itself was not important. What they sought was what it would lead them to. The star was a sign of the Beyond. It rested over a house. They went in and saw the child and his mother Mary. Faith is a commitment to the distant, dimly perceived Beyond that has come into our midst in this child at Bethlehem.

The wise men brought gifts of gold for a king, frankincense for a priest and myrrh for the embalming of one who would die for his people.

The gifts we bring to God at Epiphany are symbolised by the gifts of the magi.

The gold we bring is our commitment to the kingdom of God established by Jesus on earth: this means a commitment to the Christian ideals for society ... justice, peace and joy in the Holy Spirit.

The frankincense we bring is our recognition of Jesus Christ as the true priest or authentic way to the Father. All our prayer is in his name. The Eucharist, as the prayer of Christian memory, is the pinnacle of our journey to God.

The myrrh we bring is our belief and trust in Jesus Christ who has conquered death. We now dare to hope even when all the omens are bad and everything else points to defeat. With these gifts of faith and trust, we fall on our knees and pay homage.

God is in our midst.

Emmanuel.

The Baptism of the Lord

On the First Sunday in Ordinary Time the gospel story of the baptism of Jesus is a bridge between the hidden years at Nazareth and the days of his public ministry. What happened on that day at the Jordan may be understood as the divine call to commence his mission.

Mark 1:7-11

In the course of his preaching John the Baptist said, 'Someone is following me, someone who is more powerful than I am, and I am not fit to kneel down and undo the strap of his sandals. I have baptised you with water, but he will baptise you with the Holy Spirit.'

It was at this time that Jesus came from Nazareth in Galilee and was baptised in the Jordan by John. No sooner had he come up out of the water than he saw the heavens torn apart and the Spirit, like a dove, descending on him. And a voice came from heaven, 'You are my Son, the Beloved; my favour rests on you.'

Good News

The heavens are opened as the Spirit of God descends upon Jesus, confirming him with divine power for his ministry to the world.

First Reflection
The Credentials of Jesus

Today's gospel grows out of the preparatory season of Advent, through the promise of John the Baptist that someone greater would come after him. The spirituality of Advent drew us into recognising the wild, unredeemed areas of our lives. We were challenged to face up to our inability to solve our problems: in other words, to recognise our need of a Saviour.

Christmas focused on the coming of the Saviour. He was revealed to the nations at Epiphany but settled into family life at Nazareth for thirty hidden years. In coming from Nazareth to the Jordan waters Jesus was emerging from obscurity to step into the limelight of his public ministry.

The Baptist's work was to prepare the way. Jesus accepted his cousin's role by stepping into the water and submitting to John's ceremony of washing. It expresses how fully human Jesus was, that he should join with sinners in the river of repentance.

But Jesus was more than human. He was divine. And his divine nature was affirmed in a two-fold testimony from heaven. The evidence of two witnesses was required by law. The descending Spirit and the voice of the Father were the two witnesses that day.

The coming down of the Spirit in the form of a dove recalled the text in Genesis which described the Spirit of God brooding like a bird over the waters as God drew order out of the primitive chaos. In later days the Spirit came with power upon the great judges, kings and prophets. But the Jews of Jesus' day were conscious that many centuries had passed since such an occurrence. Isaiah had predicted that the Spirit of Yahweh would rest upon the messiah, filling him with those seven virtues which are known to us as the gifts of the Spirit.

Jesus saw the heavens 'torn apart' as the Spirit descended in the form of a dove. After long centuries of waiting, the prayer of Isaiah was answered: 'Oh, that you would tear the heavens open and come down.' (Is 64:1)

The second witness was the voice of the Father: 'You are my Son, the Beloved.' It could also be translated as: 'You are my only Son.' This testimony implies that Jesus is more than a human messiah. He enjoys a unique relationship with the Father.

Mark uses this two-fold testimony from heaven to establish the credentials of Jesus' ministry. Over the course of the Sundays in Ordinary Time we will read of his public life and mission. From the outset Mark is establishing for his readers that this will be the mission of someone vastly greater than John the Baptist. For Jesus is empowered by the Spirit of God, and in an unique sense is the Son of God.

That day at the Jordan, God stepped into the rivers of human history to transform our lives with divine power. A mission was about to commence which would elevate the condition of humanity forever.

Jesus Christ is the centre of human history. Rightly do we enumerate our years from his life, calling each year AD, *anno Domini*, a year of the Lord. May this year truly be, for you and for me, a year of the Lord.

Second Reflection
Called to Ministry

The baptism of Jesus marks the day of his divine affirmation and his empowerment for public mission. It is an appropriate day to reflect on our own baptism as a call to participate actively in the mission of the Church.

The Second Vatican Council recognised the need to foster the active role of the laity in the Church's mission of salvation. Calling up the laity is not some strategy devised merely to counteract the falling number of priests and religious. The call to ministry is rooted in baptism and developed in confirmation. 'The apostolate of the laity is a sharing in the saving mission of the Church. Through baptism and confirmation all the baptised are appointed to this apostolate by the Lord himself.' (Vat II, Church, 33)

We have tended to regard baptism too much in terms of personal salvation ... as something necessary for the salvation of one's soul by the cleansing of original sin. It must also be seen as a sacrament of belonging to the family and mission of the Church. It imposes the duty to participate actively in the Church's mission of carrying on the work of Christ's kingdom.

For too long we, the clergy, have hogged the power and were happy to let the laity stand up, pay up and shut up! We did not recognise the charisms of the lay baptised, much less foster their growth. It is time for the sleeping giant of the laity to awake. The vocations crisis of today is principally about our failure to nurture the vocation of all the baptised to active mission.

But let us return to the baptism of the Lord which marked his emergence from obscurity to begin his public mission. It is very significant that his ministry began after he had received the two-fold testimony from heaven. He was divinely affirmed in his identity. One of the most mysterious areas of faith is the interplay between the human and divine natures in the person of Jesus Christ. We believe that Jesus felt with a human heart and thought with a human mind. And he had to pass through the normal stages of personal growth to maturity.

In Erikson's stages of growth, before a life is generative (as Jesus was in his public ministry), one must previously have achieved a strong sense of who-I-am (identity) and developed the capacity for intimacy. The word intimacy may well be rooted in the Latin word for fear. Intimacy means being ready to share with another in the areas of risk and fear. It demands that one is sufficiently self-secure to relate now in full trust with others in the risk of a give-and-take relationship.

A revelation from heaven confirmed for Jesus his divine identity. And the intimacy of his relationship with the Father was clearly heard: 'You are my Beloved Son; my favour rests on you.' With his identity clearly established and his relationship with the Father to reassure him, Jesus was now ready for a ministry which would generate divine life in others.

The pattern is the same for all Christians who are called to follow Jesus in ministry. I am speaking of ministry in the wide sense of any apostolic activity, rather than in the restricted areas proper to those who are ordained. Ministry is another word for serving others in the love of Christ.

The call to Christian ministry begins in finding out who I am in relationship with God. That means understanding my baptismal identity. For most Catholics this comes through a gradual process of encounters with God in prayer and the sacraments. Our faith and trust grow as God's loving relationship with us is increasingly revealed to us. There may be one special, overwhelming encounter like a weekend reteat, or some moment when we are taken beyond ourselves by the beauty of creation, or some crisis that is surmounted, when our faith crashes through a barrier and grows appreciably. In some charismatic circles they call this the experience of being born again or of receiving baptism in the Spirit.

Whether my personal history is of a dramatic breakthrough (born again) or of gradual growth (born again-and-again) is beside the point. What matters is coming to know in my heart and mind what it means to have been baptised.

Like Jesus I learn identity.

I too am a beloved child of God the Father.

I too have received the power and gifts of the Holy Spirit.

I am so loved by Jesus Christ, the Son, that he entered the murky waters of human existence to embrace me. This is my Christian identity.

And when I prayerfully bring this light to shine on my daily experiences, I will grow in confidence. For God is always with me. I will be ready to go, with God, into the areas of risk and fear ... intimacy.

When this courage grows my life will be generative and apostolic. I will be ready to share with others in Christ's name. It may be in a service of family responsibility, of working for justice, of feeding the hungry, of helping in retreats and growth programmes, or of liturgical ministry. In a great diversity of ways we are called to witness to our faith.

In Christian ministry it is not myself that I give to others, but Christ who lives in me. If I were to give of my own sinfulness and inadequacy it would be of little service to others. But the call to Christian ministry is to give what is not my own. What I give is whatever God's Spirit will use me for.

Most people will initially react in fear when asked to participate in ministry. But this fear comes from thinking that it depends totally on my own abilities.

Jeremiah, when he received the call to give God's word, recoiled in fear: 'Ah Lord Yahweh; look, I do not know how to speak:I am a child.' But God reassured him: 'Do not be afraid of them, for I am with you to protect you.' (Jer 1:4,8)

If I am called to any ministry or service in the Church it is not a reward for being a good parishioner. In Christian ministry I am called to give what is not my own: to give of Christ who lives in me by the grace of baptism. All I need to do is offer my emptiness to the Holy Spirit to fill me and use me for God's purposes.

The voice of the Father speaks in my heart:

'My Spirit tears open the heavens and pierces the clouds to come and rest on you. Be not afraid.'

Note: The text for next Sunday, The Second Sunday in Ordinary Time, will be found on page 142.

First Sunday of Lent

The gospel readings chosen for the Sundays of Lent this year develop the theme of dying with Christ to the old ways of sin so as to enter the new way of God's life and kingdom. Today's gospel tells of Jesus waging war on the evil spirits before proclaiming the victory of the reign of God upon earth.

Mark 1:12-15

The Spirit drove Jesus out into the wilderness and he remained there for forty days, and was tempted by Satan. He was with the wild beasts, and the angels looked after him.

After John had been arrested, Jesus went into Galilee. There he proclaimed the Good News from God. 'The time has come,' he said, 'and the kingdom of God is close at hand. Repent, and believe the Good News.'

Good News

Jesus entered into battle with the evil one and then proclaimed the advance of God's reign on earth. God reigns in our lives when we repent of evil ways and live according to the gospel.

First Reflection
Good News of Victory

Mark's account of the temptation of Jesus in the wilderness is much shorter than the versions of Matthew and Luke. He makes no mention of the three specific temptations which the others describe. Despite its brevity, Mark's version opens up some very important theological themes as an introduction to the public mission of Jesus.

The first point to note is the role of the Holy Spirit in this episode. Immediately after the baptism of Jesus, the heavens were torn apart and the Spirit like a dove descended upon him. The Spirit then drove him out into the wilderness. There is a great sense of urgency here as the Spirit has filled Jesus with zeal and energy to commence his mission to recall mankind from the ways of sin and restore their hearts to the rule of God.

We have to appreciate the mentality of the time. It was commonly accepted that the world was under the rule of the spirit of evil but that in the messianic times God would intervene and wage a great war to win back the hearts of people to the divine will.

Eager to commence his mission, Jesus, as it were, declared war on the devil by venturing into the wilderness. The wilderness, an untamed area which supported no useful forms of life, was regarded as the home territory of the evil spirit. By entering this territory Jesus was taking the battle to the enemy on his home pitch. He remained there for forty days, a period of fulness, for this was to be no passing skirmish but a declaration of total war.

We read that Jesus was tempted by Satan. Tempted here means being tried and tested like a contestant in the boxing or wrestling ring. Satan is the name given in scripture to the chief enemy of God. The first engagement in this battle is a contest between the champion warrior of each side, like the old matching of David and Goliath as champions of the Israelites and Philistines respectively.

The result of this first bout was victory for Jesus. We are told: 'He was with the wild beasts, and the angels looked after him.' The angels represent God's support and care during the struggle. And the most likely meaning of the wild beasts is that they are with Jesus in peace, having lost their distrust and ferocity. For this presence of Jesus in the untamed wilderness is the first indication of the restoration of the peace of paradise.

One connects this restoration of harmony with the stories of Christ's faithful follower, Francis of Assisi, who enjoyed a remarkable relationship with animals, even the wildest of wolves. When his biographer, Saint Bonaventure, reflected on this, he wrote that Francis 'showed a return to the state of original innocence through universal reconciliation.'(Major Life,8,l) Another great biographer, Thomas of Celano, comments that the brotherly relationship of Francis with all things advanced him to paradise ever before he was dead: 'he already had escaped into the freedom of the glory of the sons of God.' (l Cel 81)

Isaiah dreamt of the time of perfect reconciliation when the wolf would lie down with the lamb. The time of God's peace had now begun when Jesus confronted Satan in the wilderness. In the chapters of Mark which follow, there are many stories of the evil spirits being routed and cast out.

What follows this first victory is its proclamation. 'He proclaimed the Good News from God.' When we reflected on the opening line of Mark's gospel on the Second Sunday of Advent, we noted that originally the word *evangelion* meant the cry of the king's herald to proclaim some great news like a victory. In this instance the proclamation of Jesus is not on behalf of any earthly king but that God's power had intervened in human history. 'The time has come ...', the long years of waiting and expectation are over. 'The kingdom of God is at hand ...' God's victorious intervention has commenced.

The first bout was over with victory to Jesus, but the war was to continue. The evil spirit was to fight back with all the ferocity of desperation. And the struggle for God's kingdom continues to this day in the hearts of all of us. The call of Jesus is to join him in his victory: 'Repent and believe the Good News.' To repent is to break our ties with evil in our thoughts, words and deeds. And to believe means to move more and more towards the mind of Jesus.

Lent is the liturgical season when we pay special attention to the on-going struggle against sin in our lives. We prepare for the renewal of our baptismal covenant with God through forty days of self-discipline and training. At the imposition of ashes we hear the Lord's battle-cry: 'Repent and believe in the Good News.'

Second Reflection
The Ashes of Repentance

Lent commences with the imposition of ashes, a sign of destruction and decomposition. In one sense the ashes are a reminder to us of our bodily mortality. 'Remember that thou art but dust and unto dust thou shalt return.' So, why should we spend all our energy on the service of the body destined to perish, while neglecting the things of the spirit destined for eternity?

The ashes are also a sign of fire, in this case the fires of purification. Accepting the ashes at the start of Lent is an expression that one is making a commitment to a season of self-discipline and purification in preparation for the renewal of our baptismal covenant at Easter.

The first two readings in today's liturgy refer to the story of Noah. In Noah's time the evil ways of mankind brought down a flood of destruction upon the earth. Many people feel today that the immorality of our world is close to drawing a similar flood of disaster upon the globe.

Mercifully, as I write, the threat of an East-West confrontation, which might well wreak the total destruction of life on this planet, is rapidly receding.

But the threat from industrial greed continues to grow. Fear of another Hiroshima or Chernobyl puts only a slight brake on the daily destruction of our environmental balance. At least one species of plant or animal life is lost to the world each day. Science and technology are powerful monsters which need the guidance of caring hearts and responsible consciences.

Equally terrifying is the flood of immorality which is sweeping away the quality of life, particularly the stability of family life. Security and tranquillity have been destroyed by urban terrorism, violent crime and organised gangsterism. Unemployment increases and brings a train of problems in its wake. The gap between rich and poor countries is constantly getting wider. The sacredness of human life is under constant threat through pornography, sexual promiscuity and the availability of abortion. Lives are being destroyed by unhealthy lifestyles, smoking, over indulgence in food and drink, and the abuse of drugs.

We do not need to wait for heavenly warnings to tell us that unless we repent we are doomed for destruction. It will not require any punishing action of God's hand because the way we are living at the moment we are the agents of self-destruction.

In today's gospel we hear the words of Jesus which call us to share in his victory over Satan: 'The kingdom of God is close at hand. Repent, and believe the Good News.'

To repent is to turn away from the ways of destruction ... environmental, family, personal. It means overcoming the evil ways of selfishness, lust, violence, greed and envy.

To believe the Good News is to turn towards the way, the truth and the life offered to us in Jesus Christ. It means to work towards a better world by means of reconciliation and peace.

The evils of the world and the injustices of society will not be redressed by violent revolution but by conversion of ways. History shows that revolutions tend to bring in even more injustices than previously existed. What is needed is conversion of heart to Jesus and the values of the gospel.

May the ashes of Lent remind us to favour the things of the spirit which are eternal, over the pleasures of the body which are passing.

And may these ashes spur us on to repentance of sinful ways so as to make wholehearted commitment to the ways of Jesus.

Repent and believe.

Second Sunday of Lent

Lent takes us from last Sunday's encounter with Satan in the wilderness to today's vision of the transfigured Lord on the mountain. The transfiguration was a glimpse of glory given to the three disciples who would later experience Jesus at his lowest in Gethsemane. God will not lead us into a hard testing without first strengthening us with his blessing.

Mark 9:2-10

Jesus took with him Peter and James and John and led them up a high mountain where they could be alone by themselves. There in their presence he was transfigured: his clothes became dazzlingly white, whiter than any earthly bleacher could make them.

Elijah appeared to them with Moses; and they were talking with Jesus. Then Peter spoke to Jesus: 'Rabbi,' he said, 'it is wonderful for us to be here; so let us make three tents, one for you, one for Moses and one for Elijah.' He did not know what to say; they were so frightened.

And a cloud came, covering them in shadow; and there came a voice from the cloud, 'This is my Son, the Beloved. Listen to him.' Then suddenly, when they looked round, they saw no one with them any more but only Jesus.

As they came down from the mountain he warned them to tell no one what they had seen, until after the Son of Man had risen from the dead. They observed the warning faithfully, though among themselves they discussed what 'rising from the dead' could mean.

Good News

Jesus is the beloved Son of the Father who speaks the word of God to us. He will lead us out of the dark ways of sin into the light of God's glory.

First Reflection
The Day on the Mountain

Mountains are great places for offering us a wider view of the surrounding countryside. The experience invites the mind to take on a broader perspective on our everyday preoccupations. 'Great things happen when men and mountains meet.' Not surprisingly, in the bible mountains are associated with divine encounters and with visions which inspired life.

Students of Mark note that he was a writer who arranged his material with the same deliberate care that an architect gives to the symmetry of a construction. The transfiguration is placed exactly in the middle of Mark's composition. It comes like a halfway resting stop on the journey. Jesus had just made the first prediction of his rejection, death and rising. The second half of his journey would be towards Jerusalem and rejection.

The inner circle of three disciples, Peter, James and John, who would witness the weakest moment of Jesus in Gethsemane, were prepared for that dark night by the experience of a day of light on the mountain. It was a glimpse of the future power and glory of the kingdom. It was a day of blessing.

Peter, not yet understanding how Jesus was to be the Suffering Servant of God, wanted that wonderful experience to last. 'It is wonderful for us to be here; so let us make three tents, one for you, one for Moses and one for Elijah.' Mark tells us that the cloud covered the disciples too. The overshadowing cloud is a scriptural way of expressing the presence and action of God's power. It was a moment of great blessing in their lives.

But this midway mountain was not to be the end of the journey. They had to come down from the heights. God was asking them to let go of their own satisfaction and in the light of this blessed experience to journey forward in total trust. They discussed among themselves what the future might be, and particularly what 'rising from the dead' might mean.

It is always advisable to read any Sunday's gospel in conjunction with the first reading of the liturgy. Today we read of Abraham, another man who was given a great blessing from God but was asked to let go of his personal satisfaction.

The blessing of Abraham was in the birth of a son many years after his wife Sara had passed the normal years of childbearing. They called their son Isaac, a name expressing the smile of God on their lives. Today's reading picks up the story at the harrowing test of Abraham's faith. He was asked to offer in sacrifice his little son, the very smile of God in his life. The most important line in the passage is the opening sentence. It was God who put Abraham to the test. The greatness of Abraham is seen in his unquestioning acceptance of God's will. To give back the smile of God, Isaac, was the most severe sacrifice possible to him, but he did not question God's right to ask for it. He was willing to take God on his terms.

In the weakness of our faith we often resemble Peter there on the mountain, trying to dictate our own terms to God. We want to

55

stay for all time in the experience of God's power and consolation. We want every day to be an Easter Sunday. But we fear to go with Jesus through the Friday of suffering and the Saturday of lying in the darkness of the tomb. We want the resurrection without the crucifixion, the crown without the cross, the new life without dying to the old.

The spirituality of the time before Vatican II was, perhaps, excessively centred on the cross and did not give sufficient place to the resurrection. It had its limitations but it did prepare people to persevere with the Lord through suffering and through long periods of darkness in faith or dryness in prayer.

Nowadays one meets many people who have no understanding of the ways of God who tests us so as to deepen our faith. Yet we must always remember that before God tests the soul he will first have given his smile and joy.

The bread is blessed before it is broken. Abraham enjoyed the smile of God before he was tested. The three apostles glimpsed the glory of Jesus before they experienced his rejection and humiliation.

The view on the midway mountain was a blessed moment of light to sustain them in the darkness of Gethsemane and in the days after the life of Jesus. We use this reading in Lent to encourage us to persevere in our Lenten programme of repentance.

Second Reflection
Listen to him

'This is my Son, the Beloved. Listen to him.' These were the words of the heavenly Father, heard through the cloud of divine presence on the mountain. As a project for Lent it would be hard to think of a better resolution than to give time every day to the prayer of listening to God.

Lent is about repenting and believing. We express our repenting in what we give up for Lent. We can show our believing in what we take on. Many of us are better at the giving up than the taking on.

Back in the time of Jesus it was the same. The religious sort of people were put off Jesus because he was not big into fasting like John the Baptist and their own preachers. But Jesus replied that it is much more important to take on the works of mercy and the enjoyment of God's presence. The joy of knowing God as the bridegroom of my soul is far more pleasing to God than the gloomy face which scowls the word penance to all we meet. Lent should never mean a resolution which puts us into bad form and impossible to live with!

'Listen to him.'

Give yourself the time and the chance to appreciate his presence. He is with us since our baptism. But are you with him? If you think that you are a million miles from God, guess who moved!

Perhaps we need to move away from multiplying words in prayer and consider prayer in terms of desiring God.

'My soul is thirsting for God, the God of my life.'

Our desire for God will be seen in the amount of time we make available to prayer.

A serious Lent will mean cutting back on the time we give to wasteful, empty distractions. The hours wasted before the television. The vapid, empty reading of novels and endless newspapers. Even apart from what one would classify as bad reading, so much of what we read does nothing to help us listen to God. And then there is the compulsive radio listener who lives with a mind swirling in the fog of a million words of empty chatter.

T.S.Eliot comments that we have,

'Knowledge of speech, but not of silence
Knowledge of words, and ignorance of the Word.'

And he asks us,

'Where is the Life we have lost in living?
Where is the wisdom we have lost in knowledge?
Where is the knowledge we have lost in information?'

(Choruses from 'The Rock', 1.)

Cutting back on the inflow of words is the necessary beginning for listening to God. Then we must try to identify what form of prayer suits us best.

For one person it will be a time of adoration before the Blessed Sacrament. The Eucharist becomes a focus point for our attention to God's presence.

'My body pines for you
Like a dry, weary land without water
So I gaze upon you in the sanctuary
to see your strength and your glory.' (Ps 62, Grail)

Another person finds it easier to listen to God by meditating with a page of scripture. Approach the sacred word as God's special word to you today. Listen, wait and listen. Wait again and listen. Our willingness to wait is an expression of our desire for God.

Sometimes our own deep feelings or agitations are so strong that we cannot concentrate on any holy symbol. Then we must let our feelings, worries or agitations surface in our minds and pray out of them as a source. Bring them to God and find how God is present in your stressful life. If you persist in the usual approach to meditations you will regard these thoughts as distraction. But if you pray from where you are in life, then instead of being bothered with distractions you will be learning to listen to God in the pressures of life. We can learn what God is saying to us through what we previously regarded as distractions.

Lenten fasting is important. But it is more important to savour the presence of the Bridegroom of your soul and to listen to him. It is good to work hard and to offer the service of a Martha. But at times the better part is to sit with Mary and listen to him.

'God our Father, help us to hear your Son.
Enlighten us with your word, that we may find the
way to your glory.' (Prayer of the Day).

Third Sunday of Lent

The Lenten gospels of this year develop the theme of dying to the old ways of sin so as to rise to the new life of Christ. Today we commence a block of three Sundays from John's gospel. Each week we will have a story which illustrates the challenge of the new life that Jesus offers. Jesus cleared the merchants and money changers from the Temple in a gesture which challenged the Jews about the role of the Temple. The question he put was whether the Temple was serving or hindering true worship.

John 2: 13-25

Just before the Jewish Passover Jesus went to Jerusalem, and in the Temple he found people selling cattle and sheep and pigeons, and the money changers sitting at their counters there. Making a whip out of some cord, he drove them all out of the Temple, cattle and sheep as well, scattered the money changers' coins, knocked their tables over and said to the pigeon-sellers, 'Take all this out of here and stop turning my Father's house into a market.' Then his disciples remembered the words of scripture: Zeal for your house will devour me.

The Jews intervened and said, 'What sign can you show us to justify what you have done?' Jesus answered, 'Destroy this sanctuary, and in three days I will raise it up.'

The Jews replied, 'It has taken forty-six years to build this sanctuary: are you going to raise it up in three days?' But he was speaking of the sanctuary that was his body, and when Jesus rose from the dead, his disciples remembered that he had said this, and they believed the scripture and the words he had said.

During his stay in Jerusalem for the Passover many believed in his name when they saw the signs that he gave, but Jesus knew them all and did not trust himself to them; he never needed evidence about any man; he could tell what a man had in him.

Good News

The risen Lord Jesus is the new Temple: he is the true meeting place with God the Father; and it is only through him that true worship is offered to the Father, in the power of the Holy Spirit.

First Reflection

The New Temple

The action of Jesus, when he made a whip out of some cord and drove the moneychangers and sellers out of the temple courtyard, was a grand, symbolic gesture. In no way should it be seen as a resort to physical violence. A little whip made from cord can hardly be regarded as an effective instrument of physical force. During the busy days before Passover there would have been thousands of animals and birds with several hundred drovers and sellers there. Would one man have driven them all out? Hardly likely. You may be sure that an hour later the dust had settled and everybody was back where they started with business as normal.

I well remember our Dean in boarding school herding us forward with the symbolic threat of his white Franciscan cord. It could do little damage but it was enough to get his point across.

Many great leaders have known the power of a symbolic gesture to challenge the system and to arouse the slumbering energy of peoples' consciences. It was Ghandi's greatest weapon. He once challenged South Africa's racialism through burning identity cards. In imperial India he challenged the occupying power through the refusal to pay salt tax and by burning all clothes manufactured in England. His spinning wheel became the symbol of national independence.

The picture of Jesus clearing the Temple is a grand gesture to express the end of that religion which emphasised the worship of God by sacrifices in the Temple.

The Temple was intended to express God's presence with his chosen people and to be the sacred place where all their prayer and worship reached its climax. However, over the course of years, the ceremonies and regulations took on such an importance of their own that the prayerful heart of Temple worship was obscured. When Jesus was twelve and celebrating his bar-mitzvah by going in pilgrimage to the Temple, he was deeply disappointed at what he saw there. He resolved that day to be busy about the Father's business: to work towards restoring the pure meaning of Temple worship.

What was wrong there? First of all the place was too crowded and pressurised for any proper worship. The business of sacrificing birds and animals had grown enormously. Rather than drive their own animals on long pilgrimage, pilgrims could buy them on the spot. And with a wink here and a tip there, it was far more likely that the animal bought in Jerusalem would pass the ritual inspection required before acceptance of the animal for sacrifice.

Then again, the Temple emphasised the exclusion of non-Jews from the area beyond the Court of Gentiles. The prophets' dream of all nations coming to the Temple was blocked by legislation. Coins of foreign currency were not to be used for the purchase of sacrificial animals lest the effigy of a pagan ruler on a coin profane the sacred area. Hence the business of the money changers.

As a result of all the transactions the sacred area was at once a cattle mart, a huge abattoir and a bureau of change. You can imagine the squawking of birds, the bellowing of cattle, the noise of sheep and goats, the hustling of people and the heavy smell of blood. It was everything except a place of prayer.

The reactions to the gesture of Jesus were significant. The disciples understood it as a return to the original meaning of the Temple as a place of prayerful worship: 'Zeal for your house will devour me.' The Jews – here John means the religious leaders – interpreted the action of Jesus as a claim to be the Messiah. They remembered the prophetic texts which promised that the Messiah would come and take possession of the Temple. So, if Jesus were claiming to be Messiah, they wanted a sign.

He answered: 'Destroy this sanctuary and in three days I will raise it up.' In Jesus' eyes the sanctuary was already destroyed because it had lost its purpose. It would be replaced by the new sanctuary which is suggested by the phrase, 'after three days I will raise it up.'

At this point of the story John is taking liberties with his readers by using words which the reader can understand but which the participants could not possibly have understood on the same level. John's readers are asked to believe that the new Temple is the risen body of the Lord Jesus: 'He was speaking of the sanctuary that was his body.' Many people came to believe in Jesus but he did not trust himself to them, for he could tell what a man had in him. They were as yet only beginning the journey of faith, a journey which could not be completed until after the resurrection.

John intends his readers to understand the entire Temple episode in the light of the resurrection. In the new age of risen life Jesus brought the old religious institutions to fulfilment. No longer would people require multiple sacrifices of lambs and cattle, for Jesus is the Lamb of God whose sacrifice is perfect for all time.

Nor would people need the crowded bedlam of the old Temple system, for the new Temple of divine encounter is by relationship with the Father, through the risen Lord Jesus, by the power of the Holy Spirit. The risen Lord Jesus is with the Father and is ever living to intercede for us.

'Through him, with him, in him, in the unity of the Holy Spirit, all glory and honour is yours, almighty Father, for ever and ever.'

Second Reflection
Lenten Renewal

Jesus came to raise us up to new life: to move beyond the old frontiers of human experience: to offer us a new vision of life.

But he found the greatest opposition coming from those who were stuck in the old religious systems. They resisted all attempts at renewal. He spoke of the problem of putting new wine into old wineskins. He pointed to the diseased fruit trees which were incapable of renewal and should be cut down.

The whole Temple system upset him from the first contact he had with it. Originally the Temple was a great idea. It added a new dignity to worship. It was a sacred place which people could mentally associate with God: a focal point of pilgrims' desire: a sanctuary removed from the pressures of everyday living. It became the very special place for offering sacrifice, answering the need of the human heart to make some tangible return of life to the Creator.

But the simple atmosphere of sacred worship gradually gave way to the growing complexity of numbers and noise. The institutional regulations had become a parasitical growth which now weighed down and choked the parent tree.

Jesus made a little whip of cord as a gesture to indicate the need to clear out and renew this Temple system. In fact the system had been destroyed beyond renewal. It would have to be replaced. He would restore worship in spirit and in truth.

The lesson must be taken to heart by every religious institution and each individual Christian. Lent is the season of self-examination before the renewal of our commitment to Christ at Easter. We have to cut back any parasitical growth which chokes our fruitfulness.

The self-destroying process which affected the Temple system represents a tendency which can recur in any religious institution. It applies to the Church as a whole which can become so caught up in protecting its own institutions that it neglects to serve the kingdom. Rules which were once framed to protect some value are sometimes retained even when they are producing the counter effect. Bishops and priests too easily become so weighed down under financial problems, administrative tasks and personnel management that they no longer have any energy for their primary function, the preaching of the good news.

Religious orders and congregations drift away from the

passionate spirit of their founders. They become museum-keepers treasuring the fossils of former vitality. They are preoccupied with self-preservation. And it shows in the growing number who become neurotically attentive to finicky details or dietary practices.

Parish communities too can lose their missionary generosity and their ability to respond to the needs of the locality or to the trends of changing requirements. Then Sunday liturgy will be a perfunctory ritual with little sense of celebration. If the community shows no vitality in its faith, then it will have nothing to celebrate on Sunday.

The challenge of Jesus is to examine our religious institutions and ourselves as individuals. Are we strangled by red tape or preoccupied with preserving our selfish interests? Are we capable of responding with a fresh commitment to Christ each day?

May the gesture of Christ in clearing out the Temple challenge us to destroy the temple of self-preservation so as to discover the true temple of the risen Lord.

Fourth Sunday of Lent

Today we read the second of the three extracts from John which were chosen for the Lenten theme of dying to the old ways so as to be reborn in the new life of Christ.

Nicodemus came to Jesus by night and Jesus spoke to him of the need to be born again in the life of the Spirit: he is invited to leave behind the ways of darkness so as to live in the light of Christ's way.

John 3: 14-21

Jesus said to Nicodemus: 'The Son of Man must be lifted up as Moses lifted up the serpent in the desert, so that everyone who believes may have eternal life in him. Yes, God loved the world so much that he gave his only Son, so that everyone who believes in him may not be lost but may have eternal life.

'For God sent his Son into the world not to condemn the world, but so that through him the world might be saved. No one who believes in him will be condemned; but whoever refuses to believe is condemned already, because he has refused to believe in the name of God's only Son.

'On these grounds is sentence pronounced: that though the light has come into the world men have shown they prefer darkness to the light because their deeds were evil. And indeed, everybody who does wrong hates the light and avoids it, for fear his actions should be exposed; but the man who lives by the truth comes out into the light, so that it may be plainly seen that what he does is done in God.'

Good News

God loved the world so much that he gave his only Son, so that everyone who believes in him may not be lost but may have eternal life.

First Reflection
Lifted Up

Jesus spoke to Nicodemus of the need to be born again on a higher plane of life. He spoke of life according to the Spirit of God as being higher than the natural life of the flesh. This higher life is now called supernatural life or a sharing in divine life.

'How can this happen?' asked Nicodemus. And his question is the lead into today's gospel. The answer of Jesus is a summary of the whole economy of salvation in three movements:

Jesus came down from above to our level of life in order to raise us up to share in his divine life;

the great power behind all this is God's love for the world;

our cooperation with God's grace is required, through our willingness to walk in the light of Christ's way.

First comes the picture of Jesus being lifted up. It has the double application to Jesus of being lifted up on the cross and then in his resurrection. The upright cross, once the sign of curse and disgrace, became the instrument of healing and grace. It was like that strange story of Moses and the snakes. The people were subjected to a plague of serpents. Moses told them to fashion a bronze serpent and to raise it aloft. And all who looked up at this serpent of bronze were cured of the effects of snakebite. It is certainly a strange sort of story, but it was a symbol of healing. John uses the story to illustrate how Jesus came to lift up and help our sick world.

With the picture of lifting up in mind, John then proceeds to tell us that the power behind all this healing is God's love for the world.

'Yes, God loved the world so much
that everyone who believes in him may not be lost
but may have eternal life.'

What a memorable statement! Surely one of the greatest sentences of hope ever written!

The wonder of mercy is that God's love reaches down to us most of all when we are fallen to our lowest point. Today's first reading shows God reaching out in compassion to the people in exile in Babylon. And in the second reading Paul says: 'When we were dead through our sins, he brought us to life.'

The love of God reaches down to us in our sick, bruised and hurt world, and invites us to rise up with Jesus to share in his divine life. On the cross Jesus took the full brunt of evil and hatred upon himself. But he did not react in bitterness or a return of hatred. He conquered through divine love. And so the cross of disgrace was changed into the ladder to glory. The tree of death became the tree of life.

Jesus did not come to condemn. People were already condemning themselves. Last Sunday we saw that he did not come to destroy the Temple system: it had already been destroyed and needed to be replaced. Jesus came to call people to his way so that they might be lifted up from the quagmire of condemnation.

However, God does not force his grace on us. He respects our

65

free will. The choice to cooperate with God's invitation or not is ours. We are called to step out of the ways of darkness into the light of Christ. John reflects with sadness that,

'though the light came into the world
men have shown they prefer darkness to the light
because their deeds were evil.'

Those who refuse the morals and standards of Christian life have already condemned themselves to the way of death. They remain prisoners of vengeful thoughts, uncontrolled anger, unbridled lust, gluttony and every other form of selfishness.

People are often troubled by the question of how can a loving God condemn anybody. The answer is given here. God does not condemn anybody. People condemn themselves according to the way they accept or reject the way of Jesus Christ. And the shrewd observation is added that everybody who does wrong hates the light and avoids it. Light hurts the sore eye. It is only to be expected that those who have fallen away from the Christian way will hate the light of Christ's Church.

This year's Lenten gospels call us to leave behind the ways of darkness and sin so as to rise with Christ in newness of life. The love of God reaches out to our fallen world to raise us up with Christ's rising. We are invited by God to come and be lifted up in healing and glory with him.

Second Reflection
The Eternal Triangle

The words of Jesus to Nicodemus contain a wonderful summary of the outreach of God's love to us in the story of salvation. God bent down to our fallen race, embraced our condition and raised us up to share in divine life.

I picture the movements of God in our regard as the three lines of a triangle. The topmost point, the apex of the pyramid represents the Father. Draw the first line of the pyramid down from the apex to show how the Father so loved the world that he gave his only Son.

No other reason but love and compassion could explain this sending down from heaven. It was not as if we had deserved this gift of love. The Father had pity on sinful, straying humanity.

Putting it in very human terms you can imagine the Father saying to the Son one day:

'Son, would you ever do a job for me? Would you become Jesus, a Saviour? Would you go down there and show them how to live? Bring them back to my will, restore my kingdom.'

Thus did God love the world in mercy and give his only Son that we might not be lost. The downward line of the triangle is the sending of Jesus.

The baseline of the triangle represents the life of Jesus among us. The word was made flesh and dwelt among us. He journeyed along our level of life. He nursed the sick patient with such intimacy that he was eventually infected with the leprosy he had come to cure. For the forces of evil so hated the light that the people of dark minds conspired against him. They concocted a plot, rigged a sham trial, compromised a weak governor and brought Jesus to the cross.

Now the phrase 'gave his only Son' took on a sacrificial meaning. Thinking they had triumphed, the forces of evil and minds of darkness lifted up their booty when the torn body of Jesus was raised for all to see. How they gloated in their dark minds!

Then, enter the Holy Spirit. The Father who had sent down his Word as he breathed out now draws back his Breath. Jesus is raised up in the Breath's return. This is the third line of the triangle, the line of return from the baseline to the apex.

The Good News is that all who believe in Jesus Christ are raised up in him. They live now on a lifted-up plane of life. It is higher than natural life: for it is supernatural, already a sharing in divine life.

'The Son of man must be lifted up...
so that everyone who believes in him
may have eternal life in him.'

The triangle is completed when, at death, we finally return to the Father with Jesus by the power of the Holy Spirit.

St John speaks of eternal life in the present tense. In his mystical thinking, eternal life has already begun in anyone who is a true believer and committed Christian.

Our sharing in divine life is a tiny seed sown in baptism. If the seed is nurtured in a Christian environment with prayer and good works it flourishes gradually.

Some people experience a dramatic day of growth in the sudden realisation of what supernatural life and union with Jesus means. It is a moment of great grace. They call this experience a new birth and they will speak of having being born again. But for most Catholics who pray and draw sustenance regularly from Reconciliation and the Eucharist, the experience of Christ's energy within us is a more gradual growth. And our joy at being saved is always tempered by the realisation that we are still prone to sin and might easily fall away.

Lent is the season when we look at our lives in preparation for renewing our baptismal commitment during the Easter Vigil. As Jesus died before he was raised up in the power of the Spirit, so too the pattern of our baptism is in daily dying to sin so as to live a Christ-like life.

'The man who lives by the truth comes out into the light so that it may be plainly seen that what he does is done in God.'

Fifth Sunday of Lent

For the third consecutive Sunday we have a reading from John to develop the Lenten theme that it is through our willingness to die to selfishness that our growth in divine life develops.

John 12:20-33

Among those who went up to worship at the festival were some Greeks. These approached Philip, who came from Bethsaida in Galilee, and put this question to him, 'Sir, we should like to see Jesus.' Philip went to tell Andrew, and Andrew and Philip together went to tell Jesus.

Jesus replied to them:
'Now the hour has come
for the Son of Man to be glorified.
I tell you, most solemnly,
unless a wheat grain falls on the ground and dies,
it remains only a single grain
but if it dies,
it yields a rich harvest.
Anyone who loves his life loses it;
anyone who hates his life in this world
will keep it for the eternal life.
If a man serves me, he must follow me,
wherever I am, my servant will be there too.
If anyone serves me, my Father will honour him.
Now my soul is troubled.
What shall I say:
Father, save me from this hour?
But it was for this very reason that I have come to this hour.
Father, glorify your name!'
A voice came from heaven, 'I have glorified it, and I will glorify it again.' People standing by, who heard this, said it was a clap of thunder; others said, 'It was an angel speaking to him.' Jesus answered, 'It was not for my sake that this voice came, but for yours.
Now sentence is being passed on this world;
now the prince of this world is to be overthrown.
And when I am lifted up from the earth,
I shall draw all men to myself.'
By these words he indicated the kind of death he would die.

Good News

The wheat grain is a parable of how death opens up an expansion of life. It was the path taken by Jesus in obedience to the Father. And it is our way to eternal life.

First Reflection
An Appointment with Jesus

In the plan of John's gospel this passage marks the end of the public ministry of Jesus before the evangelist starts the narrative of the Last Supper.

Some Greeks come and ask to be introduced to Jesus. Their coming marks the end of a ministry which was restricted in time and place to the Jews. The time of preparatory signs has ended and so Jesus announces:

'Now the hour has come
for the Son of Man to be glorified.'

He takes the wheat grain as an example of the expansion of life which can occur only through death. The one grain which is buried will grow to become many. The life of Jesus which was restricted within the husk of his body would become available to many through the coming of the Holy Spirit. It would be a rich harvest. To avail of this sharing in the life of Jesus, the disciple must imitate the pattern of Jesus by dying to one-centredness in order to become love-centred and focused on many. One seed can eventually fill the whole field. And the life of Jesus is destined to fill the whole world. Those who follow Jesus and serve him will be honoured by the Father.

However, there would have to be a time of pain and dying before the bursting forth of new life: a winter before spring. Jesus admits to the agony in his soul. As a young man in the full flowering of vitality his whole human system recoils in shock at the looming prospect of death.

'Now is my soul troubled', he openly confesses.

Unlike the other evangelists, John did not write any account of the agony in Gethsemane. This text is his reference to the turmoil within Jesus. The Gethsemane agony took place in the darkness of night. But the agony mentioned by John is openly admitted and under broad daylight. Jesus is not depicted as weak in any sense but as fully in control of the situation. He is, as it were, fully assessing the cost before clearly submitting himself to the Father's will.

'Father, glorify your name!'

In today's second reading, the Epistle to the Hebrews has a

70

remarkable statement about the humble submission of Jesus to the will of the Father: 'Although he was Son, he learnt to obey through suffering.'

Obedience comes from the Latin word for hearing. It means listening to God as the voice which directs one's life. In this episode the Father's voice is heard to confirm the divine pleasure at what Jesus has done and is about to do.

'I have glorified it, and I will glorify it again.'

John then tells us of the different levels on which people heard this. Some thought it was a clap of thunder: these were the people who witnessed the signs worked by Jesus but saw them as no more than extraordinary physical happenings and made no move towards faith.

Others thought it was a angel speaking to Jesus: they accepted that the works of Jesus were beyond human power but they did not yet accept Jesus in faith.

Jesus knew that it was the voice of the Father for all to hear. The true disciples saw the hand of God in the works of Jesus and they heard God's voice in his words. They accepted Jesus in faith.

Jesus, observing these different reactions, announces:

'Now sentence is being passed on this world.'

As we saw in last week's reflection, people are their own judges in so far as they reject or accept Jesus. In each person's own response will be his/her own sentencing.

The hour of Jesus had come and it would be the climax of world history.

'Now the prince of this world is to be overthrown.'

The episode began with some people from an outside nation seeking an appointment with Jesus. And it ends with Jesus announcing that the hour has come and he is ready to receive all people of every nation. Like the grain, his death would mean an expansion of life. In opening his arms on the cross Jesus would embrace the whole world.

'When I am lifted up from the earth,
I shall draw all men to myself.'

The word DRAW can be an aid to remember the work of Jesus for us. The mystery of our faith is that Christ Died, Rose, Ascended and Will come again to take us to himself in glory.

Second Reflection
Drawn to the Crucified
We are near the time of year when our thoughts are drawn very

much towards Jesus on the cross. Indicating the kind of death he would endure, Jesus said:

'And when I am lifted up from the earth,
I shall draw all men to myself.'

As the career of Jesus progressed he was aware of the mounting wave of opposition. He could sense the intensity of the hostility. As he reached Jerusalem the inevitablility of the cross imposed itself more and more upon his thoughts. His mind was torn in two directions.

His young life and passion for all about him recoiled at the prospect of a sudden goodbye to it all. He openly admitted to the agitation in his innermost being: 'Now is my soul troubled.'

And he was afraid. He felt all the apprehension one experiences in the anticipation of suffering. Fear can act on us in two opposite ways. Sometimes it paralyses us and drains us of all energy. At other times it plunges us into a frantic threshing around as we seek to be distracted and diverted from the fearful prospect.

But the thoughts of Jesus also took account of the Father's will in what he was about to face. He could see it written in the law of growth apparent in every field around him. The seed must die before it multiplies. We must move on from where we are in order to advance. In the mind of Jesus his abandonment to the Father's will was deeper than the human fear he was experiencing.

The importance of motivation is expressed by Victor Frankl in his reflections on the harrowing experiences of people in Auschwitz: 'He who has a why to live can put up with any how.' The great why (or motive) for Jesus was always the Father. He was totally united with the Father's will.

In Lenten prayer we come before the crucifix. We see Jesus lifted up before our eyes. Totally given to the Father's will. And totally given up for love of us. Greater love no one can show than to give up one's life out of love for others.

He opened his arms on the cross ... a worldwide embrace ... for having loved his own who were in the world, he loved them to the end. His open arms invite all to come to him.

He is utterly defenceless, clutching no weapon of retaliation and clenching no fist in anger. He prays for forgiveness for his persecutors. Love has triumphed over hatred and bitterness.

In the weakness of death he shows the divine power of resurrection. In the foolishness of love he proves the wisdom of God.

Lenten prayer casts a light of examination on my conscience. For if the cross of Christ carries the greatest manifestation of love, then the greatest contradiction of the cross is selfishness. In the shadow of the cross I see how mean and selfish I am. How proud and arrogant. Bossy and tyrannical. Insensitive and hurtful. Judgmental and unforgiving.

I built unnecessary walls to keep others and their problems out of my reach. I make use of others for my own purposes and manipulate them by flattery or deceit.

I colour their motivation according to my own point of view and interpret everything to my own advantage. Sometimes I am in love with my own martyrdom and hold on to bitter memories long after the hurt was done to me.

True Christian love must be the crucifixion of selfishness before I am raised up to let Jesus love others through me.

> Lord Jesus, I see you lifted up before me, crucified to all self-ishness and abandoned to the Father's will.
>
> Draw me up out of my fears and selfish preoccupations.
>
> Help me to let go of all that I hold on to ... to empty my hands so that they can receive from you.
>
> Draw me into your heart so that my heart may lose its selfish-ness and be absorbed in your union with the Father.
>
> May I know what it is to abandon myself, as you did, to the glory of the Father.
>
> In me too, Father, glorify your name.

Passion Sunday

Because of the length of this passage, Mark 14:1 - 15:47, the reader is requested to take it from the lectionary or bible.

The Passion According to Mark

Mark's account of the Passion can be regarded as the drama of the Crucified Messiah. Jesus is the main character around whom the action revolves. Other characters come and go on the stage. Subplots crop up, are dropped and come back again to serve the main plot. The drama unfolds in four acts.

Act I: The Conspiracy 14: 1-25

In the first act Mark is setting the scene by introducing the various strands which will eventually be pulled together.

First we are told of the timing of the event. It will prove very significant. It is Passover time. Whether or not the Last Supper was a true Passover meal is debated by the scholars, but at least the events of these days must be interpreted in the light of the Passover.

There is a brief introduction to the conspiracy to get rid of Jesus (14:1-2) The stage is then taken over by the meal at Bethany (14:3-9). The unnamed woman comes in and anoints the head of Jesus. People were expecting the Messiah to receive a great royal anointing to mark his solemn entrance into Jerusalem. But this humble anointing reverses all the grandiose schemes. This is one of Mark's recurring themes – how the plans of God were for a humble servant whereas the people were expecting a great outward show of power and prestige.

The anointing sparks off a controversy which only shows how much the disciples were out of touch with the magnitude of what was about to happen. Some consider it a waste of money which should have been given to the poor. But the answer of Jesus lets us know that the story which is about to unfold has a significance for all times and for all peoples. Only a small mind would confine it to feeding a handful of people for a week.

As the scene changes there is a brief mention of Judas, one of the twelve, who was negotiating with the conspirators to betray Jesus. (14:10-11)

The focus light then rests on Jesus. He is making arrangements for the Last Supper. One small detail which may be quite significant is the mention of the man carrying the pitcher of water (14:13).

Fetching the water was a job usually done by women and jealously retained as their daily opportunity for meeting others at the well. And if men did carry water it was usually in a water-sack rather than in a pitcher on the head. Perhaps this man who was doing the woman's job had no wife. Could it be that he was an associate of the celibate Essene community near the Dead Sea? What is significant about this conjecture is the fact that the Essenes followed an ancient calendar which differed from that of the priests in Jerusalem. The Essene Passover meal would have been held that year on the Tuesday whereas the Jerusalem celebration was on the Friday. Jesus, who had no great alliance with the Pharisees, may have followed the Essene calendar by celebrating the Passover on the Tuesday. But according to the Jerusalem calendar the time of his death coincided with the slaughtering of the Passover lambs in the Temple. It allows more time for fitting in all the events and trials which took place before Friday morning. It all makes for a very interesting theory though it has not received much backing from the scholars.

At the Last Supper there are two happenings related to the main story: the prediction of betrayal and the institution of the Eucharist. As Judas is opting out Jesus is arranging to stay.

Our attention is brought back to Judas, one of the twelve. 'Alas for that man by whom the Son of Man is betrayed! Better for that man if he had never been born!.' (14:21) We must not regard this as a curse of condemnation on the part of Jesus. Rather, it is a statement of fact about the betrayer's self-inflicted condemnation.

Then follows the action of Jesus with the bread and wine. We must keep in mind the ritual of the Passover meal. The youngest of the family would ask why they were eating unleavened bread. The head of the household then explained that it was a reminder of the haste with which their forefathers left Egypt, the land of slavery, on the night of their liberation. At the Last Supper Jesus explains the meaning of the bread and wine. 'This is my body', he says of the bread. And taking the wine: 'This is my blood, the blood of the covenant, which is to be poured out for many.' The meal is thus interpreted as an enactment of the new liberation from slavery and the new covenant between God and humanity.

Act II: Jesus is Deserted 14: 26-52

The main themes of the story have been introduced. Mark now focuses our attention on the central character, Jesus.

Throughout the gospel Mark has emphasised how much Jesus has been misunderstood by those around him. Now at the moment of crisis he is totally alone. He will be abandoned by all, betrayed by one of the twelve, denied by Peter and feel alienated from the Father.

Jesus quotes the prophet Zechariah about the scattering of the sheep when the shepherd is attacked. Peter arrogantly says that he will never turn his back. But Jesus warns him of his forthcoming denials.

They reach Gethsemane. This is the third time that Mark mentions Jesus at prayer. In all three instances it is a time of pain and crisis. Mark holds back nothing of the human anguish in Jesus. 'And a sudden fear came over him, and great distress.' His soul is sorrowful to the point of death. In his loneliness he reaches out for companionship and support. Three times he comes back to the three closest disciples only to find them asleep. When he speaks to Peter he addresses him as Simon, for at this moment he does not deserve the name of the rock of support.

Marching footsteps crunch the gravel, coming closer. Flickering lights dance fitfully through the olive trees. Soldiers have come to arrest them, guided by Judas. For a third time Mark calls him one of the twelve. They all desert him and run away. Jesus is left alone in the midst of enemies.

Act III: The Trials 14:53 - 15:15

Mark tells us of two trials of Jesus: first before the Jewish High Council (Sanhedrin) and then before the political court of Pilate. There is no mention of going before Herod.

The Sanhedrin have their minds made up already that he is to be found guilty and given the death-sentence. But finding a charge that will stick proves tricky. They try him first about threatening to destroy the Temple. The efforts of the witnesses are so pathetic that Jesus does not even attempt to answer them. His silence indicates that it is impossible to communicate with people whose minds are closed by prejudice.

The high priest quickly sees that they cannot get away with any trumped-up charge so he has to come out with the crunch question which he would rather not have had to face. The words must have been ashes in his mouth: 'Are you the Christ, the Son of the Blessed One?'

Jesus replied: 'I am, and you will see the Son of Man seated at the right hand of the Power and coming with the clouds of heaven.' At this the high priest goes through a charade of righteous indignation, pronounces it as blasphemy and calls for the sentence of death.

Before the political trial, Mark has the interlude of Peter's denials. Each one is stronger than the preceding one. Again we note that Mark has the storyteller's instinct of relating an episode in three steps. At the third denial Peter starts to call down curses on his own head. How this chosen and blessed man has fallen to a cursed condition!

The cock crows once, twice ... and Peter remembers the Lord's prediction. He goes outside and bursts into tears. And that's the last time we meet Peter in Mark's gospel. He certainly made no effort to portray the apostles in any sort of flattering light. The other evangelists, writing later than Mark and when the position of the various apostles was highly regarded, were far more sympathetic towards them. But Mark's brutal honesty can help us to cope with any sinful humanity we meet with in the church. If that is what the first apostles were like, why be scandalised by anything today!

Night yields to morning and the Jewish leaders waste no time in pursuing their scheme. Jesus is led to Pilate. Mark is very sparing in his description of the trial. Pilate quickly concludes that there is no threat to be feared from Jesus as a king, but the problem is the jealousy of the chief priests. The mob has been worked up and Pilate lacks the courage to go against them. He tries to play them with irony, making the gesture of offering the release of a captive in honour of their feast. 'Do you want me to release for you the king of the Jews?' But the conspirators are not going to back down in the face of irony. The name of Barabbas is mentioned and the mob take it up and cry for his release. Pilate's weak effort has misfired. Anxious to pacify the crowd he releases Barabbas, orders that Jesus be scourged and hands him over to be crucified.

Act IV: Crucifixion 15: 16-39

The spare words of Mark carry us very quickly through the soldiers' burlesque of crowning Jesus in a cap of thorns.

He is led out carrying the cross, or at least the crossbeam. The passer-by, Simon from Cyrene in North Africa, is commandeered to help. Mark mentions that Simon is the father of Alexander and Rufus who must have been known to the local church where Mark was writing. Perhaps they are mentioned as two witnesses who could legally verify the authenticity of his story. They reach Golgotha, the place of the skull.

Mark notes the passing hours. It is the third hour (9am) when the nailing begins. Jesus refuses the narcotic drink which was allowed to lessen the pain. The charge is nailed above his head for all to read. His cross is raised between those of two robbers.

In addition to the physical pain, the taunts and mockery continue. The passers-by jeer and the chief priests and scribes lose any shred of dignity that was left to them as they join in the mockery. But Mark sees a tremendous irony in their jibes. Their three taunts are precisely the areas of accomplishment by Jesus, could they but see it. They taunt him about destroying the Temple and it is the very moment when the Temple religion is being surpassed and left redundant. 'Save yourself' they cry ... and he is in fact saving the whole world just then. They ask him to come down from the cross, but throughout the gospel he has insisted on being understood in relationship to this cross.

There is nobody to understand him or support him in his pain. Even the two robbers join in the mockery. Mark says nothing of the repentance of one thief, as Luke, the evangelist of mercy, does.

The clock has ticked on and it is midday, the sixth hour. It ought to be the hour of maximum light but a strange darkness envelopes the land. There is no further mention of mockery in this darkness.

The ninth hour (3pm) arrives. The drained lungs and dry mouth of Jesus find the energy of utter desperation to cry out: 'My God, my God, why have you deserted me?' These are the opening words of Psalm 21 which eventually becomes a prayer of trust and hope. But there are no grounds here in Mark's gospel for saying that Jesus anticipated the final note of hope. According to Mark, the desolation and abandonment felt by Jesus is total.

Once again we meet with Mark's habit of inserting a little detail which delays the progress of the main drama. The Hebrew word 'Eloi' which Jesus used, is misunderstood as a reference to Elijah. 'He is calling on Elijah.' Someone tries to offer him a soothing drink to delay his dying so that Elijah might eventually arrive to his assistance. There is no mockery at this stage, only fear and awe at what was happening on this day of darkness.

Then Mark is back to the main drama. 'Jesus gave a loud cry.' It has all the drama of the operatic stage where the consumptive soprano somehow manages to reach notes of sheer brilliance in her dying breath. Unreal perhaps but ever so dramatic!

'Jesus gave a loud cry and breathed his last'.

Full stop. End of story. Or is it?

A moment's pause and Mark continues. 'And the veil of the Temple was torn in two from top to bottom.' The veil had been there to prevent people from entering the sacred place. But now the rending of that veil shows that Jesus has opened up access to God for all people. The birds of mockery have come home to roost.

And Mark has a further point to make. Out of this moment of apparent tragedy comes the climax of the entire gospel: 'In truth this man was son of God.' Mark had opened his gospel as the Good News about Jesus Christ, the Son of God. At the end of the story it is an outsider, the Roman centurion, who is the first person to say who Jesus really is ... Son of God.

Conclusion 15: 40-47

The drama is over. All that remains is to clean up the stage, as it were. Mark's dramatic haste now changes to a quiet, dignified account of the burial of Jesus.

We are left in silence to ponder before the bare cross. How strange the ways of God which allowed the Beloved Son to suffer such violence and humiliation, such abandonment and alienation. Mark has let the reader know in no uncertain terms that Jesus has served us with an absolute, unlimited giving of his life.

To be a disciple of Jesus does not mean having divine magic at one's command. It means sharing in the cross of Jesus but knowing that no matter how bad the experience we suffer, Jesus has been there before us.

Mark would agree with Paul in his discovery of how to meet Christ in the experience of darkness: 'My grace is enough for you: my power is at its best in weakness.' (2 Cor 12:9)

Mark's point is that the way of discipleship is the way of the cross. It is a teaching which is not readily accepted in our pampered culture today.

'If anyone wants to be a follower of mine, let him renounce himself and take up his cross and follow me.' (Mk 8:34)

Holy Thursday

The liturgy of Holy Thursday grows out of two commandments of the Lord.

'Do this as a memorial of me.' (1 Cor 11:24) – from which our eucharistic celebration originates.

'Copy what I have done to you.' (Jn 13:15) – the divine life which we share in through the Eucharist must be brought outside the church building by taking Christ's love and service to other people.

John 13: 1-15

It was before the festival of the Passover, and Jesus knew that the hour had come for him to pass from this world to the Father. He had always loved those who were his in the world, but now he showed how perfect his love was.

They were at supper, and the devil had already put it into the mind of Judas Iscariot, son of Simon, to betray him. Jesus knew that the Father had put everything into his hands and that he had come from God and was returning to God, and he got up from table, removed his outer garment and, taking a towel, wrapped it round his waist; he then poured water into a basin and began to wash the disciples' feet and to wipe them with the towel he was wearing.

He came to Simon Peter, who said to him, 'Lord, are you going to wash my feet?' Jesus answered, 'At the moment you do not know what I am doing but later you will understand.' 'Never!' said Peter. 'You shall never wash my feet.' Jesus replied, 'If I do not wash you, you can have nothing in common with me.' 'Then, Lord,' said Simon Peter, 'not only my feet but my hands and my head as well.' Jesus said, 'No one who has taken a bath needs washing, he is clean all over. You too are clean, though not all of you are.' He knew who was going to betray him, that was why he said, 'though not all of you are.'

When he had washed their feet and put on his clothes again he went back to the table. 'Do you understand,' he said, 'what I have done to you? You call me Master and Lord, and rightly; so I am. If I then, the Lord and Master, have washed your feet, you should wash each other's feet. I have given you an example so that you may copy what I have done to you.'

Good News
The Lord Jesus Christ lives in us through the sacraments and works for people through our charity.

Reflection
One is surprised on first learning that John's gospel contains no account of the institution of the Eucharist. However he devoted the whole of Chapter 6 to the theme of the bread of life. His theology of what the sacrament means is beautifully developed there. Later this year we will spend five Sundays with that chapter.

Today's extract from John 13 represents another aspect of Eucharist. The act of humble service performed by Jesus is an example to us of how to live up to the challenge of the Eucharist. If we are nourished on Christ's life in the Bread of Life, then we are given the mission of bringing his life and love to others.

The time-context mentioned is very significant, the festival of the Passover. This feast recalled the journey of the Hebrews out of slavery into freedom (cf First Reading). They passed safely through the waters of the Red Sea. The other evanegelists seem to regard the Last Supper as a Passover meal. But John clearly states that the meal he writes of took place before the Passover. In his mind the true Passover sacrifice of that year was not in the killing of the many lambs in the Temple but in the sacrificial death of Jesus, the lamb of God, on Calvary. This fulfilling of the Feast of Passing is indicated by John: 'Jesus knew that the hour had come for him to pass from this world to the Father.' The journey from slavery in Egypt to freedom was a prefigurement of our passing from this world to God.

John then makes the point that love is the only motive which can explain the actions of Jesus, first in washing the feet of the disciples and then in laying down his life in sacrifice. His love was perfect, that is it went the whole way to the utmost expression.

What takes place at that supper is a story on two levels. On the human level of events, the progression towards Calvary is advanced when John mentions the intention of Judas to betray Jesus. But on the divine level this is understood as part of the great story of how Jesus was going back to the Father from whom he had come. The good news for our lives is that Jesus draws all people to himself in his own rising up. This new life is manifested in living no longer in a self-ish way but in a manner resembling the humble service of Jesus.

Jesus performed the service which pupils might sometimes offer their rabbi. He reversed the roles in a startling lesson.

The mention of water should be pondered a while since it is

such a rich symbol of divine life in this gospel. Jesus is to be the Lamb of God who takes away the sin of the world, and the water he uses in this instance is a sign of purification. The picture of Jesus on his knees washing feet anticipates the service he was to perform in laying down his life to cleanse us from sin.

A literary device often used by John is to have somebody misunderstand Jesus and this offers an opportunity for further development of an idea. Here it is Simon Peter who objects. Trust Peter! Always the one to put his foot in it except this one occasion when Jesus wanted him to put his foot into something!

But Jesus insists: 'Unless you let me wash you, you can have no share in me.' Jesus is speaking of the great spiritual washing and renewal through sharing in his life. But Peter is still thinking in a limited, literal sense of washing. 'Then, Lord, wash not only my feet, but my hands and head as well.' Jesus has to explain that this is not a matter of physical washing. It is like the old story of entering the Red Sea and passing into new life with Jesus. A new life and a new way of thinking and behaving in the humble service of love, as Jesus is showing them.

'Do you understand what I have done to you? Do you understand that I have given you the headline to follow if you want to follow me?' Love is not just an emotion or feeling. It must be practical and expressed in action. That is why Jesus gave a lesson of practical service.

The challenge of receiving the Eucharist is to live out the example of Jesus. In the sacrament we receive an infusion of divine energy. Each time we receive we grow more like Christ. Our passover from selfishness to humble love is developed. Our feet are washed of the dust of self-centred journeys.

In the celebration of the Eucharist we recall the death and resurrection of Jesus in his return to the Father. Lifted up in glory, he draws us up to a better life.

We remember so that we might re-member: that we might be the members of Christ's body on earth today, carrying on his loving service in our own time.

He has no hands now but ours.

Good Friday

The Passion According to John (18:1 -19:42)

It is hardly surprising that Christian art should have depicted the crucifixion in so many different ways since the four evangelists differed considerably in their respective attitudes towards the story of the Passion.

On Palm Sunday we reflected on Mark's account of the Passion. It was remarkable for the physical violence done to Jesus, the humiliation and mockery he had to endure, his loneliness through abandonment and betrayal. There was no comforting support there from his mother or relations. He suffered under darkness and cried out in the pain of alienation from the Father.

How different is the picture given by John! The emphasis is taken from the human suffering of Jesus and placed on his regal nobility. John makes no mention of anything that would suggest weakness on the part of Jesus. He omits the anguished loneliness of Gethsemane, the need of help from Simon of Cyrene, the weeping women who offer consolation, the offer of a narcotic drink to lessen the pain, the hours of darkness and the utter dereliction of Jesus's cry to the Father.

While there is frantic movement and activity all around him, Jesus at the centre is serenely in control of the situation. It has been remarked that in John's account there is no passion, for Jesus freely allows everything to happen. The other evangelists call us to weep before the sufferings of Jesus, but John invites us to contemplate the great saving actions of that day when Jesus passed from the lowest point of human weakness back to the Father. 'Jesus knew that the hour had come for him to pass from this world to the Father.' (Jn 13:l) John emphasises the freedom of Jesus throughout, even at the final moment when the Father's will is perfectly completed: 'It is accomplished,' Jesus announces triumphantly.

There are several little details which suggest an eye-witness account, such as giving the name Malchus to the servant whose ear was cut off, the identification of the paved courtyard (Lithostratos) where Pilate sat in judgment, and the charcoal fire where Peter went to warm his hands. Yet the concern of John is not so much about detailed accuracy as the theological importance of the whole event. It is the hour of at-one-ment when the Son of God, who has bent down to the lowest point of the human condition in dying, now rises up in glory and draws all of humanity up with him.

Jesus once described his mission as a movement down from heaven and then back up in return.

'I have come from the Father and have come into the world and now I leave the world to go to the Father.' (Jn 16:28) Throughout the Passion he is both king coming down from above and priest rising up from below.

As king, he is the one who has come from God and is always in perfect union with the Father's will. As priest, he represents humanity in our desire to offer a fitting sacrifice to God.

1. Jesus as King

John makes no mention of the Jewish trial of Jesus before the Sanhedrin or the charges relating to destroying the Temple. These matters have been adequately dealt with by John already. But the trial before Pilate, which is on the issue of kingship, is related at some length. There is great strength in Jesus's reply to Pilate: 'Yes, I am a king. I was born for this, I came into the world for this: to bear witness to the truth.'

Pilate, who respects the ways of military power and political bargaining, is cynical about truth. But the light of truth which is in Jesus shows up the true standing of all the other characters. The soldiers who came with torches and weapons to arrest him are shown to be weak as they are thrown back and fall to the ground. Caiaphas is shown to be no true priest but a small-minded conspirator protecting the interests of his own circle. Pilate who thinks he is the judge with power is in fact the one who is being judged: he is seen to be a weak politican who yields to the pressure of the threat to blacken his name before Caesar.

John shows his typical use of irony ... when a character says something which is far more true than he realises. The chief priests have fallen so much from all they ought to stand for that they eventually insist: 'We have no king except Caesar.' By their behaviour they had cut themselves off from having God as their king. The opposite side of the coin has Pilate, the Roman Governor, stubbornly insisting that Jesus is the king of the Jews. In fact he has it written in Hebrew, Latin and Greek so as to proclaim it to the universe. Little does he realise how true it is.

Even on the cross Jesus remains in control. He makes provision for the care of his mother. He knowingly fulfils the words of scripture, saying: 'I am thirsty.' Even the moment of death is described as the free choice of Jesus. 'It is accomplished,' he said and then, 'bowing his head he gave up his spirit.' Death on the cross usually came when the lungs of the victim could no longer function as the head and chest increasingly weighed down. John has depicted Jesus freely deciding to bow his head and when to return his final breath (spirit) to the One from whom all breath is borrowed.

Throughout John's account then, Jesus is free, noble and kingly to the very end.

2. Jesus as Priest

If Jesus as king is God bending down to our human condition, then Jesus as priest represents humanity rising towards God in offering sacrifice. A priest intercedes with God on behalf of humanity and offers gifts and sacrifices.

The theme of priesthood is woven into the story by the recurring references to the Passover and to sacrifice. The sentencing of Jesus took place at 'about the sixth hour' on the Passover Preparation Day. There were but six hours remaining for the slaughtering and cooking of the paschal lambs for the Passover of the following day. John heightens the sense that Jesus is the true Lamb of God whose sacrificial death took place as the lambs in the Temple were being slaughtered.

And as the true Lamb, the law was fulfilled when his legs were not broken. In this instance and throughout the story the soldiers are participants in the great plan of God, even though they do not know it.

When the side of Jesus was pierced, blood and water poured out. This is medically possible, but John's interest is in the significance of the blood of sacrifice and the water of new life. It leads him to recall the words of the prophet: 'They will look on the one whom they have pierced.'

John's story invites us to look at the events of the day and to meditate on their significance. It is the hour when Jesus is finally lifted up from the earth. As king divine and as priest for us, he lifts us up with him. He draws all people to himself. John's crucifix is no instrument of torture but a royal throne and the tree of life.

Abroad the regal banners fly
Now shines the Cross's mystery;
Upon it Life did death endure,
And yet by death did life procure. (Sixth Century Hymn)

After the reading of John's Passion, the liturgy extends the priestly and kingly roles of Christ. In the power of his priesthood, intercessions are made for all the people of the world. And then his kingship is recognised when we, his subjects, come in veneration before the royal throne of the cross.

85

Easter Vigil

The Easter Vigil is the high point of our year. The ceremony is in four stages:
— the symbolic victory of light over darkness;
— the story is told in the liturgy of the readings;
— the renewal of our baptismal commitment to the risen Lord;
— in the Eucharist we receive the Bread of Life to strengthen us to live up to our commitment.

The liturgy of the word is extended with several readings which enrich our understanding of all that Christ's resurrection fulfilled. The story of creation is recalled to set the context for the elevation of creation to the new life in the risen Christ. Then we hear of the covenant with Abraham which is surpassed in the new family of God which the resurrection inaugurates. The story of how Moses led the people out of slavery is a key reading, setting the background for the liberation won by Christ. A selection of readings from the prophets look forward to renewal of the covenant in the messianic age. After the Gloria of the Mass, we hear Paul telling the Romans that baptism means a life of dying to sin so as to live in a Christ-like manner.

Mark 16:1-8

When the sabbath was over, Mary of Magdala, Mary the mother of James, and Salome, brought spices with which to go and anoint him. And very early in the morning on the first day of the week they went to the tomb, just as the sun was rising.

They had been saying to one another, 'Who will roll away the stone for us from the entrance to the tomb?' But when they looked they could see that the stone—which was very big—had already been rolled back. On entering the tomb they saw a young man in a white robe seated on the right-hand side, and they were struck with amazement.

But he said to them, 'There is no need for alarm. You are looking for Jesus of Nazareth, who was crucified: he has risen, he is not here. See, here is the place where they laid him. But you must go and tell his disciples and Peter, "He is going before you to Galilee; it is there you will see him, just as he told you." ' And the women came out and ran away from the tomb because they were frightened out of their wits; and they said nothing to a soul, for they were afraid.

Reflection
The Proclamation of the Resurrection

There is no attempt here, nor indeed anywhere in Sacred Scripture, to give a physical description to the mystery of the resurrection. What Mark offers us is the testimony of 'a young man in white' who tells the women that Jesus of Nazareth, who was crucified, has risen from the dead.

Mark's Passion Narrative is framed between two stories about women anointing the body of Jesus. The sabbath was over at sundown on the Saturday evening. The women then bought the spices and ointments that they needed. Very early next morning, on the first day of the week, they went to the tomb. It was the first day of the new age of re-created humanity. The rising sun signified the light of God smiling on the renewed earth.

There is a nice little human touch in the way that the women were so preoccupied bringing all that they would need that they forgot about rolling back the large, circular stone which acted as a door to the tomb. But to their surprise, the job was done. They were even more surprised at the sight of a young man in a white robe seated at the right-hand side. Obviously this was no ordinary mortal. 'There is no need for alarm', he said to them. Messages from God were invariably introduced with an encouragement to let go of all fear. And what was this divine annunciation? 'I know you are looking for Jesus, who was crucified. He is not here, for he has risen, as he said he would.' It is the proclamation of the resurrection of Jesus.

But who was that young man in the white robe? Matthew writes that it was an angel who gave the news of the resurrection to the women. Mark however says it was a young man, using the same word as he had used for the young man who had witnessed the arrest of Jesus but who had run away naked, leaving his garment in the grasp of the soldier who tried to grab hold of him. (Mk 14:52)

If Mark intends a connection between the two young men, then it is a symbolic reference to baptism: the young man who has cast off the old garment and is now clad in white is the herald of the good news of the resurrection.

A further step with this conjecture attempts to identify this herald with the author himself. Since Mark alone mentions the young man at the arrest of Jesus, many commentators suggest that he was Mark. So, the baptismal figure in white who proclaims the resurrection of the crucified Messiah may be a symbolic reference to Mark's own mission as an evangelist ... the herald of the resurrection of the crucified Servant of God.

This mysterious herald of the resurrection instructed the women to tell the disciples and Peter to head for Galilee. Mark has already flown in the face of religious convention in having an outsider, the Roman centurion, as the first to call Jesus 'Son of God'. He does so again in writing that the women were the first to be asked to proclaim the resurrection. However, they were frightened out of their wits, and they said nothing, for they were afraid. They were given a message for the disciples and Peter: 'He is going before you into Galilee: it is there you will see him, just as he told you.'

Peter is mentioned especially because of his denials. All of them are rehabilitated as followers of the one who is going before them. Back to Galilee where Jesus was accepted, unlike Jerusalem where he was rejected. Galilee was where he crossed the sea over and back to unite Jewish and Gentile sides. Galilee now stands for the universal mission of the rehabilitated disciples.

'You will see him there, just as he told you.' This seeing could refer to apparitions of the risen Lord or even to the expectation of his final coming. But most likely it is seeing in the sense of faith... that the disciples will finally understand Jesus and his mission. Now at last they will see and understand that Jesus was the true Messiah in his act of total servanthood on the cross.

Darkness has yielded to light in the sunrise of the first day of the week. The days of blindness and misunderstanding are over as the disciples finally see and believe. Now they are restored and, in believing, they accept the crucified Messiah who has risen.

In our Easter Vigil we proceed from Mark's proclamation of the resurrection to the renewal of our baptismal commitment to Jesus Christ who died and rose again. In our baptismal life we are summoned, like the first disciples, to follow him who goes before us. We undertake a life of crucifying our sinful passions, promising to live the new life of the Christian way.

Then, after this renewal of baptism, we proceed to the Bread of Life. There we receive the divine strength to live up to our promises and to carry on as true disciples.

Easter Sunday

'The resurrection is the unique and sensational event on which the whole of human history turns'. (Pope Paul VI) It is so central to our Christian belief that St Paul stated: 'If Christ has not been raised then our preaching is useless and your believing is useless.' (1 Cor 15:14)

John 20: 1-9
The tomb of death is empty: Jesus Christ is risen, and the story of humanity will never be the same again.

It was very early on the first day of the week and still dark, when Mary of Magdala came to the tomb. She saw that the stone had been moved away from the tomb and came running to Simon Peter and the other disciple, the one Jesus loved. 'They have taken the Lord out of the tomb,' she said, 'and we don't know where they have put him.'

So Peter set out with the other disciple to go to the tomb. They ran together, but the other disciple, running faster than Peter, reached the tomb first; he bent down and saw the linen cloths lying on the ground, but did not go in. Simon Peter who was following now came up, went right into the tomb, saw the linen cloths on the ground, and also the cloth that had been over his head; this was not with the linen cloths but rolled up in a place by itself. Then the other disciple who had reached the tomb first also went in; he saw and he believed. Till this moment they had failed to understand the teaching of scripture, that he must rise from the dead.

First Reflection
The Third Day

We believe that 'Christ died for our sins, in accordance with the scriptures; that he was buried; and that he was raised to life on the third day, in accordance with the scriptures.' (1 Cor 15:3-4)

There were many incidents in Old Testament history where people were rescued on the third day. If you think of it, the third day is part of the storyteller's stock in trade. On the first day the problem arises: on the second day there is no way out of it: but on the third day the unexpected arrives and all is changed.

The most beautiful third day text is where Hosea urges the people to repent and to return to God.

Come, let us return to Yahweh.
He has torn us to pieces, but he will heal us;
he has struck us down, but he will bandage our wounds;
after a day or two he will bring us back to life,
on the third day he will raise us
and we shall live in his presence. (Hos 6:1-3)

The events of the passion and resurrection of Jesus are told in the story of three days. The Jewish day was measured from sunset to sunset. The first day began on the evening of the Thursday and lasted until sundown on the Friday. It carries us from the Last Supper into Gethsemane, the arrest and trial of Jesus, his crucifixion and death. His burial occurred just before sundown.

The second day was the sabbath, from Friday sunset until Saturday sunset. We can regard it as our time of waiting for the coming of God. The Apostles' Creed says of Christ that he descended into hell. This is not suggesting that he experienced the state of damnation. The word hell originally meant the hiding place of the dead. The phrase in the creed is a way of saying that Christ, who came down for all, embraced unto himself all those who lived and died before his time on earth. The second day is when it seems our problems are insurmountable, that there is no way out of the tomb, that life itself is dead. But the lesson is to stay there in hope until the power of God will come to visit us in our place of darkness.

The third day emerges out of the darkness of very early Sunday morning. It was still dark when Mary of Magdala came to the tomb. More significant was the darkness of mind that enveloped the faith of Magdalen, Peter and the beloved disciple. They could see but they did not understand.

Magdalen saw that the stone had been rolled away from the tomb. But her mind concluded, 'They have taken the Lord out of the tomb, and we don't know where they have put him.'

Simon Peter and the beloved disciple then ran together to the tomb. Peter entered the tomb. It was empty. And he saw the linen cloths lying on the ground and the cloth which had been over Jesus's face. Peter noted where the cloths were placed: like a detective amassing a dossier of facts. But as yet all he understood was emptiness: empty tomb and empty linens.

Then the beloved disciple went in. And in the place of human emptiness he discovered divine fulness. 'He saw and he believed.' Jesus had to visit the place of death if the full demands of the incarnation were to be met, but now this tomb is empty, for he has gone through death to new life.

The linens are empty, not just to prove that the body wasn't stolen, but to show that he had cast off the clothing of physical flesh. He has passed beyond the need of material adornments. He is not here in one place only because now he is everywhere.

The words of Hosea have acquired a new depth of meaning: 'On the third day he will raise us and we shall live in his presence.' It was an old Irish custom to rise early on Easter morning to see the sun dancing, for all creation rejoices in the conquest of death and in the new life that the Lord has brought.

The third day is when we awake from the sleep of darkness and begin to see with understanding. On the third day we are woken up with light and a song of joy. We are called to rise up and to walk in God's presence for the rest of our days.

John notes that the third day was really the first day of the week. It is the first day of the rest of our lives.

Second Reflection
Risen in us
In the darkest days of Stalinist Russia a special League of the Godless was established to stamp out the last vestiges of religion from peoples' lives. One Easter Sunday morning the Commissar of this League addressed a huge rally in Moscow's Red Square. He ranted along his usual lines that religion is the instrument of the bourgeoisie and the opium of the proletarait. At the end of his harangue he generously offered the microphone to anybody who wished to debate with him. Nobody there wanted a one-way ticket to Siberia until one old man made his way forward. He surveyed his huge audience, cleared his throat and began to sing: 'The Lord is risen.' It was the traditional Orthodox Easter greeting. Moved by the old man's courage, voices from the square swelled up in reply: 'He has truly risen.'

Religion in Russia was not dead as long as belief in the resurrection of Christ was not dead in people.

Easter is not just the annual commemoration of a past event as a nation might commemorate some great victory. Easter must always be our realisation that Christ is life: alive in the Father's glory but also alive in us.

Jesus said that when he was lifted up from the earth he would draw all people to himself. He draws us up to participate in supernatural life. We are called to live according to standards and values which are more noble than those which the natural life can ever attain. This is where secularistic humanism falls short. It does not recognise the lifting up of human life in Christ's resurrection. It does not understand supernatural life, nor the meaning of sanctifying grace.

Sanctifying grace is the gift of God to us which lifts us up to participate even here on earth in divine life.

This new life is planted in us as a tiny seed in baptism. The tiny plant is nourished in a supportive climate of prayer, instruction and good example. The divine energy within us is wonderfully increased by the Eucharist. And it is restored to us in the healing of our failures in the sacrament of Reconciliation. When this baptismal life within one grows, it will bear fruit in a mind that sees things from Christ's perspective and in a behaviour which is increasingly a true imitation of Christ.

No writer has given us better descriptions of baptismal life than St Paul. In today's second reading he tells the Colossians: 'You have died, and now the life you have is hidden with Christ in God.' He goes on to exhort them to live up to the rhythm of baptism by always dying to the ways of sin and living by the behaviour of Christ. 'You have stripped off your old behaviour with your old self, and you have put on a new self which will progress towards true knowledge the more it is renewed in the image of its creator.' (Col 3: 9-10)

Easter day, according to the gospel, was the first day of the week ... the first day of a new age ... the first day of the human race lifted up in the beginning of divine participation.

And Easter is celebrated not only one day in the year, but every day in the soul of any person who is alive in Christ ... thinking, behaving and loving as he did. The Lord has truly risen and he is alive and working through every follower who walks in his footsteps.

Second Sunday of Easter

Today's gospel passage is in three parts:
the commissioning of the disciples in the power of the Spirit;
Thomas' act of faith;
the purpose of the evangelist is to lead people to faith in
Jesus Christ.

John 20: 19-31

In the evening of that same day, the first day of the week, the
doors were closed in the room where the disciples were, for fear of
the Jews. Jesus came and stood among them. He said to them,
'Peace be with you,' and showed them his hands and his side. The
disciples were filled with joy when they saw the Lord, and he said to
them again, 'Peace be with you.

>'As the Father sent me,
>so am I sending you.'

After saying this he breathed on them and said:

>'Receive the Holy Spirit.
>For those whose sins you forgive,
>they are forgiven;
>for those whose sins you retain,
>they are retained.'

Thomas, called the Twin, who was one of the Twelve, was not
with them when Jesus came. When the disciples said, 'We have seen
the Lord,' he answered, 'Unless I see the holes that the nails made in
his hands and can put my finger into the holes they made, and unless
I can put my hand into his side, I refuse to believe.'

Eight days later the disciples were in the house again and
Thomas was with them. The doors were closed but Jesus came in
and stood among them. 'Peace be with you,' he said. Then he spoke
to Thomas, 'Put your finger here; look, here are my hands. Give me
your hand; put it into my side. Doubt no longer but believe.' Thomas
replied, 'My Lord and my God!'

Jesus said to him:

>'You believe because you can see me.
>Happy are those who have not seen and yet believe.'

There were many other signs that Jesus worked and the disciples saw, but they are not recorded in this book. These are recorded
so that you may believe that Jesus is the Christ, the Son of God, and
that believing this you may have life through his name.

Good News
The days of the ministry of Jesus may be over but his work continues. The Risen Lord sends out the disciples, in the power of the Spirit, to bring forgiveness and divine life to the whole world.

First Reflection
The transition of Thomas
The story begins in a dark atmosphere which has not been penetrated by the light and joy of the resurrection. The disciples are locked away physically behind closed doors and mentally in fear. But the risen Lord comes in a power which penetrates all physical and mental barriers. His victory is announced in his greeting ... Peace ... Shalom ... all is well, God is in control.

As he shows them his wounded hands and pierced side they can be sure of his identity. The one who was crucified is truly risen. Everything changes for them and they are filled with joy.

Jesus then speaks to them of the two missions. First was his own mission when he was sent by the Father. His mission was now completed and the second mission was about to commence. 'As the Father sent me so am I sending you.'

They are commissioned to carry on his work. He breathes on them and prays over them as they receive the divine Spirit who had inspired his own ministry. And their work will be for the forgiveness of sins, just as the name of Jesus indicated one who would save the people from their sins.

In this bestowal of the Holy Spirit we can see the beginning of the Church, which is the human community of the risen Lord, carrying on his work on earth. The sacrament of Reconciliation can be traced to this gift of the Spirit with the power of forgiveness. But, indeed, the mission of salvation is not restricted to the sacraments but is carried on in all apostolates of Christian education, ministries of caring, and works for justice and peace.

The second episode in this passage occurs a week later, on the eight day. Our attention is drawn to Thomas who had missed the earlier appearance. Thomas, cautious in the extreme, refused to believe the others. He could see all the reasons for not accepting their excitement. This is quite in keeping with the other episodes where we meet him. For instance, at the time when Jesus went towards Jerusalem to visit Lazarus, all Thomas could forsee was certain death facing them all. But to his credit he was loyal despite his fears: 'Let us go too, and die with him.' (Jn 11:16)

Cautiousness and loyalty are often found together in the one character. These people will be slow to join your cause, but slower still to desert you. A sort of misguided loyalty kept Thomas back in the old days of the first mission, when Jesus was physically with them. His doors were stubbornly closed until the risen Lord came personally to him to invite him to come forward into the new age.

The Lord appreciated the caution of Thomas and knew of his loyalty. And it is from Thomas that we hear the purest act of faith in Jesus on the lips of anybody in the gospel: 'My Lord and my God!' He proclaimed Jesus as the one, true God of Israel.

The story of Thomas is used by the evangelist to exemplify the transition from the days of the physical life of Jesus to the era of the risen Lord. In this new age, faith in Jesus is no longer based on physical contact and witnessing signs, but on hearing the word that is preached by the disciples.

'Blessed are those who have not seen and yet believe.'

This leads into John's concluding reflection on the signs given by Jesus. As an evangelist, he is performing the work begun when the Holy Spirit commissioned the disciples to carry on the mission of Jesus. They proclaim the word so that others might hear and receive the grace of faith: 'that you may believe that Jesus is the Christ, the Son of God, and that believing this you may have life through his name.'

The era of closed doors and paralysing fear is over because the victorious Lord Jesus is inviting us to rise up with him to share in the gift of the Spirit and to come into divine life.

Second Reflection
The divine breath

He breathed on them and said: 'Receive the Holy Spirit ... be filled with the breath of divine life ... be born anew into a life above this world.'

Long, long ago, in the very early days of human development, our primitive forebears sought to understand that secret force which caused life and governed the cycles of nature. It must be something very like our breath, they thought. Breath is invisible but vitally necessary. When we stop breathing we die. Maybe a great breath or spirit is the power behind life.

And so, the oldest name for God was the Great Breath or Spirit.

You don't see the wind itself but in its effects. You see the clouds flying, the rain slanting, the smoke trailing, and you know how the wind is blowing.

Old stories in the Bible about creation picture God breathing life into the bodies of clay which he had fashioned. And the thought is carried on in the words of a psalm:

'You send forth your breath and things are created
and you renew the face of the earth.
Then you take back your breath and they die,
returning to the dust from which they came.'

The people of the time considered the breath of life as something we have on loan from God. When we die we are returning the breath to its divine owner.

In the new age of the risen Lord the Breath of God came anew. There was a new creation. There are two versions of this coming, Luke's story of Pentecost and John's story in today's gospel.

We are more familiar with Luke's version because our calendar of feasts follows the plan of separating the events of Christ's glorification into distinct happenings over a certain period of time. But John's theology is above and beyond all laws of time, so in his writing the entire glorification belongs to the first day, meaning the new   age.

In Luke's story of Pentecost it sounded like a mighty wind from heaven which shook the house where the disciples were gathered. But in John's story the holy wind is as soft as a human breath.

In the silent warmth of this holy breath each disciple is born to a new level of life. There will be no more groping in tombs, hiding behind closed doors, or cowering in fear. This new life is above all natural experience. It is supernatural. Hence it cannot be proved on the score of physical evidence. It belongs to the realms of a faith.

The second reading in today's liturgy (1 Jn 5:1-6) tells us about this supernatural life. It means that one is begotten by God and becomes a child of God. It 'overcomes the world', that is, it moves beyond the limitations of the physical world. Just as we see how the wind is blowing in its effects, so this divine life will be seen outwardly in two great effects – love of God and observance of the commandments.

The sources of this new life are three – the water, the blood and the Spirit. We can identify these in the sacraments of Baptism, Eucharist and Confirmation. Collectively these are known as the Sacraments of Christian Initiation.

It is by faith in this new life that
we have the courage to call God 'Our Father',
that we can trust in divine forgiveness,
and that we believe in the presence of Christ in the Eucharist.
And it is in the living warmth of the Divine Breath
that we break down barriers and open the closed doors,

move out of fear and show the light of joy,
and reach out to others to share God's love with them.

Third Sunday of Easter

Last Sunday we read John's story of the risen Lord sending out the disciples, in the power of the Spirit, to continue his own mission of salvation. Today we read Luke's account of the risen Lord calling them to be witnesses in his name. The other two readings at Mass expand on the theme of repentance and forgiveness.

Luke 24:35-48

The disciples told their story of what had happened on the road and how they had recognised Jesus at the breaking of bread.

They were still talking about this when Jesus himself stood among them and said to them, 'Peace be with you!' In a state of alarm and fright, they thought they were seeing a ghost. But he said, 'Why are you so agitated, and why are these doubts rising in your hearts? Look at my hands and feet; yes, it is I indeed. Touch me and see for yourselves; a ghost has no flesh and bones as you can see I have.' And as he said this he showed them his hands and feet.

Their joy was so great that they still could not believe it, and they stood there dumbfounded; so he said to them, 'Have you anything here to eat?' And they offered him a piece of grilled fish, which he took and ate before their eyes.

Then he told them, 'This is what I meant when I said, while I was still with you, that everything written about me in the Law of Moses, in the Prophets and in the Psalms, has to be fulfilled.' He then opened their minds to understand the scriptures, and he said to them, 'So you see how it is written that the Christ would suffer and on the third day rise from the dead, and that, in his name, repentance for the forgiveness of sins would be preached to all the nations, beginning from Jerusalem. You are witnesses to this.'

Good News

As followers of the risen Lord we are called to be fed at his table and we are then sent out in his name to be his witnesses.

First Reflection
Witnesses to Christ

This is the only Sunday of this year's cycle when the gospel is taken from Luke. Even in this extract we meet many of his favourite themes – joy in the Lord, table-fellowship, fulfilment of the old figures, the mystical sense of Jerusalem, divine forgiveness, and the call to be witnesses.

We can see the story in three acts: the experience, the teaching and the mandate.

1. The Experience

We pick up the story immediately after two disciples recounted their encounter with the risen Jesus on the Emmaus road, when they had recognised him at the breaking of the break. Their talking was abruptly halted as Jesus stood among them. He greeted them: 'Peace be with you.' This is true to the style of divine encounters, for God must first relax all fears and doubts and agitations which would threaten anybody whose familiar experience of the world is suddenly overturned at a divine encounter.

There were doubts rising in the minds of the disciples. This is an important piece of information for it helps us to see that they did not lightly come to believe. The Lord invited them to establish for themselves the reality of his presence. 'Touch me and see for yourselves.' Furthermore he showed them his wounded hands and feet, so that they could be sure that he was the crucified one.

Luke always notes the inner emotions of people. Here it is a joy beyond words.

Then we have the great eucharistic theme which dominates Luke's gospel. 'Have you anything here to eat?' In this gospel the greatest sign of community is to share a meal with somebody. The greatest scandal of Jesus in the eyes of the religious leaders was the way he sat to table with people who were regarded as sinners. Now when the risen Lord eats with the disciples they know that he is truly with them.

Meals are very important in Luke's gospel because he wants his readers to understand how their Sunday 'breaking of the bread' sustained their relationship with Jesus Christ.

2. The Teaching

Part of every Eucharistic liturgy is the teaching of Sacred Scripture as the foundation of our faith. They had touched Jesus physically: this helped them to identify him as the one they had known. But touching did not bring about their faith in the resurrection. He had to teach them and open up their minds to understand the scriptures. These stories of old, these figures of history and patterns of behaviour established a context in which they could understand the death and resurrection of Jesus. It was a familiar pattern of God's way ... to take, bless, break and give.

The life of Jesus was the centre of time, between the old testament era, which he fulfilled, and the new era of the Church, which he was inaugurating.

3. The Mandate

The Church is given the mandate to continue the saving work of Jesus Christ: 'In his name, repentance for the forgiveness of sins would be preached ... You are witnesses to this.'

The work of Jesus had been limited in time, restricted to the pace of his disciples and confined to a very small territory. Jerusalem, the centre of the Jewish world, is Luke's image for this confined mission.

The mission of the Church, however, would engage many feet, many hands and many mouths. It would spread out from Jerusalem far and wide. 'You will be my witnesses.' It would truly be the continuation of the work of Jesus. That is the significance of the phrase 'in my name'. To act in the name of Jesus is to bring the reality of his presence and power to the people.

Luke has recounted a resurrection experience for us. In our Christian liturgy, every Sunday is a resurrection day. In the liturgy of the word our faith is nourished as the sacred texts fill up our understanding of Jesus, his background and his message.

We are then invited to the sacred act of sitting at table with Jesus. In this sacred eating we are sustained with his own divine energy.

Then at the end of Mass we are sent out in his name to be his witnesses wherever we go.

Second Reflection
In his name

'In his name ... you will be his witnesses.'

From this point on, to invoke the name of Jesus Christ is the same as invoking the name of God. The divinity of Jesus Christ is implied in the phrase.

It is a great honour as a Christian to bear the name of Jesus Christ. Yet to hear the way that many Christians abuse his name makes one wonder about their understanding of it.

Nowadays names have nothing like the depth of significance they held in olden days. Sometimes it seems that there is more sense in the names of racehorses than in the names taken by groups of people who band together for musical or sporting purposes.

Many people know the sound of the name of Jesus but obviously they do not know the person. Otherwise they would not use the sacred name as they do. Father, forgive them for they do not know what they are saying.

In the name is the presence and the power of the person.

The second commandment protects the sacredness of God's

name. Forbidding that God's name be taken in vain means that God's presence should not be invoked for wrong purposes, such as witnessing to an untruth in perjury; nor should God's power be invoked for destructive or evil purposes. What applies to God's name is equally applicable to the name of Jesus Christ.

The popular abuse of the sacred names is hardly intended as an invocation of God's presence and power. But it does betray a serious irreverence and insensitivity to God.

On the positive side we should deepen our awareness of the power of goodness that is available to us in the name of Jesus Christ, risen from the dead. He is with us and his power is within us. In the Acts we read how Peter and John believed in the presence of Jesus within them. To the crippled beggar Peter said: 'I have neither silver nor gold, but I will give you what I have: in the name of Jesus Christ the Nazarene, walk!'

In the name is the presence and the power.

The sacred names should never be used without due reverence. In the name of Jesus Christ we invoke his presence. For what? To witness to our frustration, our displeasure with the referee, or to the inadequacy of our vocabulary!

The name of Jesus should be the centre of our prayer as Christians. In the name is the presence. The Orthodox Church has long treasured the rhythmic repetition of the sacred name in the Jesus Prayer. This practice is very different from the use of the mantra in oriental meditation. The oriental mantra is supposed to be meaningless and is used to quieten the mind. But the prayerful repetition of the name of Jesus in some short formula is not a hypnotic murmur but a living response of faith to Jesus who is present to us in divine grace. It is an alertness to his presence: not just a sort of cosy drowsiness which relaxes the busy person. The Jesus Prayer is a means towards constant prayer, the way of the pilgrim towards the fulness of divine presence in the mystical Jerusalem.

Out of Jesus-centred prayer comes truly Christian action: the life and action of an authentic witness to Jesus Christ. 'In his name ... they will be his witnesses.'

If my prayer centres on the presence of Christ-with-me and Christ-within-me, then my life will be an extension of the mission of Jesus into the time and place where I live. Out of Jesus-prayer emerges Jesus-witness.

Through my baptism, confirmation and eucharist, the power of Christ is already in me to teach, to heal, to reconcile people and to bring them the peace of divine forgiveness. This seed of divine presence and power has been planted but it will grow only in the atmosphere of prayer.

In the name is the presence and the power.

A resolution for the Easter season might be to walk every day in his name with this little prayer never far from your mind:

Christ with me. Christ within me.

In the name is the presence and the power.

Fourth Sunday of Easter

The gospel for the Fourth Sunday of Easter is always taken from the Good Shepherd chapter of John's gospel. The image of the shepherd's dedication to the flock is the basis for choosing this day as Vocations Sunday.

John 10: 11-18
Jesus said:
'I am the good shepherd:
the good shepherd is one who lays down his life
    for his sheep.
The hired man, since he is not the shepherd
and the sheep do not belong to him,
abandons the sheep and runs away
as soon as he sees a wolf coming,
and then the wolf attacks and scatters the sheep;
this is because he is only a hired man
and has no concern for the sheep.
I am the good shepherd;
I know my own
and my own know me,
just as the Father knows me
and I know the Father;
and I lay down my life for my sheep.
And there are other sheep I have
that are not of this fold,
and these I have to lead as well.
They too will listen to my voice,
and there will be only one flock,
and one shepherd.
The Father loves me,
because I lay down my life
in order to take it up again.
No one takes it from me;
I lay it down of my own free will,
and as it is in my power to lay it down,
so it is in my power to take it up again;
and this is the command I have been given by my Father.'

Good News

The love of God has been manifested to us in the total self-giving of Jesus on our behalf, and in his call to us to follow in his way.

First Reflection
The Good Shepherd

Whenever John tells us that Jesus said 'I am', we must pay very close attention to what follows. 'I am' is an echo of the answer given by God to Moses when he asked for the divine name. God called himself: 'I am'.

John recounts seven statements of Jesus which echo this divine title. Each of these statements tell us something different about how God, in Jesus Christ, is reaching out to us to draw us more intimately into divine life.

'I am the Good Shepherd,' he said.

The image of the shepherd is one of our most popular concepts of God. And the psalm of the shepherd is one of the most popular prayers of all time. But an overly sentimental picture of the shepherd might well obscure the strength of this divine title. Our sentimental concept comes from the countless pictures we have seen of misty-eyed shepherds, handsomely bearded and immaculately groomed. And the pastures in our mind are a combination of Alpine postcards and lush grasslands, with pretty lambs gambolling about.

The reality was that sheep territory was anything but lush grassland. The good land was reserved for other agricultural purposes and the sheep were out on the rocky outbacks where they had to scavenge for survival.

And as for the shepherds in Our Lord's time, they were regarded as robbers dressed in smelly sheepskins, too dirty to be admitted to the local synagogue.

Two features of the shepherd which Jesus took up were the dedication of the shepherd's life to the flock, and his one-to-one relationship with the sheep.

Sheep are particularly timid and stupid animals, always needing a leader to show the way, a searcher when they stray and a healer when they are cut and bruised. The oriental shepherd gives his whole time, 'lays down his life', for the flock, for he had to leave home for very long periods to lead the flock to far off pastures. The sheep become his family and he gets to know each of them as an individual. This expresses the desire of Jesus that each individual person would grow in intimate relationship with him.

104

Jesus called himself the good shepherd in contrast to the hired man. The hired man was concerned only about his own job or what he was getting out of it: the genuine shepherd had the concern of the sheep at heart.

Originally the statement about the false shepherds was a criticism of the Jewish leaders who were failing to give proper leadership. But the criticism is valid for all time as there will always be false shepherds trying to beguile people away from following the voice of Jesus Christ.

The situation is particularly true today when traditional Christian culture is under attack from the media advocates of secularistic humanism. When authority is under attack, then people are more easily beguiled by clever gurus and misled by constant propaganda.

Self-appointed shepherds are using the Sunday newspapers as an alternative to the Sunday pulpit. They are leading people away from the voice of Christ to a different understanding of life, to different values and standards of behaviour. But in many cases it is surely the blind leading the blind for these teachers of life are themselves no paragons of virtue or models of stability.

Whose voice do you follow? Whose values do you respect and aspire to?

Does your shepherd offer a comprehensive meaning to life ... a meaning which will carry us through the dark valley of suffering and across the bridge of death?

Jesus said that there will be only one flock and one shepherd. This expresses his own unique position as the only true way to salvation, the only name in which we can be saved. A contemporary confused person regards all religions as more or less the same. But this is to underestimate the unique role of Jesus Christ, the one whom God raised from the dead, in which name alone is healing, and who is the keystone of all human history (cf First Reading).

Jesus calls us to follow his way and this leads directly to the Father. His will was always perfectly united to the Father's, as he demonstrated when he freely laid down his life in obedience to the Father's will.

In today's second reading St John asks us to reflect on the love of God which raises us up to be children of God. To follow Jesus as our shepherd is the same as belonging to his family as a brother or a sister. Only heaven will reveal what all this means.

For the moment we follow our risen Saviour day by day on our journey of life. We are strengthened in prayer as our minds delight in the psalm's description of what the shepherd does for us.

There is nothing I shall want ... he gives me repose ... he revives my drooping spirit ... he guides me along the right path ... he is with me in the valley of darkness ... he has prepared a banquet for me ... my head is anointed with oil, my cup is overflowing.

Second Reflection
Vocations Sunday

The image of Jesus as the shepherd leading his flock forward has prompted the Church to dedicate this Sunday to vocations. We are asked to reflect on the need for shepherds or leaders in the Church of our own day and we are reminded of the need to pray for vocations.

A vocation is a call from God to offer oneself for some form of service in the Church. It may be in one's role as a lay person or it may be in the ministerial priesthood or in the consecration of one's life as a religious.

The greater recognition of the charisms of baptism and confirmation is one of the most significant fruits of the Second Vatican Council. It's a bit like the idea of Sport For All. Marathon running used be regarded as a specialised occupation for a few nutcases and the role of the thousands was to deride or applaud as they thought fit. But the concept changed when thousands took to the streets and recognised that sport is more about participating than spectating.

Similarly, ministry or service in the Church used be regarded as the preserve of the ordained clergy while the laity were reduced to passive spectators ... called to stand up, to pay up and to shut up. The image of the stupid sheep of the flock was being extended a bit too far.

But little by little over the past twenty-five years the awareness has been growing of the gifts of the Spirit which are part of baptism and confirmation, and which entitle all the faithful to an active and responsible participation in the Church's mission.

Pope John Paul II, drawing on the collective wisdom of the 1987 Synod of Bishops, issued a letter on the vocation and mission of the laity. His stated purpose was 'to stir and promote a deeper awareness among all the faithful of the gift and responsibility they share, both as a group and as individuals, in the communion and mission of the Church.'

Christian action is an expression of the divine energy of Christ-life which is bestowed on us in the sacraments. The Pope's letter expresses it: 'The participation of the lay faithful in the threefold mission of Christ as Priest, Prophet and King finds its source in the anointing of Baptism, its further development in Confirmation and its realisation and dynamic sustenance in the Holy Eucharist.' The crisis of vocations in the Church today may well be in the area of recognising and encouraging the vast potential of the laity in the service of the Church.

Yet this greater recognition of the vocation of the laity must not result in underestimating the special vocation to the ministerial priesthood. In his letter to priests for Holy Thursday (1990) Pope John Paul II wrote: 'The priesthood is not an institution that exists 'alongside' the laity, or 'above' it. The priesthood of Bishops and Priests, as well as the ministry of Deacons, is 'for' the laity.' Priesthood is a special form of service or ministry for all the Church. It is principally through the sacraments, which are ministered by the ordained priests, that the laity are served with the means to Christian life. Without ordained priests who dedicate their lives to the gospel and to Church ministry, an essential witness in the life of the Church would be missing.

The vocation to religious life also offers an essential witness in the Church. Religious life is a full-scale consecration of life to God's love and to the service of people according to the model of Jesus' life in the gospel. The Church would be very much the poorer without the prophetic stance of those who risk all on their faith in God's love.

In the gospel there are very few specific intentions that Jesus told us to pray for. That makes it all the more significant that he did tell us to pray for vocations: 'The harvest is rich but the labourers are few, so ask the Lord of the harvest to send labourers to his harvest.' (Mt 9:37)

One often hears that in a democracy people get the government they deserve. Perhaps in a similar way we can say that the Church will get the vocations it deserves, both in regard to quantity and quality. Whenever I hear anybody criticising the bishops and priests I feel like asking the critic if he/she has ever prayed for vocations in the Church. The government we have is the government we deserve. And the clergy we have are the clergy we've deserved.

As we prepare for the third millennium of Christianity, our concern for the future of the Church must be real and practical. All baptized-confirmed members of the Church must be aware of their responsibility to carry the light of Christ into society. We must support and pray for those who generously dedicate their entire careers to being shepherds of the flock, in imitation of Jesus Christ, the Good Shepherd.

And we must pray for the vocations which will ensure the future well-being of the Church.

Fifth Sunday of Easter

The risen Lord Jesus continues to be present and operative in the world today through the community of his disciples. This is beautifully expressed in the allegory of the vine and the branches.

John 15:1-8
Jesus said to his disciples:
'I am the true vine,
and my Father is the vinedresser.
Every branch in me that bears no fruit
he cuts away,
and every branch that does bear fruit he prunes
to make it bear even more.
You are pruned already,
by means of the word that I have spoken to you.
Make your home in me, as I make mine in you.
As a branch cannot bear fruit all by itself,
but must remain part of the vine,
neither can you unless you remain in me.
I am the vine,
you are the branches.
Whoever remains in me, with me in him,
bears fruit in plenty;
for cut off from me you can do nothing.
Anyone who does not remain in me
is like a branch that has been thrown away
—he withers;
these branches are collected and thrown on the fire,
and they are burnt.
If you remain in me
and my words remain in you,
you may ask what you will
and you shall get it.
It is to the glory of my Father that you should bear much fruit,
and then you will be my disciples.'

Good News
If we belong to Jesus Christ and follow his teaching, he will live
in us and continue his saving work in the world through us.

First Reflection
The True Vine

Initially Jesus said, 'I am the true vine and my Father is the vinedresser.' As the true vine, he is the fulfilment of all that was said about Israel being the chosen vineyard of God. These things were but shadows cast back from Christ, who is the reality. Jesus is truly the Beloved Son of the Father, the Chosen One in a unique sense.

One of the features which adorned the Temple was a golden vine, and rich businessmen considered it a great honour to have contributed in gold to its extension. But Jesus, who had previously called himself the new temple or meeting-place with God, now declares himself the true vine beloved by God.

The intimate relationship between the Father and Jesus is then extended to the disciples. 'I am the vine, you are the branches.'

This is an allegory as distinct from a parable. In a parable only the main point is strictly intended for application to life. But in an allegory all the details are applied. As the allegory of the vine is told, the disciples hear many aspects of Christ's relationship with them.

The main themes of the entire Last Supper discourse are summed up here:
– although Jesus is about to depart physically, his work will continue;
– the disciples will be commissioned to carry on his work;
– they will receive divine energy or sap for the task.

The pruning of the vine is applied to life. The vine is a plant that grows rapidly and has to be pruned drastically if it is to bear fruit. One type of pruning involves lopping off the shoots which will not bear fruit. The community of true believers are separate from those who have been cut off from Christ through unbelief.

Another type of pruning involves cutting back the branches which do bear fruit. This is more of a purifying or cleansing process. It reminds one of the washing of the feet before the Last Supper when Jesus told Peter: 'If I do not wash you, you can have nothing in common with me.' But now Jesus reassures the disciples that they have already been cleansed by means of his teaching ... 'by means of the words I have spoken to you.'

The next point in the allegory is the beautiful truth that the disciple is at home in Christ. 'Make your home in me, as I make mine in you.' The disciple is as much at home in Christ as the branch is in the tree. Home is where you belong and where you come back to all the time. That is how the disciple finds that his life is rooted and grounded in Christ and is always coming back to Christ for meaning, light and sustenance.

'Whoever remains in me, with me in him,
bears fruit in plenty;
for cut off from me you can do nothing.'
What sort of fruit is meant? We get our answer in today's second reading:
'His commandments are these:
that we believe in the name of his Son Jesus Christ
and that we love one another.' (1 Jn 3:23)
To believe is to have your mind enlightened by the teaching of Jesus, to have all your confidence rooted in him, and to find your peace of mind in his divine forgiveness. When we are so rooted in Jesus, then we willingly open out our lives in practical love to others. No longer living a self-centred life, our great desire will be to love others with something of the love of Jesus.

'If you remain in me and my words remain in you, you may ask what you will and you shall get it.' The answer to prayer is guaranteed ... but note the condition: 'If you remain in me and my words remain in you.' The fact is that whoever is so firmly rooted and grounded in Christ will ask only for whatever is the divine will.

The final point concerns the extension of the glory of the Father. There is a sense in which God's work is not complete until we extend his kingdom to every part of society.

The allegory of the vine brings home to us what a noble calling it is to be a disciple of Jesus Christ. We are challenged to be his fruit-bearing representatives in our world today. But we are wonderfully reassured that success in this task is due to the divine energy which is in us when we live in Christ.

Second Reflection
Fragile little twigs
At this time of year the naked branches of trees are all curtained in a haze of tender blossoms. This unfolding greenery and all these blossoms of white, pink and crimson are not growing on the solid trunk or sturdy branches but out at the very tip of the tender, fragile twigs. In the Southern Hemisphere it is fruit-picking time, but the lesson is the same, for the fruit too is borne on the weak, little tendrils.

When we reflect on our vocation from God to be the bearers of the mission of Christ, our first reaction must surely be a sense of our inadequacy. God must be joking, picking me to represent him! However, the fruit tree shows that the weak little twigs are what must bear the blossoms of Spring and the fruits of Autumn.

When Jeremiah was called to be God's prophet to the nations he was overcome by the thought of his own childish powerlessness. 'Ah, Lord Yahweh,' he protested, 'look I do not know how to speak: 'I am a child!' But God told him not to be thinking along those lines but to consider how God would be his strength. 'Do not be afraid of them, for I am with you to protect you.' (Jer 1:4-8)

The call to serve in any form of Church ministry is to bring to others what is not our own. For if all we had to bring was our own contribution it would not be much of a help to them. What we are asked to bring is something from Christ. Apart from him we are the dead twigs of winter. But when our source of life is the sap of Christ, then what we can bring others will be the fruits of his presence and power at home in us.

The vine and the branches must be one of our great anchor points in prayer, a safe harbour to return to in times of storm in temptation and darkness. It is back home to Christ we must come when we are severely tempted to give up because of our failures, or when we feel ashamed of the duplicity which has us showing the pious face and brave front before others while all is torn apart within.

In mid-life we may feel we've been only a failure when we are far more aware of what we have not done and never will do, than of what has been achieved through us.

We are but fragile, vulnerable twigs far removed from the unshakable bole of the tree. Yet the sap of the Holy Spirit will reach out through us if we remain in Christ, holding on to our belief in the power of his name.

Once St Paul appreciated where his success came from, namely from Christ abiding within him, then he learned to smile at his own human deficiencies. He saw that God deliberately chooses the foolish and weak of this world to confound the worldly wise and strong ... 'those who are nothing at all to show up those who are everything,' so that it may be plainly seen that whatever fruit is borne must be due to God's work rather than to human powers.

If we are bringing Christ's life and power to people, it is a most precious treasure that we bear. But Paul is well aware of the earthly frailty of the ministers. 'We are only earthenware jars that hold this treasure, to make it clear that such an overwhelming power comes from God and not from us.' (2 Cor 4:7)

The great secret of ministry ... whether in teaching, parenting, works of compassion, the pursuit of justice, liturgical service ... is keeping in contact with home. And home means Jesus Christ.

Prayerful contact every day with Jesus is how we weak, vulnera-

111

ble twigs, can keep in touch with the life-giving sap of the Spirit. In morning prayer we begin our day by attuning our mentality to the word of God.

And at the end of a day's activities it is good to sit with our tiredness in God's presence and let whatever pain or joy that is deep within us now surface with God.

The great message of the resurrection continues week by week:

'As the Father sent me so am I sending you.'

We are sent ... but he is in us and we are in him.

Christ with me ... Christ within me.

Sixth Sunday of Easter

On the last Sunday before the Ascension our readings today stress how Jesus Christ remains in the community of disciples who believe in his love and know that it is their mission in life to pass it on to others.

John 15:9-17
Jesus said to his disciples:
'As the Father has loved me,
so I have loved you.
Remain in my love.
If you keep my commandments
you will remain in my love,
just as I have kept my Father's commandments
and remain in his love.
I have told you this
so that my own joy may be in you
and your joy be complete.
This is my commandment:
love one another,
as I have loved you.
A man can have no greater love
than to lay down his life for his friends.
You are my friends,
if you do what I command you.
I shall not call you servants any more,
because a servant does not know
his master's business;
I call you friends,
because I have made known to you
everything I have learned from my Father.
You did not choose me,
no, I chose you;
and I commissioned you
to go out and to bear fruit,
fruit that will last;
and then the Father will give you
anything you ask him in my name.
What I command you
is to love one another.'

Good News

Love begins in God the Father. It has been manifested to us in Jesus Christ who loved us to the end. And his love has been planted in us by the Holy Spirit.

First Reflection

Remain in my love

The gospel continues the lessons of the vine and the branches. What is in the main trunk of the tree passes out into the branches and into the outermost little twigs. Jesus is thus explaining that the life which is in him is passing out into the souls of the true disciples.

What is most special about Jesus is his relationship with the Father. He is the Beloved Son, the Word of the Father. The Father's great love for the Son is now being passed out into the branches and twigs. 'As the Father has loved me, so I have loved you.' The whole secret of Christian life is to 'remain in my love.' The love of God, as shown to us in Jesus Christ, is the basis of our philosophy of life: it is the foundation of all our hopes: it is the home we come back to, where we know we are understood and accepted.

Divine love comes to us in three stages. All begins in the Father's creating of life. Why did God bother with creating us? St Thomas Aquinas offered this reason: love did not permit God to remain alone. Beautiful, isn't it! So, the very beginning of human life ... of my life ... is a creating act by the Father.

The second stage of divine love is the showing of God's love to us in the life of Jesus Christ. He loved us to the end and called his disciples into intimate friendship.

The third stage is the gift of the Holy Spirit who implants God's love in our souls so that we might pass it onto others. 'The love of God has been poured into our hearts by the Holy Spirit which has been given us.' (Rom 5:5) We can sum it up like this: love begins in God the Father; it is shown to us in Jesus Christ; and it is implanted in us by the Holy Spirit.

Love must be practical. Throughout John's writing he shows his concern about a certain sect who were full of theories about God but considered ideas without action to be sufficient. God-talk is empty unless it passes into God-action. And in John's understanding of things, what Christian life is all about is letting God act through us. And the only proof of true God-action is the fruit of love.

God's love is not just a comforting theory. It is more than a matter of nice words. God's love is a constant event, a never-ending action which permeates every moment of our lives. Oh, if only we could fully believe all this! And remain in this love ... believing that God's love is what is underneath everything, through everything and the ultimate repose of everything. 'Remain in my love'... be at home in this belief, be rooted in it and draw all your energy from it.

'This is my commandment: Love one another as I have loved you.' What we are called to is something more than natural love. It is super-natural love, a sharing in divine love. In today's second reading John says: 'This is the love I mean: not our love for God, but God's love for us when he sent his Son to be the sacrifice that takes our sins away.' (1 Jn 4:10) What charity really means is not our natural sort of love but the love of God living in us and acting through us.

Natural love needs a basis in attraction, shared interest, complementarity of characters or even pity, which makes me reach out towards the other person. It is characterised by a reaching towards the particular person. Supernatural love is characterised by where it comes from: its source is God's own love which is living in the soul by the indwelling of the Holy Spirit.

Hence, true Christian love will show the characteristics of Christ's own love. His love was not limited to the people he liked. Like the Father whose sun shines on and rain comes to good and bad people alike, so the love of Christ did not discriminate between people. His love refused to be poisoned by the wrongs of others and their hurts. His forgiveness overcame any sense of personal hurt. He gave to the point of total self-sacrifice in laying down his life for our salvation.

The pattern of Christ's love is the model for all Christians. 'Love one another, as I have loved you.'

Natural love is always limited to certain people: it excludes others and finds total forgiveness virtually impossible. But supernatural love, since it is a participation in divine love, can surpass these limitations and restraints. It draws from divine understanding and compassion to find the ability to forgive those who have hurt us.

If you are finding it impossible to forgive somebody it shows that you have not yet discovered the Holy Spirit within you, the Spirit given to you in baptism. Your natural love is focussing towards that person whom you can't love. Supernatural love thinks less of towards and more of from ... the source of divine love within us. Hand over this problem of forgiving to God-within-you. Confess to God that your natural ability has reached its limits. Invite God-with-you to think in your mind and to love through your heart.

Jesus called the disciples to be purified or pruned by his teaching and thus enter into his mental viewpoint. In this way they would not be like hired servants but true friends of his. 'I call you friends', he said. They were chosen by him and commissioned to carry on his work and extend his love throughout the world.

'What I command you is to love another.'
Love begins in the creating Father.
Love is shown in the total self-giving of the Son.
Love is planted in us by the sanctifying Spirit.
Christian life is in knowing what we have received ... making our home in it ... and passing it on to others.

Second Reflection
You are my friends
Nobody in the world today is better known for working with the poor and hungry than Mother Teresa of Calcutta. When she visited the affluent western world she was appalled by the other type of hunger she experienced, hunger of the spirit. This famine of loveless lives sees increasing numbers of suicides and abortions, life-escaping addictions, people feeling alien even in their own homes.

The words of Jesus at the Last Supper are so full of love, affirmation and encouragement that we should keep on reading them, memorising them and proclaiming them. See what beautiful statements he makes:

'As the Father has loved me, so I have loved you.'

'That my own joy may be in you and your joy be complete.'

'A man can have no greater love than to lay down his life for his friends.'

'You are my friends, if you do what I command you.'

It is one thing to say 'I am your friend', but there is even more affirmation in hearing 'You are my friend.' Friends with whom he shared and communicated all that he was thinking and planning.

'I chose you ... and I commissioned you to go out and to bear fruit.' In the light of these affirmations he can now give them his final command: 'What I command you is to love one another.'

We cannot give to another what we ourselves do not have. It is impossible to love others unless we have first received love. That is why Jesus so affirmed them in love and friendship before he asked them to share love. Not only to share love ... to share his love.

The famine of lovelessness comes out from the underdeveloped hearts of people who have always received more blame than affirmation, more criticism than gratitude, and more hurt than healing.

A behaviour-scientist called James Dawson did an experiment

with a particularly voracious fish called a wall-eyed pike. In his glass aquarium he fed the pike with some little minnows. In a few seconds the pike had savagely devoured the lot. Then he placed a glass panel in the aquarium and threw in some minnows on the far side. The pike sprang into action but smashed into the glass panel and hurt itself. It came forward again only to be hurt again. Each time it advanced with increasing caution. Eventually Dawson took out the panel. The minnows swam around the pike but it made no move to devour them. Going after the minnows was now associated with hurt and failure. Eventually the pike died of starvation while the food was there to be taken.

We meet many people who are starving of love because their life-story tells only of hurt and failure. The love of God is there all around them but they cannot come forward to receive its nourishment because of all the hurt in their memory. It is the famine of lovelessness.

Keep on repeating in your heart what Jesus said to the disciples: 'I am your friend unto death ... and you are my friend.' When you know in every inch of your body that you are deeply, jealously, preciously loved, you will begin to blossom and grow and bear fruit. The love you have received will be passed on to others through you.

As one commentator, Joseph Donders, brings out, love is not so much a command as a prescription for life.

Through the Eucharist, through daily prayer, through the life-giving words of scripture, take your daily dose of God's love. Your own legacy of hurt memory, of failure and weakness, will be healed and you will find the energy to love.

You will melt with sympathy and compassion where previously you were callous and cold.

You will notice what others do and how they try, where previously you saw their failures and you criticised.

You will no longer feel the need to feather your own nest all the time, but you will discover that it is more blessed to give than to receive.

What a joy it is to hear Jesus say: 'You are my friends'.

The Ascension of the Lord

*On the fortieth day of Easter we celebrate the Ascension. Since the
fourth century the Ascension has been given its own special day of celebration in the Easter season. Three great themes run through the liturgy
of the day: the return of Jesus to the Father's glory; the mission of the
Church; and our hope of joining with the glorified Lord in heaven.*

Mark 16:15-20
Jesus showed himself to the eleven, and said to them, 'Go out
to the whole world; proclaim the Good News to all creation. He
who believes and is baptised will be saved; he who does not believe
will be condemned.

These are the signs that will be associated with believers: in my
name they will cast out devils; they will have the gift of tongues; they
will pick up snakes in their hands, and be unharmed should they
drink deadly poison; they will lay their hands on the sick, who will
recover.'

And so the Lord Jesus, after he had spoken to them, was taken
up into heaven: there at the right hand of God he took his place,
while they, going out, preached everywhere, the Lord working with
them and confirming the word by the signs that accompanied it.

Good News
Jesus has taken his place in the Father's glory but he is still
among us in the mission and power of the Church.

First Reflection
Ascension Day
Our thinking about the glorification of Jesus is restricted within
our limited concepts of time and space. It is not possible for us to
express the full truth because the glorified Lord is beyond our limitations. So we find that the various New Testament writers give us a
different timing or location for the Ascension in their attempts to express some aspect of their belief. Were they to sit for examinations
they might get honours in theology but they would fail miserably in
history and geography!

We grew up with the idea of forty days before the ascension
with the coming of the Holy Spirit on the fiftieth day. This is the
sequence of events according to Luke in the Acts (today's first reading), and it has been the basis for our liturgical calendar ever since

the fourth century. The span of forty days is the customary scriptural way of suggesting a full period of time. It was a time for the minds of the disciples to grow with the impact of the resurrection.

So familiar are we with this sequence that it surprises us when we first discover that the gospels of John and Luke include the ascension as part of the overall resurrection event of Easter Sunday. However, anybody who dogmatically insists that the ascension took place on Easter Sunday is making the same mistake as the person who insists on the fortieth day. The mistake is in trying to put an event of timelessness into the limitations of earthly time and place.

This year we read the account in Mark's gospel. In his brief account of Easter Sunday he wrote of the message given to the women at the empty tomb for Peter and the other disciples: 'He is going before you into Galilee; it is there you will see him, just as he told you.'

Mark then gives a passing reference to some of the appearances of the risen Lord before this final event of his being taken up. There are three stages in the story: the sending out of the apostles; the glorification of Jesus; and the confirmation that the apostles did go out in the Lord's power.

First is the sending out of the apostles to proclaim the Good News to all creation. The Good News is about the rising of Jesus Christ and what that implies for the history of humanity. Those who believe and are baptised receive the fruits of his rising. In the name of the risen Lord they are promised power over evil spirits, protection from harm, the gift of praise to loosen tongues in prayer, and the gift of healing the sick.

The second stage of the story pictures Jesus being taken up to heaven. At the right hand of God he took his place. Obviously this is not in the sense of a physical place but a way to suggest prestige and glory.

Finally we are told that the apostles took up their mission, went out and preached everywhere. The Lord was with them, working with them in the signs and gifts which they had been promised.

Though Jesus of Nazareth no longer walks our roads in his physical flesh, his work goes on. In heaven, at the Father's right hand, he is ever living to intercede for us. He works in and through all who answer his call. No longer is his message and healing power confined to one pair of feet, one pair of hands. Now in the Church he has a million hearts to beat with his love, a million voices to proclaim his Good News.

But a million is not enough if there are still people among your acquaintances who have not heard the Good News. They may in their freedom choose to reject the Good News. But at least Jesus wants them to hear it.

And he is counting on you.

Second Reflection
A place in heaven

The feast of the ascension is a day to think of heaven. We can bring together two gospel texts. The first is about Jesus' place in heaven: 'The Lord Jesus was taken up to heaven: there at the right hand of God he took his place.'

The second text is about our place: 'There are many rooms in my Father's house ... I am going to prepare a place for you.' (Jn 14:2-3) What we celebrate in Christ's ascension is something that involves us too. The basis of our hope for heaven is summed up in today's Preface:

'Christ is the beginning, the head of the Church,

where he has gone, we hope to follow.'

Am I right in thinking that we preachers have shied away from preaching about heaven? Perhaps we fear the accusation of selling pie in the sky when you die ... of diverting people with the opium of future hope away from their present responsibilities for this world.

In our daily living we need some purpose or ambition to give us the motivation to get up and start, the energy to persevere, and a sense of satisfaction in identifying targets and attaining them. It may be the target of tidying a room (mine, never!), preparing the dinner, getting the week's work done. But beyond our daily or weekly purpose we need a meaning to life which can hold the totality of our experiences and desires together. We need a goal which will continue to have meaning when we cross the bridge of death. I suggest that heaven is as good a name as any for that eternal goal and source of meaning.

The image of eternal rest strikes me as the most boring prospect imaginable! But then I am a compulsive activist and the idea of lying out sunbathing on a sandy beach with nothing else to do is my idea of hell. My mother tells me that I anticipated her plans by two weeks in my hurry to get going. (Before many theologians rush at me, I know that eternal rest really means the repose and fulfilment of all energies in the wonder of God, and that is a glorious prospect.) As for playing harps in the sky, I'm not too keen on the harp, but if it meant mastery of the grand piano or kingly organ, I'd be very attracted.

Pardon my flippancy but I am only trying to get beyond some common images of heaven. As for the picture of Jesus going up to the accompaniment of angelic brass bands and to be showered with honours and marks of prestige, it runs counter to the gospel portrait of the obedient servant of God or the humble carpenter from Nazareth who took to the hills when they wanted to make him king. Maybe all this betrays something about myself as someone who squirms through fulsome jubilee speeches and unctuous panegyrics. 'Not to us, Lord, not to us, but to your name be the glory.' The glorification of Jesus was in his total return to the Father.

If heaven is our eternal goal and comprehensive meaning, it will bring us to a sense of total unity. All the different pages of life will be bound together in one book.

Unity within ourselves to end all the contradictions we experience between our hot and cold feelings, our ideals and failures, our makings and our breakings.

Unity with others ... and particularly appealing is the prospect of being reunited with our loved ones who have gone before us. And getting to know the forebears who were long before our time, but whose life blood courses through our veins.

Unity with God ... total oneness in the risen Lord who is one with the Father in the love-power of the Holy Spirit.

In many different ways we experience our incompleteness: and that is important. For if we thought we had it all made here and now we would never aspire to what is greater.

Our moment of joy on the holy mountain is tinged with pain when we cannot stay in the experience but must face into the daily hassle below. The incompleteness we experience in the death of a loved one takes away a part of our heart. We experience our incompetence in sickness and when our powers and faculties begin to fail with the years.

Love makes us vulnerable to pain for the sharing of ourselves with another increases the risk of hurt. As someone called to consecrated celibacy, I can testify to its occupational hazards of loneliness and substitute diversions.

These experiences of being incomplete are very important as they make us long for the total unity of heaven. The pains of the heart taught St Augustine to say: 'For you have made us for yourself, O Lord, and our hearts are restless until they rest in you.'

In today's second reading we hear the beautiful prayer of Paul for the Ephesians: 'May he enlighten the eyes of your mind so that you can see what hope his call holds for you, what rich glories he has promised the saints will inherit and how infinitely great is the power he has exercised for us believers.'

121

With the apostles we lift up our eyes to the skies today.
And the risen Lord sends down the light of hope to brighten our countenance.

Perhaps we can describe a Christian as someone who walks the roads of life with the lightsome eyes of someone who knows the meaning of where the journey is going.

Seventh Sunday of Easter

This Sunday is part of the original novena, the nine days of prayer between Ascension and Pentecost. These are the days when we pray that the Spirit's power from on high will fall upon all disciples. The gospel of today is very appropriate as it is the prayer of Jesus for the consecration of the disciples to carry on his mission.

John 17:11-19
Jesus raised his eyes to heaven and said:
'Holy Father,
keep those you have given me true to your name,
so that they may be one like us.
While I was with them,
I kept those you had given me true to your name.
I have watched over them and not one is lost
except the one who chose to be lost,
and this was to fulfil the scriptures.
But now I am coming to you
and while still in the world I say these things
to share my joy with them to the full.
I passed your word on to them,
and the world hated them,
because they belong to the world
no more than I belong to the world.
I am not asking you to remove them from the world,
but to protect them from the evil one.
They do not belong to the world
any more than I belong to the world.
Consecrate them in the truth;
your word is truth.
As you sent me into the world,
I have sent them into the world,
and for their sake I consecrate myself
so that they too may be consecrated in truth.'

Good News
Jesus has prayed for us: that we would be kept safe from a worldly, evil spirit, and equipped for our mission with the word of truth and the spirit of unity.

First Reflection
May they be one

This reading is taken from the great prayer of Jesus which John situates in the Last Supper. It is variously known as the priestly prayer of Jesus, or his prayer of consecration, or the prayer of the shepherd for his flock.

In today's extract Jesus is praying for his disciples who would carry on his mission in the time after his departure. He refers to the disciples as those who were given to him by the Father. Isn't that a lovely thought! As a disciple I am a gift of the Father to Jesus.

'Keep them true to your name.' He prays that we may be faithful in our commitment. The danger of falling away is brought to mind by the betrayal of Judas. He made his own free choice which was permitted by God, as in the case of any sin. In his own wicked choice he played a part in the fulfilment of scriptures.

'May they be one like us.' In this beautiful line Jesus prays that his disciples might experience a one-ness or unity modelled on the intimate union of Father and Son: unity in our relationship with God, in our relationship with others, and inner harmony in our own lives.

In our experiences we feel like living contradictions. We sway from one position to the other: we give the correct advice to others and do the opposite ourselves: we put on a cheerful face before the world and hide how much we are torn apart inside. Sometimes we cope in confidence with our problems but later we are shattered again on the verge of despair. Our life is a book of many pages and it can be hard to see any relationship between one page and another. How we long for that inner unity in our lives, the integration of all the various parts and energies!

Peace between people flows out of people at soul-peace. When we are at peace with ourselves we are no longer threatened by the differences that other people represent.

The prayer of Jesus continues: 'Father, I am coming to you ... but they are staying here in the world.' The return of Jesus to the Father's glory is the perfect expression of unity. It is perfect at-one-ment. The good news for us is that Jesus has gone before us to draw us to sharing the same joy of at-one-ment. 'I say these things to share my joy with them to the full.'

But for the moment, the disciples ... we ourselves ... are remaining in this world of struggle, sinfulness and hostility. Jesus has passed on his word to us, he has commissioned us in Baptism and Confirmation, to carry on his work.

124

But light always hurts the sick eye and goodness is a threat to the life that is sold on evil ways. Jesus himself was hated unto death by those who belonged to selfish, worldly ambitions rather than to God's command of love. 'They do not belong to the world any more than I belong to the world.' Our mission is in this world where opposition is encountered, but we can draw confidence from the prayer of Jesus for us: 'Protect them from the evil one.'

Jesus is the holy one, the beloved Son of the Father. Now he prays for the consecration of his disciples: 'Consecrate them in the truth.'

Consecration of any person or object means to set it apart for God's service. The prayer of consecration of a person invokes God's grace to equip the person for God's mission.

'May they be consecrated and equipped in the truth.'

Jesus is the truth. He is the very word of God.

He is the shepherd who guides me along the right path.

He is the only way, the sole truth, and the true life.

No one can go to the Father except through him.

This beautiful prayer of Jesus for the disciples perfectly suits these days of waiting between Ascension and Pentecost. Our minds join with the apostles in the upper room, praying for the fulfilment of the promise of power from on high. Our own prayer this week will invoke the continued coming of the Holy Spirit to grant us fidelity to the truth of Jesus,

the integration of our lives in unity,

and the joy of being at-one with God.

Second Reflection
The world, according to John

What is meant by the world is a complicated affair in John's writings. In a general sense it refers to this created earth and to the human race in particular.

The first point to be noted is the love of God for the world. 'Yes, God loved the world so much that he gave his only Son so that everyone who believes in him may not be lost but may have eternal life.' (Jn 3:16)

Here already is a hint that the world, i.e. humanity, was losing its way. In fact Jesus went so far as to refer to the devil as 'the prince of this world.' (Jn 16:11) The evil spirit is the father of lies and confusion, organising the hostility to Jesus. So, it gradually develops that John uses the term, world, to express any oppostion to God. It is a secularistic mode of thought which is far removed from God's mind: a way of behaviour which is anti-God.

Near the end of his life Jesus spoke of leaving the world to return to the Father. But his mission in the world would continue through the disciples. And so, in his priestly role, he prayed for these disciples.

They are to remain in the world, but must not be contaminated by the hostile influences of worldliness. They are sent, as he was sent, on the mission of redeeming the world.

Total immersion in worldly occupations is a recipe for disaster. As Wordsworth observed:

'The world is too much with us; late and soon

Getting and spending we lay waste our powers ...'

Too easily we become enslaved to materialistic preoccupations, the pursuit of power and the grasp of sensuality. These worldly cares will be the briars which can choke even a healthy plant.

At the opposite extreme, the pretence of total withdrawal from the world is equally a disastrous plan. Anybody who tries to deny the reality of our flesh and blood existence is courting folly. Those who pretend to be angels quickly tumble from their pinnacle as devils.

Down the ages Christian disciples have worked in the world with two tactics which, at first sight, seem to be contradictory: strategic withdrawal and active involvement.

The tactic of withdrawing is practised especially in the monastic life. Here one withdraws from secular preoccupations as much as possible in order to seek God, for the sake of the world.

Any true vocation is based on love. Hating the world is no proper motivation... like that man in the country parish who confided in the fiery missioner that he thought he had a vocation to their order ... 'Because ye'r order hates women and so do I.'

A true monk is one who felt suffocated by the large world so he has to withdraw in order to come to terms with the small world which is his daily life. 'The monk is separated from everyone and united to everyone,' remarked Evagrius Ponticus of the monks in the the Egyptian desert.

The true contemplative is withdrawn only to be truly in touch with the pressures and pains, joys and celebations of the whole nation. Only the contemplative can offer the prophetic vision which challenges the assumptions which are governing this imbalanced and neurotic world of ours.

I like the old Russian belief recorded by Dostoyevsky, that the world keeps on turning, season follows season, because somewhere, at any particular moment, there is somebody in prayer before God for the world. It is our contemplatives, keeping up the 24-hour watch for the world, who have saved us from self-destruction.

The second Christian tactic, by far the more common, is to be engaged in the world but with the light of the Christian perspective. 'Consecrate them in the truth', prayed Jesus.

Pope John Paul II writes of the Church in the world: 'The Church, in fact, lives in the world, even if she is not of the world. She is sent to continue the redemptive work of Jesus Christ, which by its very nature concerns the salvation of humanity, and also involves the renewal of the whole temporal order.' This is the particular field of the lay apostolate ... in family life, business, sport, politics, culture, art and you-name-it.

They are to challenge society with the sharp salt of gospel wisdom: to expose the darkness of confusion with the light of Christ: and to raise up the daily mixture of life as the leaven in the dough.

The world is my life... your life.

Deeply loved by God and embraced by Jesus Christ.

But still infected with evil and inclined to stray from Jesus.

Come, O Holy Spirit of Truth,

Come and consecrate us in the truth,

That we may be true to his name.

Pentecost Sunday

Fifty days after the feast of Unleavened Bread, the Jews celebrated the festival of thanksgiving for the wheat harvest. In the Christian liturgical calendar this feast of the fiftieth day celebrates the Church's mission of harvesting for souls. Today we celebrate the birthday of the Church, when power from on high was given to the disciples to carry on the saving work of Jesus Christ.

John 20:19-23

In the evening of that same day, the first day of the week, the doors were closed in the room where the disciples were, for fear of the authorities. Jesus came and stood among them. He said to them, 'Peace be with you,' and showed them his hands and his side. The disciples were filled with joy when they saw the Lord, and he said to them again, 'Peace be with you.

'As the Father sent me,
so am I sending you.'
After saying this he breathed on them and said:
'Receive the Holy Spirit.
For those whose sins you forgive,
they are forgiven;
for those whose sins you retain,
they are retained.'

Good News

God has given the spirit, energy and gifts of Jesus Christ to those who belong to him in faith and baptism.

First Reflection
Perspectives on Pentecost

It would be a mistake to restrict Pentecost, or the descent of the Holy Spirit, to a one day wonder when a house in Jerusalem was rocked by a mighty wind and there were mysterious tongues of fire in the air.

The three readings in today's Mass widen our understanding of the Spirit's coming as they approach it from different perspectives. Luke's story in Acts of Pentecost day is most familiar to us since our liturgical calendar follows his timing of events. However, John's gospel tells of the infusion of the Holy Spirit as part of the Easter event ... on the evening of the first day of the new age. And in today's second reading, St Paul tells the Corinthians of the various gifts of the Spirit to the community, like parts of the one body with different functions to perform.

There were two great sendings or missions of divine power. Firstly, God the Father sent Jesus Christ ...'As the Father sent me'. Then the risen Lord Jesus sent out the disciples ...'so am I sending you.' In the breath of the risen Lord they received the same Spirit who had been the power of salvation in his own mission.

The coming of the Spirit marks the dynamic expansion of the mission to all races. So, it suited Luke admirably to set the event in the context of the harvest festival of the fiftieth day. Pentecost means the fiftieth day.

The symbols in Luke's story are the mighty wind and the tongues of fire. The wind expresses the movement of God's creative power, recalling the breath of God over the primitive chaos in the story of creation.

The tongues express the proclamation of the message. They are of fire, which is the symbol of love and the agent of purification or judgment. Luke's concern in his composition of the story is the expansion of the mission of Jesus into the universal mission of the Church.

John sees the divine gift of the Spirit in the Easter context of the uplifting of Jesus in his dying and rising.

'And when I am lifted up from the earth
I shall draw all men to myself.' (Jn 12:32)
Jesus had promised much to all those who would be raised up in his rising. He promised that believers would discover fountains of living water within their own souls. As scripture says: 'From his breast shall flow fountains of living water.' And the evangelist explains that Jesus was speaking 'of the Spirit which those who believed in him were to receive; for there was no Spirit as yet because Jesus had not yet been glorified.' (Jn 7:38-39)

Jesus later explained that his going away would result in the coming of the Spirit: 'Unless I go the Advocate will not come to you; but if I do go, I will send him to you.' (Jn 16:7)

While Jesus lived in the flesh the Breath of God was confined to his one body. But when this body was broken in death and then raised in glory, his Breath was released for all believers. And so, John tells us that on the evening of the first day of the new age, the risen Lord came to the disciples, breathed the Spirit into them and sent them to complete his saving mission over sins.

The effects of the Spirit's coming are manifold and today's three readings give an idea of their diversity.

What John stresses is the power of forgiveness of sins. Jesus is the lamb of God who takes away the sins of the world: and his disciples are given his power to remove the barriers of sin which keep people away from God. It is typical of John to speak of the two extremes of acceptance or rejection of the message. Those who accept and believe will be forgiven: whereas those who refuse to believe will be retained in their sinfulness.

In the Acts, Luke stresses the power of the Spirit in the proclamation of the good news in a manner that overcomes all the barriers of language and racial differences. There is now a divine unity of news within the human diversity of tongues.

In today's second reading, St Paul tells the Corinthians that there is a variety of gifts but always the same Spirit. Whatever gifts are given they are to be regarded as forms of service to the whole community rather than as personal favours.

At Pentecost we celebrate the birthday of the Church.

With John we celebrate our involvement in the uplifting of Jesus by the gift of the Spirit to overcome sin.

With Luke we celebrate the dynamism of the Spirit seen in the preaching of the good news and the expansion of the kingdom on earth.

With Paul we celebrate the diversity of services in the whole community and the beautiful fruits of the Spirit in individual lives.

It is the birthday of the Church ... our birthday.

Second Reflection
Confirmation
The sacrament most associated with Pentecost is Confirmation. As the scriptures allow some period of time between the resurrection of Christ and the sending of the Holy Spirit, so too do we normally have some time between Baptism and Confirmation. Baptism applies to us the death and resurrection of Christ: in its waters we die to sin and are born anew as children of God. Confirmation then applies to us the grace of Pentecost: it equips us with the Spirit's gifts for engaging us in the active mission of the Church.

There is a parallel between these two sacraments and the two comings of the Spirit with regard to the life and mission of Jesus. On the day of the annunciation, the Spirit came upon Mary and overshadowed her with divine power as the life of Jesus in the flesh commenced. Thirty years later, as Jesus emerged from the Jordan, the Holy Spirit descended upon him in the form of a dove. This put the seal of confirmation on his identity as the beloved Son of the Father, and it consecrated him for his mission. Ever after that day Jesus was led or driven by the Spirit.

The sacrament of Confirmation is conferred with the anointing of chrism on the forehead, with the laying on of hands and by the words which call upon the Holy Spirit to come.

The effects of the sacrament are many. It puts a seal, like an official stamp, on one's membership of the Church. It confers what theologians have called a character. This marks one's entry into a certain stage of belonging to the Church. There is such a finality about it that Confirmation, as with Baptism and Holy Orders, cannot be repeated.

Each sacrament confers a special sacramental grace. The particular charism of Confirmation is the Spirit's strengthening to enable a person to take up service in the Christian community. The principal forms of service are in the witness of a Christian lifestyle, generosity in love and care, the light to teach and the courage to persevere. The sacrament bestows an increase in the theological virtues of faith, hope and love.

The mission of Christ, in which we are called to share, is three-fold – it is priestly, prophetic and towards the development of the kingdom of God on earth. Our sharing in these three ministries have their source in the anointing of Baptism, their further development in Confirmation and their dynamic sustenance in the Holy Eucharist. (Pope John Paul 11)

We share in Christ's priesthood whenever we pray to the Father in his name, especially in the Eucharist. Active participation in the Eucharist is not the prerogative of ordained clergy. 'The liturgical celebration, in fact, is a sacred action not simply of the clergy, but of the entire assembly. Therefore, it is natural that the tasks not proper to the ordained ministries be fulfilled by the lay faithful.' (Pope John Paul 11) In recent years we have seen greater recognition of this priestly charism of Confirmation through the restoration of the lay ministries of reading the word and distributing the sacred host.

Our participation in Christ's prophetic mission calls on us to witness to the values of the gospel in our lifestyle. We must stand up and witness to 'the hope that is in us' and be zealous to pass on the light of Christ to others.

Our sharing in Christ's kingly anointing does not mean exercising authority over others but, in the spirit of the gospel, it is a call to serve others. We are called to represent Christ to others in our attentiveness to their needs through the spiritual and corporal works of mercy.

On a wider front we are called to the restoration or preservation of the reign of God in all affairs of the world ... to be the salt and light of Christ in our homes, our work, our social pursuits, our parliaments and law courts. Our motto throughout the world must be 'Christ's Rule is O.K. here'.

In some places Confirmation is conferred about the age of seven. It is seen as part of the process of Christian Initiation, before the reception of the Eucharist.

Here in Ireland the sacrament is usually given at the end of primary schooling. It comes then at entry into adolescence, at the time of life when the child is moving out of personal preoccupation into more social concern.

However, the present social routine associated with Confirmation is simply swallowing up the vital message of the sacrament. It is too much about dressing up, visiting relatives and 'how much did you make?'

One muses about alternatives. Might it not be better to do away with the present practice of little armies marched into the sacrament and allow for Confirmation on request when one freely desires to make a considered commitment to Christian life and to service in the church community. Perhaps in late adolescence ... early adulthood ... or later. It is just a suggestion for consideration.

Confirmation is a beautiful sacrament of grace for service in the Church and at the moment it is not sufficiently appreciated.

Trinity Sunday

We have completed the cycle of Easter and today we are invited to consider the inner life of God and the movements of God as Father, Son and Holy Spirit towards us. The mystery of the inner life of God is to be savoured and enjoyed rather than probed for an explanation.

Matthew 28:16-20

The eleven disciples set out for Galilee, to the mountain where Jesus had arranged to meet them. When they saw him they fell down before him, though some hesitated.

Jesus came up and spoke to them. He said, 'All authority in heaven and on earth has been given to me. Go, therefore, make disciples of all the nations; baptise them in the name of the Father and of the Son and of the Holy Spirit, and teach them to observe all the commands I gave you. And know that I am with you always; yes, to the end of time.'

Good News

We have been baptised in the name of the Father, and the Son and the Holy Spirit. We now enjoy a personal relationship with the Creator, Redeemer and Sanctifier.

First Reflection
In the name of the Blessed Trinity

In today's gospel we read that Baptism is to be administered in the name of the Father and of the Son and of the Holy Spirit. We must try to appreciate the weight of importance that Scripture gives to a name. In the name is the presence of the person and a sharing in all that this person stands for. It is not merely acting out of the remembrance of some inspirational figure as we do when we call a club or a street after some patriot.

In scripture, the name of a person calls up the living and active presence of that person. In Baptism we are established in a vital, dynamic relationship with God as our creator, our redeemer and our sanctifier. In the name of the three divine persons is the presence and power of the three.

Theology has been beautifully described as the art of being able to hear stories about God and to tell them in turn.

And what is prayer? Prayer is when we know that we are part of these stories of God.

133

The Blessed Trinity is the story of three movements of God towards us. First is the movement of life out from the mind of God, fathering all creation. When God saw what he had created each day, he said: 'It is good.'

However, human freedom was abused and man sold off his birthright, becoming the slave of sin. He needed to be saved from this slavery. And so, the second movement of God towards us was in sending a Redeemer, a Saviour. Nowhere has it been more beautifully expressed than in Jn 3:16: 'God loved the world so much that he gave his only Son, so that everyone who believes in him might not be lost but may have eternal life.'

The Son of God took on our human condition to enter fully into our ups and downs, our thought process, our emotions, our strengths and vulnerability... into everything except sin.

As our brother, he embraced our lot.

As our Saviour, he led us out of slavery into freedom.

As the Word of God he brought us the light of faith.

As the head of the body, where he has gone, there we hope to follow. And the basis of our hope is the third movement of God in our regard ... the gift of the Spirit.

The Holy Spirit is like the breath which always returns to the great surroundings: the power of love which draws towards unity: the power of God which drew up Jesus Christ out of death into glory. And as the glorified body of Jesus is no longer limited within physical limitations, so now the Holy Spirit has been released for all believers.

The theology of the Blessed Trinity tells us the story of God reaching out to us as Father-Creator, as Son-Redeemer and as Spirit-Sanctifier. Prayer is when we know that we are part of that story: when we are caught up in response to God's movements: when we are partners in God's dance.

In today's second reading (Rom 8:14-17), St Paul describes what it means to dance with God's movements.

To be moved by the Spirit, one knows that one is raised to new life, higher than natural life, a child of God. Gone is all servile fear of God. We no longer want to hide from God's eye but our delight is in coming closer to him ... children running towards their heavenly Father. The essential word of Christian prayer is 'Abba, Father.' Prayer is love of the Father expressed in words and sighs and waiting.

Prayer is also praise and thanks. Praise to the Giver and thanks for the gifts. The true direction of praise is from the Spirit moving within us, through the Son and unto the Father.

'Through him, with him and in him,

in the unity of the Holy Spirit,
all glory and honour is yours, Almighty Father.'

Heaven will be the completion of our Baptism. Until then we are heirs of God, having the right to heaven though we are still waiting. While we wait here on earth we still encounter sufferings, tensions and contradictions. But even these experiences are not removed from God's presence. In these crosses we will encounter Christ on the cross ... 'co-heirs with Christ, sharing his sufferings so as to share in his glory.'

We have been baptised in ... plunged into ... the name of Father, Son and Holy Spirit. In reconciliation we are absolved in the name of the Blessed Three. And at the end of Mass we are sent out in their name.

In the name is the presence and the power of the one invoked. God is ever-present to us a fatherly power, redeeming word and sanctifying love. In prayer we respond to these movements.

Glory be to the Father, through the Son, by the Holy Spirit.

Second Reflection
Sent and returning

Some four hundred years before Christ, the philosopher Plato came up with two questions which he could not answer:

'If there is only one God, what does he think about, for if God is an intelligent being he must think about something?'

And question number two: 'If there is only one God, whom does he love? And to be happy one must love.'

Not all the brains in Greece combined could offer Plato any answers. Only the revelation of the trinitarian life of God provided a solution to the questions about divine intelligence and divine will.

God is not an abstract theory but the author of a story that involves me.

God is not a static principle, but is ever moving towards us.

God is not a cold, rugged individualist, but a community of knowing and loving.

God is not distant and isolated but is a family bound in warm unity.

God is not aloof, unknown and unsociable: no, the trinitarian God is creator-provider, word and lover.

An early theologian, John of Damascus, wrote of God in beautiful imagery:

'Think of the father as a spring of life, of the Son as the river flowing from that spring, and of the Holy Spirit as the sea: for the spring, the river and the sea are all one nature. Think of the Father as a root, of the Son as a branch, and of the Holy Spirit as a fruit: for the substance in these three is one.

Think of the Father as the sun, the Son as the rays and the Holy Spirit as the heat.'

In the movements of the ocean I see the incoming tide visiting our shore like the Word coming in our flesh. And in the outgoing tide, returning to the ocean, I see the drawing of the Holy Spirit in love's return to the Father's bosom.

Simpler still is the natural rhythm of our breathing. Like the movements of the sea, our breathing is the twofold movement of taking in and returning.

From the all-present air (God the Father), we take in our breath (as we receive the Son who is sent to us).

We hold that gift of air. We make it our own for a while and let it work for our bodies. Then when its work is done we return it to its great source. The longer we hold it the more it strains to return.

If our intake of air represents receiving the Son, then our return of breath represents the Spirit returning in love to the Father.

It is a simple way to quieten our racing minds, to pray to the rhythm of the Blessed Trinity in our breathing.

Draw in breath ... and name it Jesus.

Hold it as long as you need to use it.

Then let it return to its source, now naming it as Spirit.

In and out ... Jesus and Spirit.

Sent and returning ... Jesus and Spirit.

Note: Next Sunday we will resume the cycle of Sundays in Ordinary Time. Consult the liturgical calendar for the appropriate Sunday.

The Body and Blood of Christ

The readings for the feast in this year's cycle highlight the Eucharist as a sacrifice and as the meal of the new covenant between God and humanity.

Mark 14: 12-16, 22-26

On the first day of Unleavened Bread, when the Passover lamb was sacrificed, the disciples said to Jesus, 'Where do you want us to go and make the preparations for you to eat the passover?'

So he sent two of his disciples, saying to them, 'Go into the city and you will meet a man carrying a pitcher of water. Follow him, and say to the owner of the house which he enters, 'The Master says: Where is my dining room in which I can eat the passover with my disciples?' He will show you a large upper room furnished with couches, all prepared. Make the preparations for us there.' The disciples set out and went to the city and found everything as he had told them, and prepared the Passover.

And as they were eating he took some bread, and when he had said the blessing he broke it and gave it to them. 'Take it,' he said, 'this is my body.'

Then he took a cup, and when he had returned thanks he gave it to them, and all drank from it, and he said to them, 'This is my blood, the blood of the covenant, which is to be poured out for many. I tell you solemnly, I shall not drink any more wine until the day I drink the new wine in the kingdom of God.'

After psalms had been sung they left for the Mount of Olives.

Good News

Jesus Christ has left us the perfect sacrifice in his own body and blood. The new covenant, in which we are called to be children of God, is established and sustained in the sacrifice of the Eucharist.

First Reflection
Sacrifice and Covenant

Mark's account of the Last Supper draws deeply from the background of sacrifice and covenant in the Old Testament. We will reflect on the meaning of sacrifice and covenant in order to deepen our appreciation of the historical background to the Eucharist.

We know the experience of being overwhelmed by the goodness or generosity of somebody and being left with the question,

'How can I possibly repay ... how can I show my appreciation?'

In the history of humanity, once people arrived at the sense of a supreme being or invisible spirit, they had this problem of how to relate or make a return to the unseen power.

Out of fear, they wanted to placate the anger of the spirit. Out of a sense of need, they petitioned the invisible powers for favourable results in hunting, war, or any of the great social events of life. As their notion of the deity became more personal and benign, they sought to express praise and thanks. The need is well expressed in to-day's responsorial psalm:

'How can I repay the Lord for his goodness to me?'

What developed was sacrifice. *Sacrum facere* means to make something sacred, i.e. to remove it from everyday life so as to dedicate it specially to the sacred being. Usually some form of food was chosen to represent life. And more often than not it was some animal.

They could not physically meet the deity and say, 'Here is your animal which we offer you as a present.' Instead, they killed the animal. Parts of it were burnt and the rising smoke represented the giving of the animal to God. The Greek word for God probably comes from the word for the smoke of incense which was burnt to dress up the smell with pleasant fragrance.

Two very important rituals developed: the sprinkling of people with the animal's blood and the sacrificial meal. The shedding of blood ratified the peoples' relationship (or covenant) with the deity. Those who were partaking in that particular sacrifice were then sprinkled with the blood. It indicated that they had a part in this sacrifice.

After the sprinkling with blood, they had the sacrificial meal. In many instances it was considered that the god sat at table with the participants to renew their relationship and to revitalise their energy. Those who shared a covenant meal together were bound in a very sacred bond. It was the height of treachery to betray anybody with whom one one had been united in a covenant meal.

All this basic human ritual had a special depth of meaning for the Jewish people because of their belief that God had chosen them to share in a special covenant relationship. The story of their race told of the great deeds of God at the time of Moses, when they were led from slavery to become a people and nation of their own.

Today's first reading (Ex 24:3-8) describes how God's covenant with them was solemnly ratified with sacrifice and the sprinkling with blood. Each year the great events of the Exodus were celebrated at the Passover.

Mark introduces his account of the Last Supper by linking it up with the Passover background. It was on the very day 'when the Passover lamb was sacrificed.' But at this meal there was no lamb mentioned. The body to be 'given up' in sacrifice is his own body. The blood which will ratify the covenant is his own blood. 'This is my blood, the blood of the covenant, which is to be poured out for many.' What Jesus did at the supper anticipated his sacrificial death and rising, not in the smoke of burnt animals, but in his return to the Father.

Today's second reading (Heb 9:11-15) explains that the one sacrifice of Jesus was perfect. No longer is there any need for the blood of goats and bull calves or the ashes of heifers, for the blood of Christ represented the perfect sacrifice to the Father.

As the Christian community became more distanced from the sacrifice of animals, increasingly they empahasised the inner meaning of sacrifice. The sense of praise and thanks to God came more to the forefront and the Greek term, Eucharist, meaning praise and thanks, grew in popular usage.

There is also a future, heavenly dimension to the Eucharist. It is suggested in the words of Jesus, 'I shall not drink any more wine until the day I drink the new wine in the kingdom of God.' The Eucharist anticipates the perfect praise of God in heaven. That is why we are invited to lift up our hearts to give praise and thanks to God. And in the preface we join with the choirs of heaven in their song to the thrice holy God.

The most important mental requirement in coming to Mass is a sense of thanks and praise. The most authentic way to express it is in participating in the perfect sacrifice of Jesus Christ, returning to the Father. The risen Lord Jesus Christ is the only way to the Father. No one can go to the Father except through him.

Parents sometimes feel they should insist that their unwilling offspring go out to Sunday Mass. Perhaps they can be forced out but they cannot be forced in. Only the sense of praise and thanks will bring one into the sacrifice. The grumpy face and unwilling heart have no place in this sacrifice of praise.

'How can I repay the Lord for his goodness to me ?
The cup of salvation I will raise;
I will call on the Lord's name.'

Second Reflection
Jesus, Bread of Life

Brennan Manning, an American Franciscan priest, tells this story about his mother, a lady in her mid-seventies in Brooklyn. Mrs Manning's day centred on her daily Eucharist. Because she began a voluntary stint at a drug detoxification centre each morning at 7.30 am, the only Mass she could reach each day was at 5.30 am.

Across the road from her lived a very successful lawyer, mid-thirties, married with two children. The man had no religion and was particularly critical of daily church-goers. Driving home from a late party at 5 am one January morning, the roads glassy with ice, he said to his wife: 'I bet that old bag won't be out this morning', referring to Mrs Manning. But to his shock, there she was on hands and knees negotiating the hill up to the church.

He went home, tried to sleep, but could not. Around 9am he rose, went to the local presbytery and asked to see a priest. 'Padre,' he said, 'I am not one of yours. I have no religion. But could you tell me what do you have in there that can make an old woman crawl on hands and knees on an icy morning?' Thus began his conversion, along with his wife and family.

Mrs Manning was one of those people who never studied deep religious books, never knew the big theological words, but she knew what it is to meet Jesus Christ in Holy Communion.

We have everything we need in Holy Communion. Jesus Christ is our bread of life. What more could we want?

We do not need complicated systems, big words, faraway shrines, psychological programmes or anything else if we have a simple, strong faith in the Blessed Eucharist. The Eucharist is Jesus: the Eucharist is everything.

There are two sentences in the liturgy which are worth a moment's reflection.

'Lord, I am not worthy to receive you.' Holy Communion is not a prize for being good. We do not pretend to be worthy. We come because we are struggling sinners. We come to the table, not when we are full, but precisely because we are hungry and weak. Jesus did not take a gold medal as his hiding place but bread and wine ... food and drink ... sustenance and celebration.

'Happy are those who are called to this supper.' A pity the translators did not give us the stronger word, blessed. How blessed are those who receive the Lord! How privileged!

Lord Jesus Christ in the Blessed Eucharist you come to me
as the bread to sustain me this day,

as the friend who stays beside me,
as the light to guide me.
You are my strength against temptation
my energy to work in your name,
and my challenge to bring your love to all I meet this day.

'Padre, what do you have in there?'
I pray that you will be blessed with the faith to know that
we have everything there ... Jesus Christ... our bread of life.

Second Sunday

Before we develop Mark's gospel, which will be our source through most of this liturgical year, today we have a reading from John. His account of the call of the first followers is deeply theological and serves as a sort of preface to Mark's story of the relationship of Jesus to his disciples.

John 1:35-42
As John stood with two of his disciples, Jesus passed, and John stared hard at him and said, 'Look, there is the lamb of God.' Hearing this, the two disciples followed Jesus. Jesus turned round, saw them following and said, 'What do you want?' They answered, 'Rabbi' – which means Teacher – 'where do you live?' 'Come and see,' he replied; so they went and saw where he lived, and stayed with him the rest of that day. It was about the tenth hour.

One of these two who became followers of Jesus after hearing what John had said was Andrew, the brother of Simon Peter. Early next morning, Andrew met his brother and said to him, 'We have found the Messiah' – which means the Christ – and he took Simon to Jesus. Jesus looked hard at him and said, 'You are Simon son of John; you are to be called Cephas' – meaning Rock.

Good News
Jesus invites us to spend time with him so that we might come to know him ... and to know our own calling.

First Reflection
Called by God
The evangelist John was far more interested in the theology of Christ's life than in the story as history. His purpose was to write a document of faith and he felt under no obligation to compile a detailed timetable of the events of the life of Jesus.

In today's extract he condenses the entire story of the divine calling of the early disciples into one episode. The other evangelists treat their calling as a gradual human response to what they see in Jesus. For instance, in Luke the call of the first four disciples comes only after they had seen the miracle of the huge haul of fish. And it is quite a while before Simon is given his new name, Peter.

But here in John, the emphasis is on the role of God in their calling. So, he anticipates the gradual process by which they came to know Jesus and receive a new identity and mission. From the divine perspective, which John favours, what has begun is regarded as already completed.

The call of these early disciples sets the pattern for God's call to all later disciples. There are certain elements in the call to faith which deserve deeper reflection.

(1) Faith comes from hearing

The story begins with the witness of John the Baptist who drew attention to Jesus. Although faith comes from God, some human witness is used as an agent by God, through word of mouth or through good example. As Paul wrote to the Romans: 'They will not believe in him unless they have heard of him and they will not hear him unless they get a preacher.' (Rom 9:14) The gift of faith comes from God but it is delivered to us by people like our parents, or teachers, or sources of light whom we meet on our journey.

The Baptist is a model of how the witness unselfishly hands over to Christ. The evangelist John has already written of the great calling of the Baptist. He was a man sent from God. But his role was to witness to the light, for he was not the light himself. Unselfishly he directed his own followers towards the one who was to come after him. 'He must grow greater and I must grow smaller.' (Jn 3:30) The witness of other people will draw us more to Jesus.

(2) Deepening knowledge

In several of the stories of John's gospel we find people growing into deeper levels of faith. The titles they use when referring to Jesus express their deepening faith. When the first two disciples initially follow Jesus they regard him as a teacher, a rabbi. But when they spend more time with him they recognise him as the long-awaited Messiah, the Christ.

Those who seek the Lord are invited to come to him, to spend time in prayer with him, and to grow in a more intimate knowledge of his person. The first witness, John the Baptist, was one who had 'stared hard' at Jesus. Our time of staring at Jesus is when we persevere in prayer and in our study of the Lord's word. It is only when our faith has grown and our knowledge of Jesus has deepened that we will be able to give witness to him through our lives.

(3) Sharing with Others

The witness of John the Baptist was given on the third day of the first week in Jesus' public life. The third day suggests a rising to new life. And it was early next morning, that is on the fourth day, when Andrew acted as a missionary and shared his faith with his brother. The fourth day is an expression of the mission received by the followers of Jesus to share their faith with others.

Andrew proclaimed Jesus as the Messiah: 'We have found the Messiah, the Christ.' It is in giving that we receive all the more: it is in sharing our faith that we claim it more deeply: it is in searching for the words to give to another that we clarify our own thoughts. But if we fail to grasp the challenges and opportunities to share our belief with others, then our own faith will weaken and fade away.

Faith is like love in this way. Love can be kept only by giving it away. Faith becomes more complete when we share it with another: when we invite our brother/sister to share in the relationship with Jesus which we ourselves experience. The fourth day is when we share our gift of faith with others.

(4) A new name

When he had come to know Jesus, Simon received a new name. Whoever becomes a true follower of Jesus Christ is raised to a new level of life. And in this new life one has a new identity: hence, a new name.

Abram became Abraham, meaning father of a multitude. And at the annunciation, the angel Gabriel addressed Mary by the new name, Full of Grace.

Now Simon's name was changed because his new role would be as the foundation rock of the Church community. He is known to us as Peter, the Greek name for a rock. But the original Aramaic form of the name which John here uses was Cephas.

In this episode, John has disregarded the lengthy time sequence of human growth in order to highlight the impact of the divine calling unto new life.

The story of the early disciples invites each of us to spend time with Jesus, to share our faith with our brother/sister, and to discover our own secret name which God has carved on the palm of his hand.

'To those who prove victorious I will give the hidden manna and a white stone – a stone with a new name written on it, known only to the man who receives it.' (Rev 2:17)

Simon discovered that he was to be a solid foundation rock.

What is written on your white stone?

What is God asking you to do on the fourth day

... the first day of the rest of your life?

Second Reflection
Come and see

'Master, where do you live? Where do we come to know you?' 'Come and see', he invites. Today's Old Testament reading of the call of young Samuel is deliberately chosen to extend our reflection on the gospel.The boy Samuel is instructed by Eli to respond to God's call with an open heart and a listening ear: 'Speak, Lord, your servant is listening.' We read that in the years that followed, the Lord was with him. And he deeply treasured the presence of the Lord in his life for 'he let no word of his fall to the ground'.

There are many meeting places where the lovers of Jesus come to spend time with him. They let no words of his fall to the ground: and every minute salvaged from the rest of life is jealously reserved for being at home with him.

Prayerful reading of sacred scripture is for many their favourite meeting place with the soul's beloved. Every day the soul thirsts for a living word of God. A passage of scripture is read and reread as the words are savoured and pondered. Lessons are drawn for the practical decisions of life. Words of prayer grow like fruit from the text. As in the life of Samuel, the Lord is with us as we stay with the inspired texts. And we probe the different layers of meaning lest any precious word escape us and fall to the ground.

Another way of taking up the invitation to come and see is in spending time in prayer before the Blessed Sacrament. Our racing minds are quietened as we focus attention towards the tabernacle or exposed host. Our daily frettings are calmed in the deep ocean of God's love as shown to us in the Blessed Sacrament. The moment of the Mass is prolonged for our devotion. We are reassured of the desire of the Lord to be with us always. We are strengthened in the memory that he is the bread of life, filling us with his own energy.

Word of God, made flesh of Mary, made bread for us.

The first two followers of Jesus went to where he lived and stayed on with him for the rest of the day. The faith of many followers today is greatly sustained by their house meetings and grouping for the purpose of prayer and Godly conversation. When we gather together in Christian conversation we are encouraged by the good example of others; we are supported in our weakness; and we are helped to pray. I have met many people whose spiritual lives never blossomed until they began to share with others.

'Let us be concerned for each other, to stir a response in love and good works. Do not stay away from the meetings of the community, as some do, but encourage each other to go.' (Heb 11:24-25)

Another way of spending time with the Lord is to sit at the end of the day in quietness. We close our eyes to let the story of our day create its own pictures. We attend to the feelings that come through to us after the day's pressures and pains, loves and labours, conflicts and reconciliations, losses and gains. We recognise the story of our life day by day. We lay it all before the Lord in praise and gratitude, in petition and repentance. We let everything rest for the night under the shadow of his wings.

'Master, where do you live? Where can we meet you?'

'Come and see.'

Open up the door of your life and the home of your heart to him. Treasure every moment and every word lest they spill to the ground and be wasted.

Third Sunday

Mark's gospel will be our source for most of the Sundays this year. Two of the great themes of Mark are introduced in today's passage: Jesus as the teacher of the Good News, and the call to discipleship.

Mark 1:14-20

After John had been arrested, Jesus went into Galilee. There he proclaimed the Good News from God. 'The time has come,' he said, 'and the kingdom of God is close at hand. Repent, and believe the Good News.'

As he was walking along by the Sea of Galilee he saw Simon and his brother Andrew casting a net in the lake – for they were fishermen. And Jesus said to them, 'Follow me and I will make you into fishers of men.' And at once they left their nets and followed him.

Going on a little further, he saw James son of Zebedee and his brother John; they too were in their boat, mending their nets. He called them at once and, leaving their father Zebedee in the boat with the men he employed, they went after him.

Good News

The kingdom of God is breaking in on our lives and the word of God calls on us to leave the ways of sin so as to enter his way.

First Reflection
Introducing Mark

Mark will be our guide for most of the year. He is the underestimated genius who, under divine inspiration, created a whole new form of sacred literature. He was the pioneer evangelist, the first to capture into a coherent story the encounter of God and mankind, which took place in the person and ministry of Jesus Christ.

He brought together the various spoken and written memoirs of Jesus Christ, edited them and wrote them into the form of an engaging story. His writing is simple but mysterious, consoling yet challenging. It has been maintained from the early days that he had access to the memories of Simon Peter. But as a writer he was a man with a mind of his own.

Mark never attempts literary affectation but he writes with the haste and directness of a reporter who knows that he has a good story and wants to get it out. Forty-one times we find him jumping ahead to the next phrase with a word like immediately or straightaway.

In recent years the actor Alec McCowen, by using the text of Mark for a one-man show, has demonstrated what a riveting story-teller Mark is. He avoids all superfluous details as he carries the reader along at breathless pace into vivid pictures and dramatic action. His pages are teeming with people and Mark keeps us in touch with their emotional reactions to what was happening.

Mark's storytelling ability is so good that his work is deceptively simple. The depth of theological reflection behind his story was for too long neglected. Only in recent years has Mark received due attention as a theologian.

As we reflect with Mark throughout the year we will be confronted especially with the mystery of the cross in the life of Jesus and with the struggles of the disciples in their growth of faith.

We will find here no dishonest pretence that all is easy and happy for those who follow Jesus. Mark courageously faces the growing pains, struggles and contradictions of all who follow the teacher whose way led to Calvary.

Perhaps Mark, with his stark message of the cross, is the evangelist for this pampered age when people have been given false expectations of worldly happiness and total self-gratification as much by half-baked preachers as by the allurements of advertising and the beguiling promises of technical progress. These false expectations of life have left far too many people unable to cope with hard reality. A spineless generation needs to hear again the good news of the cross: the news that God can be found on the crosses of life.

Mark gave a name to the new literary form which he had invented. In his opening sentence he entitled it 'Gospel', which means God-news. Here is the God-news, in the story of Jesus Christ, the Son of God.

Today's short passage introduces us to two of the great themes of this gospel. We begin the story of Jesus and also the story of discipleship.

The story of Jesus is of one who teaches the world with power and authority about the kingdom of God. He proclaims that the reign of God is breaking in on the world, calling us to follow his flag. This is news of a radical break from the old ways of sin before we can enter into a new way of living.

To break from the old way is to repent: and to break into the new way is to believe. First hear the word of God and then, in its light, turn away from the sinful ways of the past, just as the people of Nineveh heard the preaching of Jonah and renounced their evil behaviour (in today's first reading).

148

The first disciples lead the way because when they heard the call of Jesus they left their nets, occupations and families to follow him.

And so commences the second of Mark's great stories, the path of discipleship. This will be a long and oftentimes painful road throughout the year. But for the moment, Mark's point is that the call to discipleship begins at the very start of Jesus' preaching.

Mark will be our guide throughout the year. Week-by-week we will be carried along in the God-news of how Jesus challenged the world and how the world reacted. But all the while, as Mark spins his story, he is inviting us to put ourselves on the stage and see where we are in the story. For the story of discipleship is intended to be my story and yours.

Second Reflection
Disciples for the kingdom

The mission of Jesus was about the kingdom of God. He began his preaching with this message: 'The time has come and the kingdom of God is close at hand.'

What is this kingdom? Forget all your ideas of lines on a map or borders or armies and territorial possession. The kingdom is about the allegiance of the human heart to the mind and commandments of God.

Whose way do you follow, which value-system do you live by? Is your heart set on the ways of self-seeking and self gratification? Is your life given over to the ways of wealth, power and sensuality, even when these transgress the ways of love?

The rule of the heart which Jesus called for is a return to the ways of God. Wherever God's love is reflected in the values of life, there God is king. And that is the kingdom of God.

To establish this kingdom was the major mission of Jesus. And so, he began to preach on the need to repent and believe: to change direction from the ways of sinful selfishness and to set one's ambition towards God-centred patterns of thought and behaviour.

But Jesus knew that the establishment of the kingdom would be a process of slow growth. His own work would need to be extended in time through the voices of many others. So, from the very beginning of his own mission he began to prepare the community of disciples to continue and extend his own ministry. The kingdom would need the Church. The story of the Church, then, develops from the very beginning of the ministry of Jesus.

The call to repent and believe was given flesh and blood when

149

the first disciples left their nets and families to follow after Jesus. The road ahead of them would show up many forms of misunderstanding and many occasions of weakness. But for the moment, what is important is that the journey begins in an invitation from Jesus.

This was not the usual way with Jewish rabbis. People usually sought out the teacher, asked questions about his interpretation of the Law and might then decide to follow that rabbi. But here it is the teacher who takes the initiative and invites the disciples to follow him.

The first four to be called were fishemen. Two were casting their nets in the lake, while two were on the home-shore mending nets. He promised to make them into fishers of men.

Casting and mending ... corresponding to the twin works of the apostolate, mission and maintenence. Both works are needed.

Mission is the zeal to go to those who do not belong to the kingdom, either because they have never properly heard Christ's message or because they have fallen away.

Maintenance, mending the nets on the home-shore, means the routine tasks of serving those who are already disciples. Casting the nets will be more profitable when they have been properly maintained. And the task of mending achieves its purpose when they are ready for casting. Missionary zeal can grow only out of a well-maintained home base. But the home Church will be unhealthy if it does not share its relationship with Jesus through mission to others.

If you are today a disciple of Jesus it is because somewhere along your road of life you have heard the call to follow his way. But he did not call you to a cosy, private religion. You are called to be a disciple for the kingdom. The Church exists for the sake of the kingdom or reign of God in the hearts of all.

A disciple for the kingdom reaches out with the message of Christ to others, casting nets far and wide: and also helps to mend the torn nets and broken lives of those on the home-shore.

Fourth Sunday

Mark hurries us along with the new followers of Jesus to experience a typical day in his ministry at Capernaum. We are introduced to the two great works of Jesus, teaching and casting out demons. At the end of the gospel these same works will be enjoined upon the disciples themselves. Jesus spoke with a hitherto unknown authority: he is the prophetic voice promised in today's first reading. (Deut 18:15-20)

Mark 1:21-28
Jesus and his followers went as far as Capernaum, and as soon as the sabbath came Jesus went to the synagogue and began to teach. And his teaching made a deep impression on them because, unlike the scribes, he taught them with authority.

In their synagogue just then there was a man possessed by an unclean spirit, and it shouted, 'What do you want with us, Jesus of Nazareth? Have you come to destroy us? I know who you are: the Holy One of God.' But Jesus said sharply, 'Be quiet! Come out of him!' And the unclean spirit threw the man into convulsions and with a loud cry went out of him. The people were so astonished that they started asking each other what it all meant. 'Here is a teaching that is new,' they said, 'and with authority behind it: he gives orders even to unclean spirits and they obey him.' And his reputation rapidly spread everywhere, through all the surrounding Galilean countryside.

Good News
In Jesus Christ, God has come to us with the light of his teaching and the power of goodness which overcomes all destructive forces.

First Reflection
The power-struggle
In this account of a day at Capernaum we get the first inkling of the great power-struggle which took place when God encountered the world in the person of Jesus Christ.

Mark understands the incidents of that day as part of a much greater story. Those who witnessed the events, insofar as they were astonished at what they experienced, were getting the first glimpses of a great mystery.

It was a sabbath. And there was nothing unusual in requesting a travelling teacher to supply the homily on the day's sacred reading in the local synagogue.

Jesus began to teach. For the moment Mark does not give us any of the content of his teaching. That will come later. Here Mark wants to draw our attention to the impact of Jesus on all present. The reactions are polarised: the people are deeply impressed but the evil spirits are severely threatened.

The people sensed a new authority in Jesus as a teacher and it impressed them deeply. He was unlike the typical scribe who understood his task to be the conservation of orthodoxy at all costs. The scribes thought that what mattered in a lesson was the number of reputable scholars of the past that one could quote from. There was a freshness in the words of Jesus, for clearly they came out of his own goodness and wisdom. This was a totally new experience for the audience ... a sermon that was actually alive! The man himself was the message.

But it was not all a story of acceptance. The evil spirits felt threatened and immediately began a disturbance through a poor, demented man. If we were listening to a musical symphony based on the gospel of Mark, we would now be hearing the first statement of a major theme in the work. For Mark wrote under one great question: how is it that this great teacher and worker of wonders was rejected and eventually crucified?

Mark wrote for a community of Christians who were faced with a parallel question in their own lives. How can we claim to be following the all wise, loving and powerful God in the steps of Jesus Christ if what we are experiencing in life is belittlement, persecution and the danger of death? The events of any one day in the life of Jesus must be seen on the broader canvas of a mysterious power-struggle which was taking place for the mastery of souls.

The evil spirits were immediately threatened once Jesus appeared on the stage of the world. The first battle took place in that poor man who was possessed by an unclean spirit. His condition was a symptom of how the world at large was under the enforced possession of the alien, occupying powers. This unjust possession was challenged by the light and goodness of Jesus the teacher. Mark regards any destructive illness as being caused directly or indirectly by a hostile, anti-God, anti-life power.

The evil spirit reacted in two ways: through magical incantation and violent frenzy. In calling out on Jesus as the Holy One of God the evil spirit was certainly not involved in the prayer of adoration. Rather this was an attempt to gain magical power over Jesus by calling out his secret name, or unmasking him. Magic means trying to get some superhuman power to work on one's behalf.

The second tactic of the devil was to throw the poor man into violent convulsions. His loud cries of pain filled the air. The devil is the father of lies and a dealer in death. Diabolical power shows up in the confusion of true belief, in resorting to violence and destruction, in frenzy and loud cacophony.

How significant it is that the words of Jesus were: 'Be quiet.'

Godly power is gentle.

And true wisdom needs no shouting.

Be still, my soul, and rest in the Lord.

His gentle power urges me to be quiet.

Jesus is the teacher of true wisdom and the source of peace. He offers a quiet strength which is greater than the outer frenzies and inner frettings which too often possess us.

'Be quiet', he tells us.

Be quiet, my soul, and listen to his living voice today.

Second Reflection
Astonishment and wonder

The people at Capernaum were deeply impressed and astonished. They started asking what it all meant. Mark sees this reaction of the people as very important in the steps towards discipleship.

Astonishment and wonder open up the mind to the possibility of a greater world, still unseen, but at least faintly glimpsed. The journey to faith often begins in an honest search for meaning or in that openness of mind that sees the wonders of everyday life.

This age of scientific and technical education goes hard on the sense of wonder. Science breeds the expectation that everything can be subjected to analysis and then explained. In this way it seeks mastery and control. There are people today who genuinely believe that one day soon we will have the computer which will answer all the questions about the origin and destiny of the universe. They think that subjecting things to analysis will offer sufficient meaning to satisfy the hungers of the heart.

But under scientific domination things are torn apart without sufficient respect for nature's delicate balance. The ugliness of pollution stalks the land, poisons the waters and pierces the umbrella of the atmosphere. It breeds a companion ugliness in forms of art and music which manifest all the diabolical signs of cacophany and convulsion.

The patron saint of ecology is Francis of Assisi. Even those who know nothing whatsoever of his sanctity have heard stories of his love for animals. The highly respected psychologist, Erikson, considers Francis as the most significant example of a person grown into adult creativity, precisely because of his capacity to contemplate things as they are without feeling the need to own them or manipulate them in any way.

I grew a little towards understanding Francis in my moment of the lizard. It was in Central Africa and I was basking in a shaded verandah while the midday sun beat down dizzily and reduced the surrounding world to stillness and silence. The little lizard alone, on the wall opposite me, was busy. Could I capture him on film and bring back this little bit of an African day to show to the folks at home? The lizard could be pictured but the total atmosphere of the moment was too subtle to capture. I realised a little what it is to contemplate the moment and receive from it rather than attempt to master it. St Francis lived like that all the time and precisely through owning nothing he enjoyed the world in a passionate way that few have ever known.

As long as we are open to wonder and astonishment we can be lifted beyond the circumstances of today. We can glimpse the broader canvas of life and begin to live with mystery. Beauty will minister to us if we let it. It will elevate our thoughts beyond our day-to-day frettings. We learn that most problems are not solved: they are simply by-passed. And today's problem will be the basis of next week's joke.

Anybody who really believes in God has a youthful soul ... for God is the One who makes all things new. (Rev 21:5) The soul that is ever-young is capable of being impressed, being astonished and amazed. But the staleness of sin leaves the soul caught in the cobwebs of old memory and stuck in the routine which sees nothing but the boring sameness of things. Guilt and hatred come out of old memories, but joy and wonder are always new.

It is no surprise that this age of technological education is also the age of boredom. There is enough mystery in one small garden to stimulate the mind for a year.

Jesus made a deep impression on the people at Capernaum and he evoked their astonishment. They had made the first tiny steps towards the faith of discipleship.

From the staleness of sin ... deliver us, O Lord.

From the dead mind of boredom ... deliver us, O Lord.

With the psalmist we learn to pray:

'I thank you for the wonder of my being,

For the wonders of all your creation.' (Ps 138, Grail)

Fifth Sunday

The readings in today's liturgy come together in their portraits of people under pressure. Job offers a profound insight into the condition of one who is utterly broken and deflated by suffering. In the gospel, Mark portrays Jesus under the pressure of being misunderstood: he is the victim of his own popularity, in danger of being restricted from his wider mission. Paul, in the second reading, finds that his apostolic energy comes in no small way from the press of duty which his conscience lays on him.

Mark 1:29-39

On leaving the synagogue, Jesus went with James and John straight to the house of Simon and Andrew.

Now Simon's mother-in-law had gone to bed with fever, and they told him about her straightaway. He went to her, took her by the hand and helped her up. And the fever left her and she began to wait on them.

That evening, after sunset, they brought to him all who were sick and those who were possessed by devils. The whole town came crowding round the door, and he cured many who were suffering from diseases of one kind or another; he also cast out many devils, but he would not allow them to speak, because they knew who he was.

In the morning, long before dawn, he got up and left the house, and went off to a lonely place and prayed there. Simon and his companions set out in search of him, and when they found him they said, 'Everybody is looking for you.' He answered, 'Let us go elsewhere, to the neighbouring country towns, so that I can preach there too, because that is why I came.' And he went all through Galilee, preaching in their synagogues and casting out devils.

Good News

The life of Jesus was deeply rooted in his prayer-relationship with the Father. From that deep source came his energy to preach and to heal.

First Reflection
Morning Prayer

Mark writes in great haste. He lets us fill in many of the details for ourselves as he has a long journey to travel in his story of ministry and discipleship.

In this episode he writes of Simon and his companions: he does not as yet dare to call them disciples. They are still only beginning to move towards faith. Last week we saw that the authority and teaching of Jesus deeply impressed them. His work filled them with astonishment. They had caught the first glimpse of the greater mystery behind Jesus. They began to ask what it all might mean.

The mystery in Jesus is clarified a little in today's episode when we see him leave the crowd to go off to a lonely place to pray. It was very early morning, long before dawn. Mark lets us know that the power of Jesus, manifested in his day's preaching and healing, came from God who is encountered in prayer.

Simon and his companions set out searching for him. The verb used by Mark is not a comforting word: it suggests a police-search, or at least the upsetting intrusion of busy-bodies. They fancy they have the news he wants to hear: 'Everybody is looking for you.' But they are mistaken. Later as the story develops we will see how the apostles continually misunderstood Jesus and his plans.

Jesus knows that the crowd seek him only because they can use him as a miracle-worker. But he refuses to be a prisoner to this wave of popularity.

He has not come from heavenly glory simply to receive earthly adulation: he has come to serve: and eventually to serve with the laying down of his life. They wanted to stay in a religion which gave easy access to miracles: but he wanted to move on to the lessons of the cross.

Selfless service is the way of his ministry. And such must be the way of discipleship too. Those who are moving towards discipleship will have to learn that lesson.

Simon's mother-in-law comes into the story like a model for disciples. Virtually all the women in Mark's gospel are models of discipleship. Jesus entered her house, 'took her by the hand and helped her up.' The Greek word used by Mark could also be translated as 'raised her up.' It was a word later used with reference to the resurrection. Her cure prefigures baptism in which one is raised up to share in Christ's life by grace. She immediately began to wait on her guests. That is precisely how any disciple of Christ is called, not to a cosy, private relationship with Jesus, but to the challenge of a life of service in his name.

The way of Jesus radically questions the notion that is dear to today's extraverted world, that mass popularity and fame are prospects to be desired.

It was no shyness on his part, for he was in no way reluctant to be up front teaching and healing people. But he would not settle for celebrity status nor did he want an idolising fan-club.

His Church, whether as a worldwide body or as a local community, is not in the business of courting the popularity charts or following the opinion polls. Its duty is to proclaim the truth 'in season or out' and to wage war on the possessing spirits of society. It is called to serve the truth in charity and courage.

We must learn from Jesus who, very early in the morning, met the Father in prayer and then lived the day fully attuned to the Father's will.

In the morning we groom ourselves for the day in the mirror of prayer. There in the light of God we see our day and draw the strength to say: Thy will be done this day, on earth as it is in heaven.

Not unto us, O Lord, not unto us,
But to thy name be the glory.

Second Reflection
Prayer in time of stress
The three readings of today's Mass are about people, Job, Paul and Jesus respectively, who are under stress. The reading about Job's suffering does not easily link up with the gospel until one recognises that the context of Jesus at prayer is the stress of being misunderstood and being restricted by his own popularity.

Mark has a habit of working with incidents in threes. Three times he pictures Jesus at prayer. Each instance occurs when he is under stress regarding the true nature of his messiahship. In this first instance the stress is caused by those who would pull him away from his true mission of service.

Stress is the business of tuning a guitar or any stringed instrument. Too little tension on the string and the note is flat: it sounds dull and floppy. But too much tension and the note is sharp, grating on the nerves.

When one is insufficiently stimulated and stretched, then life is flat, stale, boring and lacking energy. But if one is overstretched, the stress will be heard and seen in a life that is sharp on the nerves, brittle at the edges, agitated and ready to snap.

Job's strings had lost all zip and energy. His life is but drudgery and slavery, with months of delusion and nights of grief, days of heavy time and hours of restless fretting. There is no hope in his heart and he will never again see joy.

In today's second reading (1 Cor 9:16-19, 22-23) we meet stress of a different kind. Paul, if anything, is too wound up. Others found him a difficult companion. His apostolic energy is nothing he can boast of, since it comes from the press of duty which his agitated conscience lays on him. He is not untypical of the converted sinner ... a bit overzealous. It is easier for him to preach than to be idle. The pains of the apostolate trouble him less than would the frustrations of inactivity. Money or payment mean nothing to him. Duty done is its own reward. But duty yet to be done puts pressure on him.

Jesus under stress needs to pray. He has been preaching and healing. He is involved in a great power-struggle for souls. These works take a severe toll on one's inner reserves. I know from experience that the preacher works at a deep, inner cost. I pity anyone who needs me as companion before or after preaching a retreat. I suspect that the cost to the healer is even more demanding on the system.

Jesus withdrew to pray. There he recovers his serenity with the Father. The parts of life come together in a totality and the strength of inner peace is restored. The best way to grow strong is to be deeply rooted. And the roots of Jesus' ministry were deeply set in his prayer-relationship with the Father.

Stress is an important part of our lives for it is necessary for our stimulation and flow of energy. But if we are overstressed and disregard it we will pay for it in frayed nerves, short temper, lack of concentration and various health problems.

Sometimes the energy that is needed for life's duties is no longer available because it has all gone inward to quieten the cries of pressure. One is left listless and goes down into the dark valley of self-pity.

When we recognise the source of our stress it is sensible to seek a diversion through the balance of an opposite occupation. If crowding is our problem the we need solitude. If loneliness is the source then we need society and companionship. If our work is mentally pressurising, then we need relaxed, physical playfulness. And physical tiredness loves to meet with gentle mental stimulation as in reading and conversation.

Beyond these ways of common sense is the way of Jesus. He leads us to prayer in times of distress.

Before God, get in touch with your stressful feeling. Listen to your body. Is it a heavy mental pressure? Or is it restlessness, agitation and gut dissatisfaction? Is it an emotional turbulence?

Seek God's light so as to discern where he is leading you through this situation. But be absolutely sure that God is with you all the way.

Seek his will in all things ... for in his will is our serenity.

Sixth Sunday

Today's gospel concludes Mark's opening presentation of the preaching and healing of Jesus. The cleansing of the leper is the final story in this section. The first reading gives us an idea of the social stigma attached to leprosy.

Mark 1:40-45

A leper came to Jesus and pleaded on his knees: 'If you want to,' he said, 'you can cure me.' Feeling sorry for him, Jesus stretched out his hand and touched him. 'Of course I want to!' he said. 'Be cured!' And the leprosy left him at once and he was cured. Jesus immediately sent him away and sternly ordered him, 'Mind you say nothing to anyone, but go and show yourself to the priest, and make the offering for your healing prescribed by Moses as evidence of your recovery.' The man went away, but then started talking about it freely and telling the story everywhere, so that Jesus could no longer go openly into any town, but had to stay outside in places where nobody lived. Even so, people from all around would come to him.

Good News

The news of God here is the revelation of the compassion of Jesus for the outcast.

First Reflection
Shunning publicity

Wasn't it ironic that an ex-leper, a man once condemned to live apart from society, became the very reason why Jesus had to stay in places where nobody lived?

Jesus took away the condemnation of the leprous man and restored him to town and family life: but the man, by not listening to Jesus, condemned his healer to absent himself from the towns. There is here a hint of what is to come in the way that Jesus took the sentence of condemnation of himself.

Mark portrays Jesus as shunning publicity. What is called the messianic secret is one of the most puzzling themes of this gospel. 'Tell nobody about all this except the priest whom you have to see to get your bill of health required by law.'

Why should Jesus want to shun this advertisement of his power? Much has been written about Mark's theme of the secrecy of Jesus. Many of today's scripture scholars hold that the secrecy theme is more of Mark's doing than based on anything in the historical life of Jesus. If that is so, then the question to be asked is why did Mark portray Jesus as shunning publicity for his miracles.

It seems that Mark wanted to move his readers away from the adulation of a miracle-worker towards a deeper appreciation of the crucified Servant of God. The cross is central in Mark's mind. It was where the ministry of Jesus reached its climax and it should be central in the minds of disciples too. Too much emphasis on the miracles only obscured the place of the cross.

Mark's insight is very relevant for this impatient age which has no understanding of the cross. We have been bred on speedy painkillers, instant everything and a technology that seems to put the whole world into our reach. We do not want to know of our limitations.

It is an age when religious charlatans try to sell healthy living and inner peace while neglecting the questions of social conscience: when 'a la carte' Christians select what they like from the religious menu but reject whatever they do not fancy: when we will happily use God to our own advantage but rebel if we feel that we are to be used by God.

The search for miracles will bring people by the busload to the prospect of a moving statue. Pictures of the divine face, or magical mittens or candles seem to mean more than the sacraments. Many popular novenas and devotions are little more than request programmes on the heavenly airwaves. God is reduced to the Almighty Aspirin. This is the sort of misunderstanding of his ministry that Jesus wished to avoid.

The culture of today favours self-fuliflment as the greatest purpose of life. And the way to self-fulfilment is usually seen in terms of what we want or according to the way that we understand things. But the doctrine of the cross is that we must die to selfishness in order to reach higher life. We must let go of what is good in order to reach for what is better. We must be ready to be broken in order to be remade in God's fashion, willing to die in order to live.

The leper disregarded the request of Jesus to keep it quiet. Oh, he knew better! So, he blazed it abroad.

And the people avid for novelty, lusting for excitement, hungry to use God, set out after Jesus. The celebrity status and notoriety which he wanted to avoid now enveloped him. He could no longer move about freely but had to stay outside the places where nobody lived.

Why can't we listen to God and try to do it his way?

Thy will, not mine, be done.

Second Reflection
The three lepers of Saint Francis

When the hand of Jesus was stretched out to touch the leper the gesture must have stunned him. Jesus was incurring defilement in the eyes of the law and automatic suspension from religious functions. But Jesus did not catch the defilement. Instead, 'the leper was infected with Jesus' purity. He caught clean.' That is how it has been described by Alec McCowan, who does a one-man show by telling Mark's gospel, word for word.

That gospel moment when compassion reached out to touch a leper was repeated in the life of St Francis of Assisi. It turned out to be the most important day in his conversion to the crucified Lord.

It happened early in his career. He had begun to give long hours to prayer but was still living with his wealthy family. Riding on horseback one day on the plain below Assisi, he came upon a leper. Francis's character was the most fastidious type of any. He had a highly refined sensitivity of smell and taste. More than other people he was totally nauseated at the sight of the leper and the smell of the putrid flesh. He spurred his horse to hurry past. But his conscience, recently enlightened by prayer, now challenged him. He remembered that he must first conquer himself if he was to become a knight in the service of Jesus Christ. He ran back to the leper who put out his hand for alms. Francis first give him what money he had. And then he kissed him.

His biographer, St Bonaventure, says that when Francis remounted his horse he looked around and although the open plain stretched in all directions, the leper was nowhere to be seen.

The leper was in no one place because in a sense he was everywhere. Francis embraced three lepers on that road.

The first leper was the actual man whose appearance filled him with revulsion and horror.

The second leper was the dark side of his own personality. This pleasure-loving young man of wealthy family was very uncomfortable in the face of ugliness, stench and handicap. Now for the first time ever he faced the fact that the horror was his. He accepted responsibility for his own unChristian reaction. He embraced the leprosy of his own sinfulness.

The third leper was the crucified Jesus Christ. This was the most important day in his journey of discipleship towards Jesus Christ. It prepared him for the mystical experience he had shortly afterwards when he heard the voice of Jesus on the cross asking him to repair his Church. His journey towards that mystical encounter began with the leper on the road. Years later, Francis wrote in his last testament that it was the Lord who had led him to the leper. And he described the change in his soul: 'What before seemed bitter was changed into sweetness of soul and body.'

The incident challenges me to face the unChristian traits, the leprous parts in my soul. If any other people are like lepers ... outcasts ... untouchables to me, then, like Francis, I am challenged to come off my high horse and own up to my responsibility for feeling that way.

Is it some superiority complex or pride in me which makes me think I am better than others ... characterwise, culturally or spiritually? Or an inferiority problem that erects a barrier of fear and shyness between me and others?

Is it an area of unforgiveness which makes me see only the short memory and never the total person? Or some inherited prejudice against a certain class ... unemployed ... different ... colour ... itinerants ... people of different language ... or culture ... or religion?

Don't say there is no leper on your road of life. For there is that one leper whom the Lord really wants you to touch. That leper is the infected person who lives in your sinfulness.

Come off your high horse and go back on the road of memory. Now touch, embrace and kiss that leper ... that part of yourself which you have always denied or hated. Accept the responsibility for your own feelings ... prejudices ... hurts ... and blind spots. Accept the ownership of your own lifestory and bring it to Jesus to be cleansed and cured.

And, like Francis discovered, what before seemed bitter will be changed into sweetness of soul and body.

Seventh Sunday

This is the first of three Sundays when the gospel tells of Jesus in dispute with some of the Jewish religious leaders. This first conflict is over his claim to have the divine authority to forgive sins. Mark presents the cure of the paralytic as a proof that Jesus had this divine power.

The paralysed man represents the condition of mankind awaiting that word of God which would blot out the sinful ways of the past and offer a new way, a new kingdom. 'See I am doing a new deed.' (First Reading)

Mark 2:1-12

When Jesus returned to Capernaum, word went around that he was back; and so many people collected that there was no room left, even in front of the door. He was preaching the word to them when some people came to him bringing a paralytic carried by four men, but as the crowds made it impossible to get the man to him, they stripped the roof over the place where Jesus was; and when they had made an opening, they lowered the stretcher on which the paralytic lay. Seeing their faith, Jesus said to the paralytic, 'My child, your sins are forgiven.' Now some scribes were sitting there, and they thought to themselves, 'How can this man talk like that? He is blaspheming. Who can forgive sins but God?' Jesus, inwardly aware that this was what they were thinking, said to them, 'Why do you have these thoughts in your hearts? Which of these is easier: to say to the paralytic, 'Your sins are forgiven' or to say, 'Get up, pick up your stretcher and walk'? But to prove to you that the Son of Man has authority on earth to forgive sins,' – he said to the paralytic – 'I order you: get up, pick up your stretcher, and go off home.' And the man got up, picked up his stretcher at once and walked out in front of everyone, so that they were all astounded and praised God saying, 'We have never seen anything like this.'

Good News

In Jesus Christ God's word is spoken to the world. His word heals sickness of the soul and restores fulness of energy to lives that were paralysed and restricted.

First Reflection

Mark concludes this story by telling us that the people were astounded for they had never seen anything like it. They were moved to praise God for his word was among them as a power to heal and to give life.

163

It is interesting that whereas Mark usually shows Jesus healing people through touch, in this instance he heals them simply with words. And they were strong words ... 'I order you: get up, pick up your stretcher and go off home.'

The first reading of the day (Is 43:18-25) is well chosen to prepare us for the gospel. The prophet appeals to the people to trust mightily in God's power. There is no need to be dragged down by memory of the past. God is ever capable of doing a new deed and of making a road out of the jungle of past complications. It is God alone, 'I it is', who can blot out everything harmful from our past.

The gospel story of this astonishing power of God to forgive and release centres on the picture of the paralysed man. Paralysis means restriction of movement and the loss of the power of feeling or sensation. The muscles are weakened, the joints stiffened and the senses diminished. The paralysed man in the story represents the many people who are no longer responding to God in a free and energetic life. You see it in individuals and institutions who have become immobile, mentally stagnated and emotionally negative.

The scribes, who were sitting there, were paralysed by the jungle of laws which had taken over their religion. They are a warning to all religious institutions of how the free-flowing charism, which once responded to the needs of the times, tends to get imprisoned and restricted in the structures which are set up to support it.

A Church community can become imprisoned in its own long history. It can be hard to get any fresh thinking accepted. Changes are resisted and new challenges are frowned upon. Apathy is prevalent and parish councils will not be set up, nor will lay responsibility emerge where it is imprisoned in long years of clerical power.

The process of paralysis can set into a marriage when love grows stale and communication ceases. The relationship no longer grows but gradually turns into a fossil.

A very common source of paralysis is fear. Many struggling souls are so afraid of falling into the sin which dominates their lives that they develop a fixation about falling: and this fixation will inevitably cause them to fall, as surely as the cyclist who strongly imagines that one hand is pulling him towards the ditch will inevitably end up there.

Even more paralysing than fear can be the effects of guilt ... blaming oneself ... feeling all dirty inside ... thinking oneself unworthy of love.

Or the restriction of life may come from the memory of past hurts. It is not unusual to meet widowed people who never recover any zest for life after the loss of a partner. Or some family scandal can leave a trail of lives that are forever emotionally blunted. The wisdom of the Church does not ask us to forget past hurts but encourages us to talk them out in the Sacrament of Reconciliation. It is in telling their story that many people have found release from their paralysis.

Back in Capernaum Jesus was preaching the word to the people. It was the message of God's kingdom, the word of renewal of life, rescuing people from the powers of evil.

The message which was meant for all time took flesh in the lifting up of one paralysed man. What God could do for one he can do for all.

His love endures for ever ... and his healing word is alive unto our own day.

Second Reflection
As Jesus saw them

There are several different groups of people in this drama of the cure of the paralytic. We can easily imagine how the eyes of Jesus quietly moved from one to the other. The first group to whom the attention of Jesus was drawn was the party of friends of the paralytic. There were people everywhere, pressing in, blocking door and window. In the house it was stifling. Enough light to see shapes and outlines but not the faces of people.

Then started the commotion on the roof. It was being stripped away. Small lumps of dried clay began to fall on those inside, dust catching in eyes and throats. A chink of light was made, then a hole and a face peered down. Smiling in mischievous apology. More thatching was torn away, the sunlight above grew blinding and then there were four heads up there.

The people inside had pushed back from the falling clay, so there was space in the centre. Two men jumped in. Two stayed on the roof (or what remained of it) and began to let down a stretcher to their friends.

'Easy now, over this way ... mind that beam ... that's it.' The two above jumped in and the four stood, one at each corner of the stretcher.

They looked at Jesus. No words were spoken but their eyes said it all. We've come because we believe in you. We've done this ridiculous thing to the house because our little friend here is so desperate.

And Jesus followed their eyes towards their friend on the pallet. Hardly a man and yet not a child. Ungrown, under-developed, stunted. Victim of the old kingdom whose sins had restricted the perfection of life. Yet this man-child was rich in his community of friends. Friends who believed and friends who carried him to Jesus.

Jesus looked down. He saw not only the paralysis of this one ungrown life but the sad state of the whole of sinful humanity. So he said to this one victim: 'My child, your sins are forgiven.'

Then everybody could hear the silence. That cold, uncomfortable sort of silence. And they looked towards the men on the seat by the wall. The Jerusalem men. Four or five of them, watching everything, listening and silent. Coldly silent.

But Jesus, looking at them, was inwardly aware of all that they were thinking.

Critics. Learned men but negative. Heresy-watchers who would never tell the story of God's love to people. Custodians of orthodoxy who would leave the people in darkness. Leaders who would have their people crippled.

It was the first time that Jesus was meeting with this kind of negativity. But it would not be their last meeting. For the challenge of Jesus would finally be answered by the insane violence of the cross. Violence is the ultimate negation of love and life.

Where do I find myself in that room?

Amond the negativity people? Always looking for the fault? An ear open to gossip: a tongue itching to pass it on. Silent about goodness. But eloquent in cynicism and criticism.

Or do I identify more with the crippled personality? Physically unenergetic: mentally stagnating: emotionally unresponsive. So bruised by the encounters in my life-story that I can no longer trust anybody. Fallen so often that I am now unable to get up. Doomed to failure at every turn.

How I need the support of friends to carry me! How I need to hear the exorcising words of divine power: 'I order you: get up.' Oh when, Lord, will your face shine on your servant?

Perhaps I am blessed to be among the faith-friends. I am willing to carry one corner of the stretcher because I have experienced how the community of Christian friends have carried me. I have experienced their love, care, support, understanding and forgiveness. I go to them now for prayers, for advice, for support ... for their Christian friendship. We have heard the word of Jesus and it has made our lives anew.

Our greatest joy now is when we can bring another friend to Jesus. We try to make a friend ... to be a friend ... and to bring a friend to Jesus.

Eighth Sunday

This is the second Sunday when we meet Jesus at the centre of a dispute with some religious leaders. The issue now is the observance of those extra fasts which devout people were expected to undertake. Jesus uses the conflict as an occasion to make the important pronouncement that he is the bridegroom of humanity, come to unify the families of heaven and earth. Fasting has its time and place but not during the celebration of a wedding. The first reading, from Hosea, enriches our meditation on the faithful love of God who opens his arms to welcome us back to union with him.

Mark 2:18-22
One day when John's disciples and the Pharisees were fasting, some people came and said to Jesus, 'Why is it that John's disciples and the disciples of the Pharisees fast, but your disciples do not?' Jesus replied, 'Surely the bridegroom's attendants would never think of fasting while the bridegroom is still with them? As long as they have the bridegroom with them, they could not think of fasting. But the time will come for the bridegroom to be taken away from them, and then, on that day, they will fast. No one sews a piece of unshrunken cloth on an old cloak; if he does, the patch pulls away from it, the new from the old, and the tear gets worse. And nobody puts new wine into old wineskins; if he does, the wine will burst the skins, and the wine is lost and the skins too. No! New wine, fresh skins!'

Good News
In Jesus Christ, God has taken humanity to himself in a loving union which ought to be celebrated in joy.

First Reflection
Something beyond fasting
Isn't it true that we experience far more trouble from those who are near to us in ideals and thought than from those who are diametrically opposed to our stance? Certainly Jesus experienced far more oppostion from religious leaders than from those who never gave a thought to God or religion.

Today's gospel shows Jesus in controversy with the Pharisees and some of John the Baptist's followers who had not aligned themselves with him.

The point at issue was fasting: or more exactly, those extra fasts which devout people were expected to observe. What the law of the Old Testament obliged regarding fasting was in fact very little. But many extra days of fasting were added on by people like the Pharisees. In time these man-made practices took on the appearance of divine law itself.

This, of course, is a situation which persists in human nature, that we become so caught up in our own inventions and projects that we may become deaf and blind to what God is asking us to do. We are then incapable of moving on to something greater.

Jesus was not against fasting as such. What he was against was any exaggeration of fasting which might lead to hyprocrisy or to a doom-'n-gloom attitude that obscures the love of God.

That he was not against fasting is obvious from his own period of fasting before commencing his ministry. He quoted the old text: 'Man does not live on bread alone but on every word that comes from the mouth of God.' While the things of the body are important, the things of the spirit are more important. And there are times when we ought to show our preference for the spirit by a deliberate choice against the gratification of the body.

Furthermore, his fasting was a way of manifesting his solidarity with all the hungry people of the world who have no option but to fast every day.

However, Jesus warned against making fasting an end in itself as if religion were a very gloomy affair with no room for people enjoying themselves. 'When you fast do not put on a gloomy look as the hypocrites do: they pull long faces to let men know that they are fasting.' (Mt 6:16)

And in one of the parables Jesus was not at all impressed by the religious man, a Pharisee, who did extra fasts, 'twice a week', but looked down on sinners.

It is a recurring temptation of religious people to think that they are very pleasing to God on the score of what they have done. They work with a Do-it-Yourself kit for holiness. They imagine that what counts with God is the score of good deeds that we achieve and all the merits we stock up in the vaults of heaven. As we exaggerate our own importance we become blind to God's doing.

So, while fasting is important in its own place, it is far more important to recognise and celebrate what God's love does for us. When Jesus was challenged about not doing the extra fasts he made the point that it was more appropriate to celebrate what God was doing for humanity. He said that it is nothing less than a wedding between heaven and earth. And a wedding is no time for fasting.

Today's liturgy, by taking a reading from Hosea, expands on this love of God which reaches out to embrace us in marriage.

Hosea's message develops out of his own life-experience. His wife, Gomer, was unfaithful to him and went off her own way. But after some years she regretted what she had done and sent out feelers to see if there was any possibility of Hosea taking her back to home and children. Hosea brought his problem before God in prayer for direction. God let him understand that the unfaithfulness of his wife was exactly how the convenanted people had betrayed God. But God's love is ever faithful and he would always take his people back.

The time of Jesus brought in this promised reconciliation between God and sinful mankind. It was nothing short of a wedding between heaven and earth. What God had initiated was far beyond what human endeavour could ever merit.

Those who trusted too much in their own merits were unable to take on all that Jesus was offering. Their old garments would be torn asunder by his new cloth. Their decrepit wineskins could never contain the powerful spirit of his message.

The message of Jesus was of a love from beyond ... beyond our merits ... beyond our endeavours ... beyond our fasting.

Second Reflection

Jesus described his time on earth as a period of wedding cele-bration. The story which best expresses this celebration is the wed-ding feast at Cana where the water for washing hands was changed into the wine of celebration. And in what abundance ... six jars each holding between twenty and thirty gallons ... on top of what they had already scoffed!

Yet, no doubt, there was some late-comer to the party who be-moaned the absence of that water. I can see him there with furrowed brow as his religious scruples prevented him from entering into the grand celebration because the water of purification was gone and he could not obey the law about washing his hands!

Like the Pharisees, we sometimes let man-made customs, tradi-tions and institutions get in the way of the pure message of the gospel.

Pope Paul VI, at the close of Vatican II, apologised to the world for the faults of the Church and for the obstacles which we Church-members put in the way of belief for others.

Sadly, there are many people who have no idea of the beauty of religion or the joy of prayer because the Church people they know have never manifested these qualities.

Doom-'n-gloom preachers give religion a bad name. Their

religion wears an anxious face and gazes out through fanatical eyes. And there are people who are so dreadfully serious about the God-stuff that they think the Lord's Day should exclude all playfulness and fun. Like the very strict family where the little boy came to his father with a serious theological problem: 'Daddy,' he asked, 'when we go to heaven will God ever let us out to play with the children in hell?' As the man said after hearing the thundering mission sermon: 'Well, if that's the sort of people who go to heaven then I'll opt for the other place.'

There was a time when learned debate took place on the question, 'Did Jesus ever smile?' There may have been times when he was angry but I'm sure that most of the time the sunshine of God's love and mercy shone on his face and welcomed the people who were broken in body and soul to him. As St Francis de Sales expressed his experience in reconciling sinners: 'A spoon of honey will attract far more wasps than a jar of vinegar.'

If God is love ... and if religion is a response to God ... then surely it must contain a lot of joy and celebration. When St Paul wrote a list of the fruits to be seen in a Spirit-filled life, he listed joy as second only to love.

Christianity is not, as some imagine, a clamping down on human development with a long series of thou-shalt-nots. It is the glorious religion that celebrates the coming of God the Son to embrace us, to take us to himself in marriage, to adopt us into the human family.

Many of us have no need to learn anything extra about the strict side of religion. We were brought up with it and it is deeply planted within us. But we do need to learn more about celebrating God ... to know what it is to eucharist ... to lift up our hearts to praise and thank God. Many know how to confess sins but do not know how to praise and celebrate. They are threatened by music or joy or any sense of fun in God. They are afraid to smile lest their faces, like decrepit wineskins, crack and tear asunder in this unaccustomed expansion of muscle and tissue.

What the Pharisees and latter-day perfectionists fail to appreciate is that religion is to be deeply enjoyed and God is to be celebrated. And if we want to find the language to celebrate, nothing will surpass the psalms as a source.

Cry out with joy to the Lord, all the earth
Serve the Lord with gladness
Come before him, singing for joy. (Ps 99, Grail)

170

Ninth Sunday

For the third consecutive Sunday our gospel has Jesus in conflict with the religious leaders. Mark uses the drama of conflict to introduce an important pronouncement of Jesus. What is at issue is the meaning of the sabbath and the authority of Jesus to interpret the law. The first reading gives us the legal background to the observance of the sabbath. By curing the man with the withered hand Jesus emphasises the need to do good deeds on the sabbath.

This concludes the opening section of Mark's gospel. Note that Mark is dropping a clear hint of where the story of Jesus will lead to ... for 'they were discussing how to destroy him.'

Mark 2:23 - 3:6

One sabbath day Jesus happened to be taking a walk through the cornfields, and his disciples began to pick ears of corn as they went along. And the Pharisees said to him, 'Look, why are they doing something on the sabbath day that is forbidden?' And he replied, 'Did you ever read what David did in his time of need when he and his followers were hungry – how he went into the house of God when Abiathar was high priest, and ate the loaves of offering which only the priests were allowed to eat, and how he gave some to the men with him?' And he said to them, 'The sabbath was made for man, not man for the sabbath; so the Son of Man is master even of the sabbath.' He went again into a synagogue, and there was a man there who had a withered hand. And they were watching him to see if he would cure him on the sabbath day, hoping for something to use against him. He said to the man with the withered hand, 'Stand up out in the middle!' Then he said to them, 'Is it against the law on the sabbath day to do good, or to do evil; to save life, or to kill?' But they said nothing. Then, grieved to find them so obstinate, he looked angrily round at them, and said to the man, 'Stretch out your hand.' He stretched it out and his hand was better. The Pharisees went out and at once began to plot with the Herodians against him, discussing how to destroy him.

Good News

On the Lord's Day we give back our time to God in praise and thanksgiving. And through holy restfulness we are re-created by God's healing power.

171

First Reflection
The Lord's Day

At the time when Mark was writing, a clear rift was emerging between the new Christian communities and the traditional Jews. The earliest followers of Jews were all Jews. In the early days after the resurrection they continued to observe all the Jewish ways, as in going to temple and synagogue: but they also began the ceremony of remembering the risen Lord in the breaking of bread on Sunday, the resurrection day. Gradually, as more non-Jews joined their ranks, they moved away from Jewish observances and the new code and cult took over.

Mark considered it important for the Christian community to highlight the pronouncement of Jesus that he was the master of the sabbath. Just as he had the divine authority to forgive sins, so too had he the authority to free them from the man-made restrictions which had become part of the sabbath. He emphasised that the sabbath was made for man ... to help us towards fuller life rather than bind us up in negativities.

The seven-day week probably came from the Babylonians who considered seven the sacred and magical number. They were great sky-watchers and they were very familiar with the seven days of each phase of the moon. Also, they considered seven planets to be of major importance, the earth, sun and moon plus the four bright stars which traversed the course of the sky each night.

The Jews borrowed much from the Babylonians and dressed it out in their own theology. In their story of creation they used the seven-day week as the framework. An important point was that God rested on the seventh day. The word sabbath means resting from labour. The law of sabbath observance was the one guarantee of rest for workers and servants. In an age when vacations were unknown and union hours unheard of, this law of rest protected the quality of life. The only holiday was the holy day.

Another theological basis for the sabbath was the injction to remember their delivery from Egypt where their forebears were slaves and appreciated a day of rest. The sabbath rest was also understood as an anticipation of the end of time when they would enjoy eternal rest in place of the endless labour of this life.

The sabbath idea, then, was based on very wholesome ideas. However, man-made laws took over the idea and changed the atmosphere of the day from freedom to restriction. Rules took over and the stage was reached when a trivial act such as plucking an ear of wheat could be regarded as breaking the law.

The early Christians gradually moved away from the Sabbath of negation to the Sunday of celebration. St Paul's letters are full of the need to throw off the slave-chains of the law so as to appreciate the glorious freedom of being children of God.

In today's world, as secularisation erodes Christian consciousness, we need to refresh our minds on the different aspects of the Christian Sunday. First and foremost, Sunday is the day to remember our risen Lord, Jesus Christ. The celebration of the eucharist is the centre of our time, for Sunday is at once the end of one week and the beginning of another. In Sunday eucharist we make a return to God in praise and thanksgiving for the past week. And looking ahead, the eucharist is our source for the energy of Christ in the days ahead: without him we can do nothing.

Our Christian Sunday retains the original sense of holy restfulness. We rest from unnecessary work and business dealings. We seek restfulness by changing occupations to allow a more leisurely pace of mind and body. Playfulness, when properly understood, is a way to re-creation.

Sunday restfulness allows time to indulge in the sort of reading which deepens our faith and helps our prayer. But what a contradiction there is in the sort of Sunday newspapers which sell at the church gates. Hardly a support to faith or source of prayer!

Sunday restfulness allows more time for family togetherness and commmunication. In our fast-moving world, where snacks replace formal meals, we easily lose the age-old benefits of sitting to table together.

When Jesus cured the man with the withered hand on the sabbath, though he could well have waited until the following day, he showed us the example of using the Lord's Day for deeds of mercy. Sunday offers the chance to visit the sick and those who need our interest.

The holy restfulness of the day which we offer back to God is beautifully expressed by St Augustine:
We shall rest and we shall see,
we shall see and we shall love,
we shall love and we shall praise.

The Lord's Day is a rest from the helter-skelter of life to allow us soul-time, family-time and God-time.

Second Reflection
Anger

The healing of the man with the withered hand is a story with a great deal of anger in it. The Pharisees were angry in a brooding, obstinate way which led them to plot the destruction of Jesus: it was an anger towards death. Jesus too was angry but a rightful reaction to their stubbornness and to the ailment of the handicapped man: his anger was an energy towards the fulness of life.

Anger is our natural reaction to a hurt received, a wrong perceived, a blow to our self-esteem or some frustration. It sets off a whole process within us that generates a great deal of energy which, as we know only too well, may be difficult to control. However this energy may be channelled to constructive purposes and then it enables us to confront an injustice or to correct a wrong. But in some instances the effect of anger is to leave one deflated, bored and cynical: this happens when the anger is not allowed to surface in honesty and then it burrows deeply into the person.

Mark does not hesitate to write of the anger of Jesus. The best-known instance is when he chased the money-changers out of the Temple. But Mark mentions several other occasions when Jesus was angry. It is an intense gut-reaction to the pains of the world around him. Translators find it hard to know whether they should translate Mark's word for this gut intensity as compassion or anger. Jesus felt this deep reaction within himself to the destructive, paralysing hold on life which the evil powers exercised. And he was angry at the withering restrictions of sabbath celebration which a warped religion produced. In this episode he is grieved at the obstinacy of his critics who have prejudged his case and refuse to see the divine authority which gave him the power to heal.

Jesus shows us that it is healthy to admit our anger. And that we have, through anger, a great reservoir of energy which can give us the determination, courage and perseverance to confront injustices, to correct wrongs, and to work towards reconciliation and healing.

In my own life I have come to appreciate the energy which anger generates. The determination and energy to write these books on the three Sunday cycles comes in no small way out of anger. I had always considered myself a fairly placid, even-tempered individual who could readily let go of any frustration through sport or manual labour. I was slow to realise how cynical and angry I had become with certain situations and the people involved there. Gently, the Lord let me to see that I was projecting my own inner frustrations onto others.

I was into my forties and after twenty-five years in religious life. But what had these years produced? I was deeply aware of the emptiness of my return to the God who had called me to his service and sent me on his mission. For my Silver Jubilee Mass I was happy to take the gospel for that day about the profitless servant who has done no more than his duty. In this emptiness and frustration I was angry and did not recognise it. I thumbed my nose at the forty milestone by running the twenty-six mile marathon ... in a very respectable time. But the inner frustration remained, thank God. It gave me the energy to undertake and persevere in research, reflection and writing, no matter how often I hit the wall.

When our anger-energy is not used constructively it becomes destructive. Eveybody recognises the open burst of temper. But less easy to spot is sideways anger. Have you ever seen the way a crab walks, sideways? Our frustration comes out but it is directed towards substitute people other than the true cause. This causes us to talk uncharitably about a third party or makes us project our own inner frustration onto some other situation.

The anger which is most difficult to see is that which does not burst out in temper, but goes inward and is repressed. The Pharisees in today's gospel are a case in point. They watch everything but they see only the faults. They say nothing when challenged. They are obstinate and death-dealing. So bent are they on the destruction of Jesus that they conspire with their traditional enemies, the Herodians, to plot against him.

The man with the withered hand was the focus of all eyes in the synagogue that day. His withered limb was a symbol of the anger that paralyses life, of the legal sabbath which obscured celebration, of the minds that plotted death.

But in the depths of Jesus's humanity his grief, compassion and anger generated the energy to order this man to stretch out his hand. And the withered hand was re-created.

The Lord's Day is a holy restfulness in which we are re-created and restored after a busy week.

In the Sunday eucharist our inner reservoir of energy is nourished by the Lord ...

that we might be purified of all withering destructiveness:
and available for the works of justice and service in the week ahead.

Tenth Sunday

In today's gospel we see how the mission of Jesus is being obstructed by misguided concern on the part of his relatives and by the malicious obstinacy of the religious experts who had come down from Jerusalem.

Mark 3:20-35

Jesus went home with his disciples, and such a crowd collected that they could not even have a meal. When his relatives heard of this, they set out to take charge of him, convinced he was out of his mind.

The scribes who had come down from Jerusalem were saying, 'Beelzebul is in him' and, 'It is through the prince of devils that he casts devils out.'

So he called them to him and spoke to them in parables, 'How can Satan cast out Satan? If a kingdom if divided against itself, that kingdom cannot last. And if a household is divided against itself, that household can never stand. Now if Satan has rebelled against himself and is divided, he cannot stand either – it is the end of him. But no one can make his way into a strong man's house and burgle his property unless he has tied up the strong man first. Only then can he burgle his house.

'I tell you solemnly, all men's sins will be forgiven, and all their blasphemies; but let anyone blaspheme against the Holy Spirit and he will never have forgiveness: he is guilty of an eternal sin.' This was because they were saying, 'An unclean spirit is in him.'

His mother and brothers now arrived and, standing outside, sent in a message asking for him. A crowd was sitting round him at the time the message was passed to him, 'Your mother and brothers and sisters are outside asking for you.'

He replied, 'Who are my mother and my brothers?' And looking round at those sitting in a circle about him, he said, 'Here are my mother and my brothers. Anyone who does the will of God, that person is my brother and sister and mother.'

Good News

Anyone who does the will of God belongs to the inner circle of Christ's family and is as close to him as brother, sister or mother.

176

First Reflection
Outsiders and insiders

Mark liked sandwiches.

He was fond of taking two slices of some story and tucking some juicy item in between them. When you get accustomed to his style you notice that the central item in the sandwich is something Mark regards as very important to his story.

At the beginning and end of today's episode we have two slices on the misguided concern of the close family relatives for Jesus. They think that this sensible, home-loving carpenter has taken leave of his senses. Imagine, giving up a steady job like that. And worse again, now being investigated by these important men from Jerusalem! To their way of thinking this insanity must be due to some form of evil possession.

At the end of today's reading we see these relatives once more, this time insensitively interrupting his teaching. Clearly they do not recognise his greater calling, that he must be busy about his Father's affairs. Their misguided concern is a warning to us about letting our natural level of thinking impede a supernatural calling. The person who follows God's call will frequently be misunderstood and regarded as slightly mad by those whose wisdom does not go beyond this world.

The meat in Mark's sandwich is a particularly spicy item: the religious experts from Jesusalem are painted for us as deliberately obstinate, even malicious, in the way that they misinterpret what Jesus is doing.

The reader knows that Mark's story is heading towards the violent death of Jesus on Calvary. Mark is offering us clues as to how that final outcome was reached.

Last Sunday we read how they began to plot his destruction. Today we see how serious is their illness of soul and mind. They are deliberately closing their minds to God's will. They are putting themselves outside the circle of Christ's associates. They are cutting themselves off from the power of the Holy Spirit.

And the irony of the situation! In their malice they misinterpret what is the central thrust of Jesus' work, as Mark sees it. Jesus is casting out devils, in order to release the world from evil, so as to set up the reign of God alone in our hearts. But they say that he is in league with the devils and is working with their power!

Jesus looks at their accusation from three points of view. First of all he challenges the common sense of their charge. 'How can Satan cast out Satan? Yet you do admit that I am casting out devils. Are you saying that Satan is rebelling against himself? You can't have it both ways.'

Secondly, Jesus portrays himself as the stronger power who has broken into Satan's territory to tie him up and carry off the souls he possessed. And finally, he gives a stern warning that their deliberate obstinacy is flying in the face of God. It is blasphemy against the Holy Spirit. And as long as a person persists in deliberate rejection of God's will he cannot be forgiven.

There is no sin that God is not willing to forgive. But those who deliberately reject God's message and call are putting themselves outside the range of forgiveness. It is not as if God will not forgive them: rather, they are refusing to accept his will, his love, his forgiveness. They never avail of God's forgiveness.

It calls to mind the observation of St John: 'He came to his own domain and his own people did not accept him.' (Jn 1:11) Or the other observation of John: 'On these grounds is sentence pronounced: that though the light has come into the world men have shown that they prefer darkness to light because their deeds were evil.' (Jn 3:19)

How does one turn away from God in that sense of preferring darkness to light? Through opting for the darkness of violence or injustice. By pursuing money in a way that makes others suffer. In belittling the sacredness of life through pornography or peddling destructive drugs. When one settles for the ways of darkness one is in the state of mortal sin.

What matters in the eyes of Jesus is our obedience to God's will. That is what is meant in practical terms by the kingdom of God, or the reign of God, which he worked to establish.

Those who do not live according to God's ways are outside his circle of family and are turning their backs on the Holy Spirit. But anyone who sets out to live according to God's will is inside his circle and will be as close to him as brother, sister or mother.

Second Reflection
Mary the lonely woman
We do not meet the person of Mary, mother of Jesus, in Mark's gospel. She is mentioned in today's extract but we are not brought close enough to meet her. She is but a cardboard figure, part of the background scenario to the drama taking place at the front of the stage.

Today's liturgy uses this passage of Mark in conjunction with a first reading from Genesis 3:9-15. This tells of the woman's part in the fall of humanity and of the ensuing conflict until the offspring of the woman will crush the head of the tempting serpent. This is the great conflict which Mark has been relating to us as the power of God in Jesus is driving out the occupying spirit from souls. The liturgical use of the Genesis passage about the woman invites us to consider Mary's participation in the conflict.

While Mark offers only a cardboard figure of Mary, we do know far more about her from Luke and John. Here, in Mark, she is a forlorn figure caught up among the fussy relatives who do not understand, and who think that Jesus is quite mad, possibly under the influence of an evil spirit.

But from Luke we know that Mary is no ordinary woman and no ordinary mother. She is 'full of grace' and mother of Jesus through the direct power of God. Many years before this, she has been introduced to the mysterious dimension of her Son and his work. He told her something about the necessity to be involved in his Father's business. And although she and Joseph did not understand what he meant, she 'stored up all these things in her heart.' We can be sure that, like her Son, she advanced in wisdom as her soul lovingly pondered the mystery which was so close to her, yet so far away.

Did Mary, like the other relatives, think that her Son was mad or possessed? It is highly unlikely. She suffers in silence among these meddlesome fuss-pots who totally fail to appreciate the depths of what Jesus has begun.

From John's gospel we know of the deep faith of Mary and of her emerging role as the woman who would be the mother of all believers. John tells of Mary in two places, at the wedding in Cana and at the foot of Calvary's cross.

It was at Cana that the disciples, on seeing the miracle-sign of water changed into wine, learned to believe in Jesus. But Mary's faith was there even before the sign for it was an active part in the miracle. She is the first believer, whose faith is passed on to the disciples by means of the first miracle of Jesus. A great theologian, Von Balthasar, writes that Mary, as well as being Mother of the Church, can also be called the Mother Church. She is the mother-cell of belief, which grows and multiplies into the community of believers, the Church.

At Cana and on Calvary, according to John, Jesus addresses his mother as 'woman'. She is now identified as the new woman of Genesis whose offspring would crush the head of the tempting spirit. She is the new Eve, the mother of all.

But today we are left to ponder on the coldness and loneliness of Mark's picture. The words of Genesis echo menacingly in the background:

'I will make you enemies of each other
you and the woman,
your offspring and her offspring.
It will crush your head
and you shall strike its heel'

As plots are hatched against Jesus and malicious minds try to trap him, it is clear that the conflict is close to climax. The devils are defeated and flee in confusion but strike back at the heel of their conqueror. Jesus is winning but is injured: and will be injured more.

If the Son suffers, then the mother suffers too. So, Mark brings her in as a forlorn figure in the background: the lonely mother whose life is messed about by the fussy relatives who do not appreciate the depths of what Jesus is doing. And in her mother's love she too will be a victim of the malicious plots which are being concocted against Jesus.

In Mark's gospel Mary is silent.

It is the silence beyond words.

The silence which bows humbly in the face of mystery.

Eleventh Sunday

Today we move away from the conflicts and controversies of the past four Sundays. We listen to Jesus teaching people about the kingdom. There are two parables about the growth of the kingdom: it is growing even when we do not see it: and growing from tiny beginnings to a huge expansion.

Mark 4:26-34
Jesus said to the crowds, 'This is what the kingdom of God is like. A man throws seed on the land. Night and day, while he sleeps, when he is awake, the seed is sprouting and growing; how, he does not know. Of its own accord the land produces first the shoot, then the ear, then the full grain in the ear. And when the crop is ready, he loses no time: he starts to reap because the harvest has come.'

He also said, 'What can we say the kingdom of God is like? What parable can we find for it? It is like a mustard seed which at the time of its sowing in the soil is the smallest of all the seeds on earth; yet once it is sown it grows into the biggest shrub of them all and puts out big branches so that the birds of the air can shelter in its shade.'

Using many parables like these, he spoke the word to them, so far as they were capable of understanding it. He would not speak to them except in parables, but he explained everything to his disciples when they were alone.

Good News
The power of God's kingdom is in our world ever since the time of Jesus, even if its growth is sometimes in the secrecy of night or from tiny, unlikely beginnings.

First Reflection
The hidden kingdom
There are many priests, teachers and parents who feel totally inadequate in the face of today's changed society. The answers of yesterday seem to have no relationship with the questions of today. Many people are finding it difficult to hold onto any faith in the kingdom. They struggle to see evidence of the Holy Spirit in our world.

Mark's gospel is very relevant to this age of faith in crisis. He was writing some forty years after the time of Jesus. The Church community was under persecution from the outside. Virtually all the apostles and direct links with Jesus were gone. They now had the new phenomenon of Christians who were relapsing and falling away. And apparently there were internal problems also from self-appointed prophets and healers who were distorting the message of Jesus to their own ends.

People were asking, 'Is this what Jesus set up as the kingdom of God? Where is the evidence of the Holy Spirit?'

Mark wrote his gospel to help this community in crisis. He gathered into one section five parables which instruct us on what the kingdom is like. Today's gospel has two of these. The kingdom is like the seed which grows in the hiddenness of night as well as in the light of day. And the mulberry seed holds out the promise of a huge expansion from the tiniest of beginnings.

At the end of this collection of parables, Mark has an intriguing comment to make: 'He would not speak to them except in parables, but he explained everything to his disciples when they were alone.'

Large crowds of people heard the story or parable but they stayed outside the circle of believers. However, those who are called disciples received the gift of further instruction and they got inside the story. They came to know that the parable was part of their life and that they were part of the parable's life.

Jesus called on people to repent and believe. To believe in the kingdom is to hear the story of Jesus and to know that we are part of that story. The gospel involves me.

These parables invite us to look at an acorn or any seed and to see how it differs from a lifeless grain of sand because of its great potential for growth. And the further marvel is in recognising that the seed of Jesus is for the soil of my life.

Yet, many people today are overcome by the extent of violence, vandalism and crime in our midst. They are appalled by the amoral standards which are accepted in entertainment. There must be a very strong diabolical power at work behind the destruction of life through the acceptance of abortion and in the culture of destructive drugs. There are parents whose lives have been shattered as their offspring casually cast off their Christian morals and expressions of faith. And many priests feel desperately inadequate in the face of questions about faith or about the relevance of Church practices.

Where is God hiding? How long is God to remain asleep? Where is that reign of God, that kingdom, which Jesus set up? But there is another side to the picture of today. Not only is it the worst of times in some ways but in many ways it is the best of times.

I see an increasing number of people deeply drawn into very close intimacy with God and who are experiencing a vibrant prayer-life. They know that they are part of the story.

There is a growing sense of responsibility for the environment and for justice throughout the world. There is admirable goodwill and generosity in answering famine appeals. Our century, for all its sins, has witnessed extraordinary advances in the elimination of unjust working conditions and standards.

And in the Church there is a growing body of laity who are conscious of their Confirmation and anxious to be actively involved in the cause of Christ.

We do well to remember the lesson of history that the darkest periods of Church life gave us the greatest saints and the most powerful religious movements.

Today's two parables call us to persevere in believing even if much of the outer evidence that we see is negative. We are called to believe that, even while God seems to be asleep and far away from us, his power is still here with us. We are asked to open our eyes to whatever is good ... even if it is very small, insignificant and removed from the centre of influence. We must believe that here is a small seed that God can bring to great growth.

We are asked to wait patiently, like the farmer. For lasting growth takes time. We wait with the sort of hope which inspired a prisoner-of-war to write:

I believe in the sun even when it is not shining:
I believe in love even when I feel it not:
I believe in God even when he is silent.

Second Reflection
Waiting on God
If you have never planted your own flower or vegetable or tree, then your appreciation of the marvel of growth and the mystery of life must be seriously lacking! Likewise, if you are not eager to scatter the seeds of God's kingdom, then you must be lacking in appreciation of what Christ means to us.

We can plant the seeds and we can help things to grow well, but we do not cause the growth. A first-year biology student can explain the laws of how things grow. But the brains of a hundred Einsteins cannot create life or actually cause life.

And the same holds true regarding spiritual growth. St Paul admits: 'I did the planting, Apollos did the watering, but God made things grow.' (1 Cor 3:6)

Today's two parables should help us appreciate God's part in spiritual growth or apostolic success. The compulsive activist in us must learn when to stop, when to share responsibility and especially when to give God a chance. The perfectionist in us must learn to recognise even the smallest signs of progress and not to be too disappointed because there is still so far to go.

The worrier learns to let go and to hand over to God ... to let go and to let God. The impatient person learns that you do not admire the blossoms and pick the apples on the same day. You must wait for God's own time ... and God's time will always be the best time. Sometimes God's time rushes in on us at an overwhelming pace. I am writing during the weeks of rapid, radical changes in the communist bloc countries. But we know from our experience that sometimes God's answer is slow in coming. 'The mills of God grind slowly.'

When our minds wrestle with a problem and clear understanding escapes us, it is sometimes advisable to sleep on it. The farmer in the parable does not stay up all night to watch if his plants are growing. Things grow while he sleeps and when he is awake.

In the field of the mind, understanding grows while the active parts of the mind sleep. The creatures of the night emerge from cover when darkness falls. And from the darker, shadowed recesses of the mind emerge the wisdom of dreams, the locked up memories, the buried hopes, the unfulfilled talents, the unexpressed ambitions and the parts of the personality which daylight living cannot cope with. Having slept on a problem, the night-staff of the mind have done their job, and often we find that morning brings a very fresh perspective on the matter.

Nature is a great teacher. That is why Jesus so often pointed to the fields to bring out his lesson. Spring growth is richer when the earth has had the chance to be enriched in winter's cycle of decomposition. Similarly, our thinking is often clarified when we stop trying to think and let sleep or day-dreaming open up other doors.

We learn that God's work ... the growth of the kingdom ... takes time. When all seems as dark as night and as cold as winter, who knows but this might eventually prove to have been a most enriching and deepening period.

Our own suffering can deepen our lives and enrich our compassion. The Church too needs periods of suffering. It throws us back on God's care as we recognise our own incompetence.

The growth of the kingdom then is a work of combined effort ... our best efforts and the grace of God. Our efforts often fail. But the love and grace of God endure for ever.

Twelfth Sunday

In today's readings we forsake the safety of land and take to the sea. The Jews were a race of landlubbers who were very uncomfortable with the sea. In the background of their minds the sea represented the pimitive chaos which God had to control before beginning the work of creation. Today's first reading, psalm and gospel proclaim the awesome wonder of God's power over the stormy sea.

Mark 4:35-41

With the coming of evening, Jesus said to his disciples, 'Let us cross over to the other side.' And leaving the crowd behind they took him, just as he was, in the boat; and there were other boats with him.

Then it began to blow a gale and the waves were breaking into the boat so that it was almost swamped. But he was in the stern, his head on the cushion, asleep. They woke him and said to him, 'Master, do you not care? We are going down!' And he woke up and rebuked the wind and said to the sea, 'Quiet now! Be calm!' And the wind dropped, and all was calm again.

Then he said to them, 'Why are you so frightened? How is it that you have no faith?' They were filled with awe and said to one another, 'Who can this be? Even the wind and the sea obey him.'

Good News

The seas may be stromy, the going may be rough, but Christ is with us in the boat of the Church. Even if he is asleep, he is with us and caring for us.

First Reflection
Church in storm

The story of Jesus calming the storm on the lake meant a great deal to the early Church communities who found themselves in storms of persecution after Jesus had entered the sleep of death.

Mark picks up this story from the Christian tradition and inserts it immediately after his collection of parables about the kingdom. Last Sunday we heard the parable of how the seed keeps on growing even when the farmer is asleep. These words of Jesus are now backed up by his deeds. He, the sower of the seed, sleeps in the arms of total confidence even through the storm of night.

There are three factors in the story, the boat, the lake and the storm, whose significance is worth developing.

First of all, the boat is very significant to Mark. It is a place where Jesus can be with the close disciples in a little group apart from the crowd. The boat represents the inner circle of disciples. Keeping in mind that the boat had been the work-place of several of the apostles, we can readily appreciate how the image of the barque of Peter became a popular name for the Church.

The Lake of Galilee, also known as the Sea of Tiberias, is also used by Mark in a very significant way. The sea is at once a barrier between two sides and the crossing between the two. Where I am blessed to live these years is beside Sheephaven Bay which is not un-like the Lake of Galilee in size and shape. I can see Rossapenna golf links scarcely a mile across the water but twelve miles distant by road. The water is a barrier. Mark is very conscious that the western side of the lake is Jewish territory whereas the other side is inhabited by pagan Gentiles. With the boat available the lake is no longer a barrier but a means of close communication between the two peoples. Mark tells of six crossings of the lake. And he portrays Jesus giving an equal share of miracles to either side.

Perhaps the most significant balancing of miracles on either side is in multiplying the loaves. After this miracle on the Jewish side there were twelve baskets left over: one for each of the twelve Jewish tribes. Whereas after the loaves-miracle on the Gentile side there were seven baskets collected, for seven was the number of fulness for these pagans.

This balancing of miracles and crossing of the lake shows that the mission of Jesus was for Jew and Gentile, all children of the one God. The boat on the lake, then, is the means of overcoming the distance between Jew and Gentile: it is a symbol of the mission of Jesus and of the Church.

The third significant factor is the storm on this lake between the Jewish and Gentile sides. When Mark was writing, the Church community was experiencing very stormy waters in the tension between its Jewish background and its worldwide expansion. The earliest Church communities had been composed entirely of Jews who continued to go to temple and synagugue though they gathered in their homes for the breaking of bread. Gradually, as Paul and others brought the message of Christ far beyond Jewish confines, the number of Gentiles began to outnumber the Jews. In his letters Paul had to deal with the problems which arose about how much or how little of the Jewish background it was necessary to retain. By the time Matthew, Luke and John were writing the definitive break between Christians and Jews had occurred. But at Mark's time the controversies and storms between Jewish and Gentile sides were very much alive.

Notwithstanding the storm, Jesus slept away soundly. Drained of energy after the day's teaching, he is out for the count on the floor of the boat, with his head on the leather cushion of the steersman's seat.

The sleep of Jesus can be considered in two ways. It represents for the Church the time after the death of Jesus. His day of active presence is completed and now the boat-church must labour through his sleeping time until he comes again.

In another sense the sleep of Jesus is an expression of total confidence and freedom from anxiety.

'I lie down in peace and sleep comes at once
for you alone, Lord, make me dwell in safety.' (Ps 4, Grail)

The step from Mark's writing to our own day demands no great stretch of the imagination. The Church-boat has had many stormy nights in recent years, even a share of mutinous dissent. What Jesus said to the sea he repeats as his message to us today: 'Quiet now! Be calm.'

When we pray through the storm the Lord opens our eyes to see the quiet, unpublicised presence of his power in the lives of his little disciples and his small groups. Then as we begin to see his presence and power we are humbled, and like the apostles, filled with awe.

Second Reflection
The storm within

Sometimes we retreat from the shore of busy-ness, the forecast promises well, but then we run into a ferocious storm. The storm comes up from within ourselves. In the picture-language of dreams water is frequently the expression of the sub-conscious part of the mind. The depths of the sea express the depths of the mind.

Leaving the crowds is pleasant. Even from the work of the Lord, or from our family, it is good to get away occasionally. The prospect is sweet of having some days away from pressures, work demands, phone calls, door-bells and regular duties. It is grand to come to some Eden of innocence where the air is unpolluted, the food is wholesome and deep sleep returns.

But by the second or third day offshore the weather has changed dramatically. Gone is the pleasantness and peace, for a storm has blown up. The storm is within. Perhaps the deep sleep has something to do with it. The deeper parts of our minds, which can never come up into the daylight awareness of normal living, now begin to surface. And when the deep eddies up, oftentimes it is stormy.

What sort of things are churned up? Henri Nouwen, a very busy priest-lecturer-writer, spent one entire summer in a Trappist monastery. He found it very challenging. He wrote: 'The first thing we discover in solitude is our restlessness, drivenness, compulsiveness, the urge to act quickly, to make an impact, to have an influence.' Perhaps we know ourselves when we are clad in the clothes of duty. But take our usefulness away and what have we left? Who am I? I have seen priests on retreat who cannot stay for three days in the retreat grounds but are compelled to be out doing good for others. Everybody coming in on opening evening comments on the bit of heaven we have here. Yet five minutes after the close of the retreat, there is not one visitor left in heaven!

When we leave the shore of busy-ness where we know what we can do, we launch out into the deep in search of the other side. The other side is our unreached life, our unanswered hopes, our unfulfilled potential. Churning up from the deep come the mountainous waves of frustration in our ministry, terrifying personal inadequacy, the poverty of our prayerlife. Sexual fantasy inevitably comes up out of the unfulfilled potentials of a celibate person. And sometimes the disturbance comes from some festering inner hurt or anger because of the way we have been misunderstood, taken for granted, used by others or unjustly treated.

In Mark's story the storm is a combination of gale and winds ... wind and water. But isn't this combination the scriptural symbol of the Holy Spirit's work? In Genesis the wind blew over the waters before creation emerged from chaos. In Exodus a strong easterly wind drove back the waters of the Red Sea for Moses to lead the people out of slavery into freedom. Then in John's gospel Jesus tells Nicodemus of the necessity of being born again in the combination of water and divine wind.

When the depths of our minds start churning up a storm it is not necessarily a destructive encounter. If we can believe that the Spirit of God is at work here we might experience a new genesis out of chaos, a new exodus out of slavery, a new fulness of life within us.

The response of no-faith is to blame some other person or circumstance for the storm. We will do anything to off-load responsibility for our own lives! Our inner frustration or anger is projected outwards and pinned onto another ... even God. Note the tone of accusation and blame as the faithless apostles cry out to Jesus, 'Master, do you not care?' They did not just wake him up but they accused him of not caring about them.

In contrast, the response of faith is to hear the words of the Lord: 'Quiet now! Be calm. Be still and know that I am God. I am with you all days ... and nights ... until the end of the world.'

If these destructive forces of frustration, fantasy or anger are lying on the ocean-bed of my subconscious, it is better to face them when they come up ... with God's help ... and the aid of a prudent director if possible.

The Lord is here, we are safe. See, he sleeps on the cushion of total confidence.

The Spirit of the Lord is here in the rich combination of wind and water. Stay with the storm and pray with it.

What is the Lord saying to me? Where is he leading me? Unto further creation, into true freedom, towards the full potential of my birth.

Thirteenth Sunday

The gospel, first reading and psalm of today's liturgy unite in the celebration of God's saving power which extends even beyond death. 'Death is not God's doing, he takes no pleasure in the extinction of the living.'

Mark 5:21-43 (longer version)

When Jesus had crossed in the boat to the other side, a large crowd gathered round him and he stayed by the lakeside. Then one of the synagogue officials came up, Jairus by name, and seeing him, fell at his feet and pleaded with him earnestly, saying, 'My little daughter is desperately sick. Do come and lay your hands on her to make her better and save her life.' Jesus went with him and a large crowd followed him; they were pressing all round him.

Now there was a woman who had suffered from a haemorrhage for twelve years; after long and painful treatment under various doctors, she had spent all she had without being any the better for it; in fact, she was getting worse. She had heard about Jesus, and she came up behind him through the crowd and touched his cloak.

'If I can touch even his clothes,' she had told herself, 'I shall be well again.' And the source of the bleeding dried up instantly, and she felt in herself that she was cured of her complaint.

Immediately aware that power had gone out from him Jesus turned round in the crowd and said, 'Who touched my clothes?'

His disciples said to him, 'You see how the crowd is pressing round you and yet you say, "Who touched me?" ' But he continued to look all round to see who had done it.

Then the woman came forward, frightened and trembling because she knew what had happened to her and she fell at his feet and told him the whole truth. 'My daughter,' he said, 'your faith has restored you to health; go in peace and be free from your complaint.'

While he was still speaking some people arrived from the house of the synagogue official to say, 'Your daughter is dead: why put the Master to any further trouble?'

But Jesus had overheard this remark of theirs and he said to the official, 'Do not be afraid; only have faith.' And he allowed no one to go with him except Peter and James and John the brother of James. So they came to the official's house and Jesus noticed all the commotion, with people weeping and wailing unrestrainedly. He went in and said to them, 'Why all this commotion and crying? The child is not dead, but asleep.'

But they laughed at him. So he turned them all out and, taking with him the child's father and mother and his own companions, he went into the place where the child lay. And taking the child by the hand he said to her, 'Talitha, kum!' which means, 'Little girl, I tell you to get up.' The little girl got up at once and began to walk about, for she was twelve years old.

At this they were overcome with astonishment, and he ordered them strictly not to let anyone know about it, and told them to give her something to eat.

Good News
In Jesus, the power of God saves the life that is wasting away and raises up the dead. He tells us to fear not but to reach out and touch him by faith.

First Reflection
Power over death
We are drawing our gospel these weeks from a section where Mark is relating the powerful deeds of Jesus which inspire the same awe that is reserved for God.

Last Sunday we saw the power of Jesus over the raging seas. After that they reached the far side of the lake. There all hell broke loose in the poor man who was possessed by an army of demons. In that fantastic story the unclean spirits are so routed at the advance of the kingdom that they surrender to Jesus and beg for a place of refuge. 'Send us into the pigs,' they cry. Pigs, to the Jews who would never eat the meat of the pig, were the lowest of the low. But even the pigs had their standards and they would not accept the fleeing legion of spirits, so they rushed headlong into the lake. Everyone was amazed.

Today we are back again on the Jewish side of the lake. Mark, who loved sandwiches, starts to tell the story of the daughter of Jairus but interrupts his account with the haemorrhaging woman before completing his story. The effect of the delay is to heighten the drama by letting us wait on the outcome.

Furthermore, there are so many similarities between the two miracles that each one helps us to understand the riches of the other. Each miracle concerns a female: a woman whose life-blood was wasting for twelve years; and a little girl whose life has apparently ended after twelve years. We note the recurrence of twelve, Mark's favourite number for events on the Jewish side.

In each story the approach to Jesus is somewhat indirect, due to the condition of the patients, but perhaps also expressing the unworthiness of woman's position. The gospel, here and in other places, implicitly challenges the accepted cultural and religious disregard for woman's equality.

Jairus, the father of the girl, comes on behalf of his daughter. The afflicted woman comes herself but only in a hidden way since a woman should not address a rabbi in public. Furthermore, her haemorrhage rendered her ritually impure and banned from religious ceremony. So, all she can do is to come up behind Jesus and touch his clothes, though not himself. But so great is her belief that she feels this will be enough. But then Jesus wants to meet her. He calls on her to stand up in the full dignity of a person. She has a life and story to tell. He calls her 'My daugher'. She is one of his family for she is a believer and a true disciple.

In both stories Mark stresses that the petitions were desperate and beyond human aid. Very bluntly he remarks that the woman was only worse off after long and expensive medical treatment. Regarding Jairus' daughter, her death has put her so far beyond human help that the messengers think it would be only a waste of Jesus's time going to the house. Human powers alone would have left everybody in their fear and lamentation. But Jesus calls on the people to let go of fear and step out in faith. The afflicted woman had done it ... and see what happened!

'The child is not dead, but asleep.' He who has the power to save a life that was wasting away can also raise up the life which has totally expired. But the unbelievers scornfully and cynically laugh at his words. They are outside the family of faith, so they are turned out of the house.

He then takes the child by the hand, tells her to get up. Up she gets and begins to walk about. Everyone is astonished out of their minds. And then, what a delightfully human touch there is to the story when Jesus tells them to give the poor girl something to eat before she collapses from hunger!

For Christians of every age these miracles show the divine power of Jesus and express who he is. He is the one who saves the life which is wasting away: and the one who raises the dead to life again. We can apply these miracles to our moral condition or spiritual life.

Our spiritual energies haemorrhage when we waste our years on empty pursuits or sinful ways: when we give time to everything except God: when, like the woman, the state of sin renders us spiritually impure and deprived of the eucharist.

If the waste of life continues, the soul is eventually dead. One is beyond human powers. Repeated failures haunt any effort to improve. Only the grace of God can now restore life to this soul.

'Do not be afraid; only have faith', says Jesus. The unbeliever laughs cynically. Yet if there is even one spark of faith left, it will reach out to touch the Lord as he passes by on his way. He has the power to save, to convert, to raise up. He calls the soul back to life and instructs the family to feed the person with eucharist and Christian fellowship.

With today's psalm we pray:

'I will praise you, Lord, you have rescued me.'

Second Reflection
Touching the Lord

Mark's story today is very homely. It is full of chatty asides like the gossip about the expensive doctors and fat lot of good they did for the woman! Or adding on that the little girl was twelve years old. And the final bit about getting the young lass a bite to eat. We can feel at home in that sort of chat.

And the story is remarkable for the atmosphere of close contact and the number of times that physical feeling is mentioned.

You can sense how the crowds were gathering in around Jesus, pressing in on all sides. No place for claustrophobia. The afflicted woman had gone through so much treatment and we are told that it was painful. Now she was reaching out for a special touch. We get the physical description that the source of her bleeding dried up instantly and she felt in herself that she was cured. Jesus felt the power going out of him. He knew that in the midst of all that pressure he had received one special touch. He looked around, seeking to make eye contact with this person.

Later, in the house of Jairus the scoffing unbelievers were sent out of Jesus's close company. The parents of the girl and the three closest apostles were brought into the room. Faith means close contact with Jesus and belonging to the family. In the room he stretched out his hand to raise up the girl in a combination of word and touch.

Mark is telling us that faith means close intimacy with Jesus. And we cannot remain hidden from his look or distant from him in an impersonal way. Our prayer must not be anonymous or mechanical ... that sort of off-by-heart formula which is more a barrier that hides us from God than a bridge to bring us face-to-face with him. Just like cliché comments pass for conversation but in reality only cover up the non-communication which ought to be faced.

193

Mark's homely style invites you to make your home in the story. He invites you into that sort of meditation where you develop awareness of your bodily feelings as the place to meet God.

You are glad that Jesus has returned to your shore again. The crowd around is large and you are happy to be among them. It's that feeling when someone you love comes around. You feel the need to draw closer him. Your life today has wasted energy ... you have reacted in pain ... you are hurt ... so now you need to draw closer to him. You reach out ... touch his garment. Not just any garment, but his. Just a touch, ever so light, lingering for a moment. It's someone you have always wanted to be near. You never told anybody. It's your secret.

How do you feel inside? Heart pounding? A cleansing wave sweeping through you. All your soreness is lifted out. You feel so much better. In this warmth you would love to stay on anonymously.

But Jesus stops and turns around. His eyes take in everybody. Who touched him? He wants to know you. Your knees are knocking but you find a courage you never thought you had. 'It is I, Lord ... it's me ... (your name)'. You feel his look. And all fear now vanishes.

The whole world has stopped revolving for only two people exist at this moment: Jesus and you. He sees into into you and behind you ... today, yesterday and tomorrow. You know that you are understood and wanted and loved.

For the eyes of truth are the eyes of love. And the truth sets you free. Free from sin, free from pain, free from pressures.

He calls you ... my daughter, my son, my sister, my brother ... for you are one of his family.

And now he waits for your reply ...

194

Fourteenth Sunday

This is one of those rare Sundays when the theme of the second reading happens to coincide with the gospel and first reading. All three are about the problems and opposition encountered in the service of God's word.

Ezechiel is called by God to stand up in the face of a defiant and obstinate people. Paul confesses to the Corinthians the opposition which comes from his own weakness. And Jesus meets with rejection in his own hometown, Nazareth.

Mark 6:1-6

Jesus went to his home town and his disciples accompanied him. With the coming of the sabbath he began teaching in the synagogue and most of them were astonished when they heard him.

They said, 'Where did the man get all this? What is this wisdom that has been granted him, and these miracles that are worked through him? This is the carpenter, surely, the son of Mary, the brother of James and Joset and Jude and Simon? His sisters, too, are they not here with us?' And they would not accept him.

And Jesus said to them, 'A prophet is only despised in his own country, among his own relations and in his own house'; and he could work no miracle there, though he cured a few sick people by laying his hands on them. He was amazed at their lack of faith.

Good News

Faith makes available to us the wisdom of Christ's words and the power of his hands.

First Reflection
Believing in Jesus

Mark, in his writing, addressed himself to a problem which was puzzling the minds of his contemporaries. How could one explain why the majority of the Jews were rejecting Jesus while the Gentiles were flocking into the Church community? This story of the rejection of Jesus in his hometown, Nazareth, is a miniature version of the larger story.

On a tour of the Holy Land our group had an unhappy reception in Nazareth. Our booking was not honoured and our liturgical arrangements were fouled up. It was obvious that the power of the shekel caused our little group to be pushed aside in favour of more

195

opulent pickings. We were disappointed, frustrated and a little angry. However, the experience added an authentic flavour to our pilgrimage, resembling in a little way the unfavourable reception meted out to Jesus in his time.

Nazareth was a surprising home for the Messiah. It was never mentioned anywhere in the Old Testament. As a town it apparently grew as a base for migrant tradesmen and artisans who were employed in the vast building campaigns of Kind Herod the Great. It had no great religious tradition, as one gathers from the remark of Nathanael: 'Can anything good come out of Nazareth?'

Mark places the return of Jesus to Nazareth after telling us of the impressive teaching of Jesus and his astonishing power over demons, desperate illness, the raging wind and sea, even over death. There can be no denying his wisdom and power.

The townfolk admit to astonishment when they hear the wisdom of Jesus in the synagogue. But the crunch comes when they face up to the consequences of going a step further than astonishment. 'Yes, the carpenter we know. We know his cousins and all belonging to him. But we must be reasonable about all this.' But Jesus wants them to take the step beyond human reasoning: the step which accepts the unseen: the step of faith. Sadly, they would not accept him. They failed the call to faith.

To believe in Jesus Christ is more than the intellectual acceptance of various teachings: the people of Nazareth admitted that the teaching was impressive, but they needed to go further.

Again, to believe is more than accepting the possibility of supernatural power in Jesus: the Nazarenes could not deny his miracles. Just as many people today accept the existence of supernatural powers but they do not have faith in Jesus Christ. Christian belief means a personal acceptance in the core of my being of Jesus Christ as the unique revelation of God to us, as the only authentic way to God, as the Saviour of my sinful humanity.

The Latin word, *credere*, to believe, comes from *cor-dare*, to give your heart to Jesus. This is what the people of Nazareth would not do. And in the absence of faith Jesus 'could do no miracle there'. Mark's comment is startling. Our hearts can be opened up to God only from the inside. The key is a combination of goodwill and openness to the goodness of God wherever we meet it. God wants to give to us: faith enables us to receive his wisdom and power; but lack of faith impedes the whole process.

Jesus is our way, our truth and our life once we accept him in faith. He is the way and the believer searches for no other direction in life. He is the way to humanity's true destiny in returning to the Father.

He is the truth. And the heart of the believer takes delight in pondering on his words and his works. Any other knowledge is limp in comparison with his truth.

And he is the life. We seek nothing that would contradict his life. We long to do everything in union with him. We strive to die to selfish ways so that his life might be ever more truly operative in us.

Second Reflection
My Nazareth
Nazareth was the home town of Jesus.

As I bring the gospel to bear on my life then Nazareth represents the hometown of my life and experiences. Have I met Jesus on the crowded streets or quiet roads of my life? Have I accepted him into my life?

The people of Nazareth were suitably astonished at the teaching of Jesus in the synagogue, the town's holy house. They spoke in hushed, reverential tones of his wisdom. In more excited chatter they swapped their stories about his miracles. Jesus was no problem to them in the holy house or so long as he worked in distant places. But now he wanted them to accept him into their everyday lives! This was too much to ask. They knew too much about him ... or so they imagined.

I can have contact of a sort with Jesus in the holy house every Sunday. I might study his wisdom at a distance through the books that other people have written. I might admire the miracles that have happened in distant places or for other people.

But will I accept Jesus into the everyday streets of my Nazareth? Am I content to leave him imprisoned in the Sunday church? Am I ready to open up every moment of my life to the light of his wisdom and the power of his presence? Do I accept that he sees me at every moment ... even in my dark moments of sin and failure? Do I trust that his divine power is here ... not only in the distant shrines ... but right beside me and within me.

Two seminarians, good friends who shared much and supported one another, were on retreat. The retreat-master asked everybody to spend an hour alone and to write about how they had met God in their lives. One of the two friends spent his hour in utter frustration and anger. Eventually he took the biro in hand and savagely wrote out one line: 'Jesus, where the so-'n-so are you?' In truth, the word he wrote was unprintable! Later he showed it to his friend.

By coincidence, his friend has also written just one line, which he now shared: 'I am right here beside you and within you.'

Sheer coincidence? I prefer to regard it as a little joke on God's part. The important conclusion to the incident is that the angry one took to heart a lesson he would never forget. Jesus is here, wanting to be accepted into the streets of my everyday life.

'Ah, but! If you only knew my shabby streets! My sins. My weakness. My double standards.'

There are no 'Ah, buts' which can stop the mercy of Jesus Christ, so long as we have the goodwill to invite him in.

St Paul, in today's second reading, had one huge 'Ah, but!' We don't know exactly what it was. He called it a 'thorn in the flesh.' It humiliated him and beat him to the ropes. He prayed for God to take it away, to change things. But God replied: 'No, Paul. You must stay with his problem. This is your hometown just as it is. Just remember I am with you here. My grace is enough for you.' And then comes the stupendous revelation: 'My power is at its best in weakness.'

Unpretentious Nazareth. Never mentioned in the holy books. No sacred shrines of its own, no religious memories. The migrant workers' town. A tough place, of people who had lost their roots.

Nazareth, God's surprising choice as hometown for the world's Messiah. Why should I be surprised if Jesus would want to know my soul too as his hometown. That he should want to set up home in me! After all, he is the one whose power is at its best in weakness.

I must accept Jesus into the everyday streets of my daily life rather than wait for a different Messiah from some other, more noble and sinless place.

'I am right here beside you and within you.'

Fifteenth Sunday

After his rejection at Nazareth Jesus turns to other places. The time has come to send out the apostles on a trial mission. Like Amos in the first reading, they go out, not of their own appointment, but by God's call and authority.

Mark 6:7-13
Jesus summoned the Twelve and began to send them out in pairs giving them authority over the unclean spirits. And he instructed them to take nothing for the journey except a staff – no bread, no haversack, no coppers for their purses. They were to wear sandals but, he added, 'Do not take a spare tunic.' And he said to them, 'If you enter a house anywhere, stay there until you leave the district. And if any place does not welcome you and people refuse to listen to you, as you walk away shake off the dust from under your feet as a sign to them.' So they set off to preach repentance; and they cast out many devils, and anointed many sick people with oil and cured them.

Good News
The strength of any Christian mission comes more from God's call and power than from human resources or qualifications.

First Reflection
Foretaste of mission
When Jesus sent out the apostles it was not yet the beginning of their great mission. They were to settle back into a passive role when they returned. But for this once they are like pupils sent from the lecture hall to field-work, getting a taste of what would come later.

The passage tells us nothing of the content of their preaching, except for the general heading of repentance. However, we are given great details of their missionary lifestyle. This indicates that the Christian message must be lived before it can be preached. Actions speak more loudly than words. 'For the Church, the first means of evangelisation is the witness of an authentically Christian life.' (Paul VI)

The first witnessing sign is that they travel in pairs. Since charity is the essence of Christian behaviour, a preacher or teacher will speak but empty words who is unable to relate comfortably with a brother or sister and co-operate with team members. Anyone who would preach in the name of Christ must be filled with Christ's love for his audience. And it is most unlikely that one would love the people out there if he does not love the people close at hand.

Maverick preachers, self-appointed prophets and bogus healers have one thing in common: they are highly individualistic operators. Close-quarter relationships do not suit them.

The second sign of the missioner is complete trust in the help of the Lord. 'Take no bread, no haversack, no coppers in your purses. Do not take a spare tunic.' This passage reflects the guarantee of oriental hospitality. It is also a sign of trusting in God's providence. Taking no baggage was a way of showing that their mission came, not from personal qualifications, but solely from the call and authority of God. In Mark's version, as distinct from the other gospels, they are allowed to take staff and sandals, indicating the need to travel long distances ... as Mark did, possibly as far as Rome.

They are instructed to stay in the same house, not to be wasting time changing about. The missioner moves with a holy haste and single-mindedness and he cannot afford time to the long formalities which were associated with oriental hospitality. They must concentrate their energies on their mission.

Perhaps the hardest part of any mission is learning to cope with failure. If the missioner acts in his own name then failure will be a very bitter pill to swallow. But the true missioner knows that since Christ himself was rejected, we have no grounds to expect perfect success and acceptance.

God is not asking us for perfect results but that we should try. People must be free to accept one's message or to reject it. It cannot be forced on people.

Getting involved in prolonged argumentation is usually a waste of time as each side only settles more solidly into their entrenched positions. The instruction of the Lord is to move on.

But as they leave the rejecting area, they are to shake off any dust that clings to their feet to show that they do not wish to be infected with the defilement of unbelief. A Jew coming back from any Gentile area would have shaken off the defiled Gentile dust before entering home.

So, the apostles were instructed and off they went on this venture from classroom into field-work. By the call and power of God they did what Jesus had been doing up to this:

preaching repentance or change of ways;

casting out many possessing spirits;

curing sick people.

They would come back to the passive learning situation as listening and observing disciples. But from this experience they would have a foretaste of the later Spirit-filled days when the mission of Christ was to become the mission of the Church.

Second Reflection
Called and sent

The apostles were called by the Lord and sent out in his name and authority. They were to preach repentance, cast out the possessing spirits of evil and to heal the sick.

Every Christian who has received the light of Christ in Baptism is called to carry that light in Christ's name. The source of all Christian mission is in Baptism: its development comes in confirmation: and its sustenance is in the bread of life, the holy Eucharist. Since the Second Vatican Council there has been an increased awareness that the entire Church is missionary. The work of evangelisation is not the special preserve of priests and religious.

There was a time when there was little mention of the call of every Christian to be missionary. Historical circumstances had something to do with this. The battlefield of the Church for several hundred years was in the matter of heresy. The specialist troops were trained theologians, the vast majority of whom were priests. It was an age for clericalism.

But times have changed. Doctrinal controversies have receded into the background, mainly because very few people know enough doctrine even to be heretics!

The battlefield of today is the society which regards God as dead: or at least, religion as irrelevant. Totalitarian communism, which once set out to eliminate all religious belief, is today being repudiated. But more subtle advocates of atheism conspire under the flag of secularistic humanism. What they offer is a diminished understanding of human nature because they choose to ignore the sacred nobility of our origin and destiny. Their ideas are earthbound, their values are of this world only and their behaviour favours permissiveness.

In this battlefield of today the frontline troops are no longer the clergy and religious but the lay faithful. It is they who are to carry the gospel ideas and values into the world of politics, finance and technology: into the areas of art, culture, sport and entertainment. They are the specialists in family values and education. A Christian and fully responsible use of the mass-media is needed.

'The more Gospel-inspired lay people there are engaged in these realities, clearly involved in them, competent to promote them

201

and conscious that they must exercise to the full their Christian powers which are often buried and suffocated, the more these realities will be at the service of the kingdom of God, and therefore of salvation in Jesus Christ.' (Paul VI)

People will not be less human because of their gospel witness. Rather, they will be more complete in their humanity when the sacred and religious values of life are no longer disregarded.

The gospel images of salt and yeast apply principally to the mission of the lay faithful because they live and work within society, just as salt and yeast find their usefulness in the mix.

One of the graces of Baptism is a sharing in the prophetic or teaching mission of Christ. This grace gives the lay Christian the ability and responsibility to accept the gospel in faith and to proclaim it in word and deed, without hesitating to courageously identify and denounce evil. (John Paul II in *The Vocation and Mission of the Laity*, 14)

The message of the gospel represents a radical challenge to many of the accepted attitudes and policies of today. The light of the gospel identifies the various possessing spirits of evil which enslave people and diminish life.

A gospel-based life will not accept the politics of violence or racial discrimination: and it will resist the pressures of consumerism which entangle lives in the rat race. It will repudiate the so-called art or entertainment which makes a multi-million pound industry out of lust and blood. It will challenge the economic systems which coldly calculate profit while millions starve through their policies. It will call out the spirit of darkness which obscures personal values under the cloak of abstract slogans: in this way, for instance, the personal crime of abortion is obscured under a slogan such as the right to choose or access to information. These are some of the evil spirits which the contemporary apostle must identify and denounce.

As in the days of Jesus Christ, the apostle of today is called and sent out on a three-fold task:

to summon the world to the way of repentance;

to rid society of the posessing spirits which enslave humanity in a condition unto death;

to bring all to Jesus Christ, the Anointed One, who alone can offer healing.

Sixteenth Sunday

Today's readings picture Jesus as the promised shepherd of God's flock who would bring back the lost and wandering sheep. He responds as compassionate shepherd to two different needs. When the apostles were subjected to too much pressure he invited them to retreat ... 'Near restful waters he leads me to revive my drooping spirit.' And to the people who were lost for leadership he is the shepherd who 'guides me along the right path.'

Mark 6:30-34

The apostles rejoined Jesus and told him all they had done and taught. Then he said to them, 'You must come away to some lonely place all by yourselves and rest for a while'; for there were so many coming and going that the apostles had no time even to eat. So they went off in a boat to a lonely place where they could be by themselves.

But people saw them going, and many could guess where; and from every town they all hurried to the place on foot and reached it before them.

So as he stepped ashore he saw a large crowd; and he took pity on them because they were like sheep without a shepherd, and he set himself to teach them at some length.

Good News

When the people were like sheep without a shepherd Jesus took pity on them. Divine compassion is the heartbeat of the ministry of Jesus.

First Reflection
Near restful waters

This is the only place in his writing where Mark uses the word apostles. Apostle means someone who is sent on a mission. But the odd thing is that this mention of the action word, apostle, does not lead up to more activity but to the exact opposite ... to withdraw or retreat from the pressure of being too busy.

In last Sunday's gospel Jesus sent out the Twelve with authority over unclean spirits. They preached repentance, cast out many devils, anointed many sick people with oil and cured them. Back they come, over the moon with excitement, thrilled at the success of all that they had done and taught. They could not wait for the next mission.

How surprised they must have been when Jesus, instead of sending them out again, actually invited them to retreat. It had become so busy that they scarcely had time to eat.

To retreat means to withdraw, to pull back from what one is doing. The Lord was showing them that the powerhouse of apostolate is divine energy. The authority they had over spirits and illness was not of human origin. All the human effort in the world is of no avail in apostolate unless it is powered from within by the divine energy of grace. 'Apart from me you can do nothing.' (Jn 15:5)

There are three phases in the Lord's invitation ... to come apart ... to an alone-place ... and to rest a while.

Busy people must recognise that if they never voluntarily come apart then they will soon involuntarily fall apart or be torn apart. Anybody who is sent on the Lord's work has to find some space in each day to come apart. And on a regular basis there should be a more thorough retreat for some days. It is virtually impossible to withdraw sufficiently in one's familiar surroundings. The mind has to be given every chance to clear out all traces of preoccupation. When going on retreat, every mile travelled is a mile from our daily routine and a mile towards a new freedom for hearing the Lord's voice.

Seeking out an alone-place is not an escape from reality. For the heart of reality is the reality of the heart, that is, the innermost centre of our being where God dwells as the powerhouse of apostolic energy. Those who are busy with the work of the Lord must return to the centre and be alone with the Lord of the work.

A retreat involves discerning where and how God has been operative in all that we have said and done. In the alone-place we encounter the Great Alone. We come to experience the difference between loneliness and solitude. Loneliness is the empty way of being alone: it is an emptiness that can tear us apart. Solitude, on the other hand, is a way of fulness when we realise that our emptiness creates the necessary space for God. We come to reflect on God's mission through our lives. We see if we have selfishly held back from the divine challenge: whether we have been serving our own ways rather than the calls of obedience: whether God's glory or our own success is our ambition.

Having come apart to be alone with God, the Lord's invitation is to rest a while and restore our energy. Today's responsorial psalm is the beloved shepherd psalm which offers some very appealing images of how God cares for us.

'Near restful waters he leads me
to revive my drooping spirit.'

Sheep need water to drink just once in the day. Apparently they have great difficulty in drinking from swiftly flowing water. The shepherd must build a dam of stones across the mountain stream or find a pool of still water.

The water is an image of our apostolic activity. God is present everywhere, but when the pace is hectic we find it difficult to drink of his presence in prayer. Like the sheep, we need to find the pool of still time. It is here that our drooping spirits are revived and true apostolic energy is restored.

It is significant, then, that the only time that Mark mentions the name apostles is not in the context of further activity, but in connection with retreating from busy-ness. The powerhouse of true apostolate is divine energy.

When we come apart to spend time with God we present our emptiness of mind, heart and hand, praying that God's spirit will be our fulness.

'Near restful waters he leads me to revive my drooping spirit.'

Second Reflection
He guides me

Our best made plans so often go astray. But it is consoling to see how Jesus was no exception. His plan for a restful, restorative retreat had to be postponed.

Whenever Mark mentions the seashore we can expect crowds. In the boat Jesus is free to be with the small group of disciples. But once they land on the seashore crowds press around him, insistent, demanding, pressurising. Anybody who is engaged in Christian apostolate today will recognise that pressure. It comes in phone calls, door bells, meetings beyond number and one-to-one contacts.

Jesus accepted that his plan for retreat had to be deferred. The purpose of the retreat was to serve the ministry, not to escape from it.

We see the needs of the people on their empty faces. They were like sheep without a shepherd. Jesus took pity on them. There's the key to ministry: divine compassion responding to a human need.

Mark develops the idea of Jesus as shepherd of the people. The shepherd leads the sheep to where they can feed. So, Jesus is first pictured as instructing the people and then he feeds them by multiplying the loaves and fishes. The shepherd-psalm expresses the teaching role thus:

'He guides me long the right path, he is true to his name.'

Times are hard on teachers and preachers today. An age when discipline is lacking is bound to be a time when discipleship is weak.

Sometimes I am asked: 'Are you still giving preached retreats?' There is a tone of accusation which says more than the words themselves. As if the preached word belonged to some dark age before the new age holistic spirituality, human development programmes or stress relieving techniques.

The popular press has no interest in the sound teaching of Christian morality. A bishop may teach sound instruction every Sunday or a preacher my travel the country and remind parish after parish of the ten commandments, but they will never be mentioned by the media for their efforts. But let them touch on some issue which some small but vocal group do not like, then they are caught up in the centre of controversy. What passes for news is controversy rather than concern for the truth.

The instruction given by Paul to Timothy reads as if it were written for today. 'Proclaim the message and, welcome or unwelcome, insist on it.' Then he lists three steps in instruction: 'Refute falsehood, correct error, call to obedience.' His words were prophetic: 'The time is sure to come when, far from being content with sound teaching, people will be avid for the latest novelty and collect for themselves a whole series of teachers according to their own tastes; and then, instead of listening to the truth, they will turn to myths.'

He encourages Timothy and says: 'Be brave under trials; make the preaching of the Good News your life's work, in thorough-going service.' (2 Tim 4:1-5)

Jesus set himself to teach the people at length. He was the shepherd who would gather together and lead the lost sheep, as foretold by Jeremiah in today's first reading.

The true shepherd 'guides me along the right path'. Being a disciple of Jesus one must accept the discipline of learning the truth of Christian teaching. One is not entitled to pick and choose teachers because of their novelty or pleasing message. 'My sheep listen to my voice,' says the Lord.

Seventeenth Sunday

For the next five Sundays we move from Mark to John for the gospel reading. Last Sunday our journey with Mark reached the stage where Jesus was acting as the shepherd leading back a lost people: 'he set himself to teach them at great length.' Immediately after that, Mark shows Jesus as the shepherd feeding his flock in the multiplication of the loaves and fishes. The liturgy of the bread follows the liturgy of the teaching. The miracle of the loaves was developed by John in a deep, theological reflection. The lectionary departs from Mark to let us avail of John over five Sundays.

John 6: 1-15

Jesus went off to the other side of the Sea of Galilee – or of Tiberias – and a large crowd followed him, impressed by the signs he gave by curing the sick. Jesus climbed the hillside, and sat down there with his disciples. It was shortly before the Jewish feast of Passover.

Looking up, Jesus saw the crowds approaching and said to Philip, 'Where can we buy some bread for these people to eat?' He only said this to test Philip; he himself knew exactly what he was going to do. Philip answered, 'Two hundred denarii would only buy enough to give them a small piece each.'

One of his disciples, Andrew, Simon Peter's brother, said, 'There is a small boy here with five barley loaves and two fish; but what is that between so many?' Jesus said to them, 'Make the people sit down.' There was plenty of grass there, and as many as five thousand men sat down.

Then Jesus took the loaves, gave thanks, and gave them out to all who were sitting ready; he then did the same with the fish, giving out as much as was wanted.

When they had eaten enough he said to the disciples, 'Pick up the pieces left over, so that nothing gets wasted.' So they picked them up, and filled twelve hampers with scraps left over from the meal of five barley loaves.

The people, seeing this sign that he had given, said, 'This really is the prophet who is to come into the world.' Jesus, who could see they were about to come and take him by force and make him king, escaped back to the hills by himself.

Good News
Jesus returned thanks to the Father and fed the people in their hunger.

First Reflection
From Passover to Eucharist
John has meditated deeply on the significance of the miracle of the loaves and fishes. His thought draws deeply from the Jewish past and reaches forward into the liturgical celebration of Christ which developed in the Christian Church. He intends us to see the clear link between this miracle and the last supper by referring to the same time-setting, 'shortly before the Jewish feast of Passover.'

Passover was the greatest feast in the Jewish year. It commemorated especially the events of the exodus. The destroying angel passed over the Hebrews' houses which were marked with the blood of the lamb. And then, under the leadership of Moses, they safely passed through the Red Sea on their journey from slavery into freedom. On the way they were fed with the manna, bread from heaven.

The miracle of the loaves and fishes took place on a hill, recalling Mount Sinai where Moses met with God. And the question put to Philip by Jesus, 'Where can we buy some bread for these people to eat?' is very similar to a question put by Moses to God. (*cf* Num 11:22)

The people sensed this parallel with Moses but they mistakenly interpreted it according to their own desires. Mistaken interpretations are often used by John as a device to enable Jesus reiterate his teaching. The mistaken understanding represents worldly or natural thinking whereas Jesus teaches a meaning which only faith can comprehend. It involves rising from the material world to the spiritual.

In this instance the people recognised in Jesus the prophet beyond all prophets, as promised by Moses. They invested the idea with their own strong hopes for a nationalistic messiah, a king who would lead them to freedom from the Roman domination, just as Moses had freed them from the Egyptian yoke. The only way out of this misunderstanding for Jesus was to escape to the hills by himself.

As John reflects, his mind reaches ahead to another Passover celebration when Jesus knew that the time had come for him to pass from this world to the Father. The last supper took place in the context of the Passover meal. Unlike the other evangelists, John does not tell of the institution of the Eucharist during that meal. However, the liturgical actions of the last supper are anticipated on the hillside as Jesus 'took the loaves, gave thanks and gave them out to all.' The word he uses for thanksgiving, *eucharistesas*, is the source for the name Eucharist which eventually prevailed over other names for the Christian community's celebration of the memory of Jesus Christ.

In today's first reading we recall how Elisha fed a hundred men with twenty barley loaves. But even that great miracle was surpassed when Jesus fed five thousand with only five loaves. Jesus took the meagre offerings of the small boy and invested them with divine power for the feeding of so many. The loaves were of barley, food of the poor. It was an anticipation of how God takes our poor offerings in the Eucharist and returns them to us in divine life.

Jesus instructed them to gather up the fragments left over. This is an allusion to the Christian community which considered itself as gathered like fragments from many hills. And the twelve baskets stand for the twelve tribes under Moses or the twelve apostles in Christ's time.

John writes like the skylark rising in song over the one area. He might start with some natural matter like water, wind, or bread, but then he rises in song up to the supernatural level. In this chapter he has begun with physical hunger and bread for the body. But over the next four weeks John will raise our thoughts up to the supernatural level of faith in Jesus and in the bread of life.

Second Reflection
Eucharist: praise and thanks

Our five weeks with John's eucharistic chapter offer us the oportunity to reflect on some aspect of the eucharist each week. We begin with a consideration of the word, eucharist. It comes from the Greek word for giving praise and thanks. John tells us that Jesus took the loaves and gave thanks (*eucharistesas*) before he distributed them.

Thanksgiving is the movement of returning to the giver. The movement is beautifully pictured by St Luke in his story of the grateful Samaritan who was cured of leprosy. Going along the road he found himself cured. One wonders had he ever found the gift of health until its loss made him so appreciative of his cure. Then he turned back on the road ... thanksgiving is the movement of return. He praised God at the top of his voice, then threw himself at the feet of Jesus and thanked him.

We can picture it as a double movement. Firstly comes the downward movement of God's giving towards us. The gift is found or appreciated. The second movement is the return upwards to God in praise and thanks.

Praise is concerned with the giver while thanks centres more on

209

the gift. One can observe how children respond to receiving gifts. The small child is delighted to be loved and special. Ever before the gift is unwrapped the small child will spontaneously hug and praise the giver. The school-going child tends to be more selfish and cute. The gift is greedily unwrapped and assessed. Then, perhaps with a prod from mother, comes the movement back to the donor. The words will express thanks more than praise, more about the gift than the giver. There may even be unspoken reservations in the tone of voice ... what I really wanted was a red one, not yellow.

In primitive religion, once people began to accept the existence of spirits or invisible powers within material things, they tried to offer something back to this power. This became known as sacrifice. More often than not the motive was to placate the angry spirits or to get this power on one's side for a successful hunt or war.

As the concept of the deity became more personal and benign, this return movement extended beyond placating anger to include movements of thanks and praise.

All pre-Christian sacrifices were but limited efforts to span the infinite distance between earth and heaven. What sacrifice could be worthy of God? The world had to wait for Jesus Christ for the perfect sacrifice. At the time of the Passover Feast, as thousands of lambs were sacrificed in the Temple, Jesus brought it all to fulfilment in his return to the Father. He described what he was about to do:

'I came from the Father and have come into the world and now I leave the world to go to the Father.' (Jn 16:28) This was his hour and the completion of his work. In his death-resurrection-ascension he returned to the glory of the Father.

The Christian Eucharist is a doing-in-memory of Jesus Christ. It is a participation in his unique and perfect sacrifice of return to the Father.

The centre of the celebration is the Eucharistic Prayer. This begins with the invitation to lift up our hearts to praise and thank God. The preface expands on the reasons why it is right to give thanks. It joins our prayers with the praises sung by the choirs of saints and angels ... 'Holy, Holy, Holy...' Then the Holy Spirit is invoked to overshadow the gifts and change them into the body and blood of Christ. The words of the last supper are repeated and the gifts are consecrated or divinised. The participants are caught up in the Son's return to the Father's glory.

The Eucharistic Prayer concludes with the great doxology which expresses this return of praise to the Father:

Through Jesus, with him and in him,
by the unifying power of the Holy Spirit of love,
we return all honour and glory to the Father.

And all who participate enthusiastically express their sharing with Jesus as they cry out or sing 'Amen'.

The first attitude in preparing for Eucharist is to grow in appreciation of God's gifts to us along the road of life. Like the leper who was cured we are to find our gifts ... and especially the gifts of redemption through Jesus Christ. Then we turn back to God on our road, praising the Giver and offering thanks for the gifts. In that attitude of praise and thanks we are disposed for the Eucharist.

'Jesus, having taken the loaves, gave thanks.'

Eighteenth Sunday

Our meditation on the miracle of bread deepens. The readings to-day call us forward from the satisfaction of physical needs to attend to the hungers of the soul which God alone can satisfy. There must be no go-ing back to the bread of Egypt. (First reading) And no returning to the old, corrupted way of life. (Second reading)

John 6: 24-35
When the people saw that neither Jesus nor his disciples were there, they got into boats and crossed to Capernaum, to look for Jesus.

When they found him on the other side, they said to him, 'Rabbi, when did you come here?'

Jesus answered:
> 'I tell you most solemnly,
> you are not looking for me
> because you have seen the signs
> but because you had all the bread you wanted to eat.
> Do not work for food that cannot last,
> but work for food that endures to eternal life,
> the kind of food the Son of Man is offering you,
> for on him the Father, God himself,
> has set his seal.'

Then they said to him,
'What must we do if we are to do the works that God wants?'

Jesus gave them this answer, 'This is working for God: you must believe in the one he has sent.' So they said, 'What sign will you give to show us that we should believe in you? What work will you do? Our fathers had manna to eat in the desert; as scripture says: He gave them bread from heaven to eat.'

Jesus answered:
> 'I tell you most solemnly,
> it was not Moses who gave you bread from heaven,
> it is my Father who gives you the bread from heaven,
> the true bread;
> for the bread of God
> is that which comes down from heaven
> and gives life to the world.'

'Sir,' they said, 'give us that bread always.'

Jesus answered:

212

'I am the bread of life.
He who comes to me will never be hungry;
he who believes in me will never thirst.'

Good News

Jesus is the bread of life: whoever comes to him will never be hungry; whoever believes in him will never thirst.

First Reflection

Hunger of the soul

The gospel here rises up from the appetite of the body to the hungers of the soul. John is the skylark who calls us to rise up with him from earthly considerations to the lofty song of the heavens. In this chapter on bread his writing ascends from physical hunger and earthly obsessions to the sublime yearnings of the soul and the thirst of the mind for eternal satisfaction.

After the miracle of the loaves and fishes Jesus had to escape from the crowd who wanted to make him their king: a king according to their political aspirations. Now they meet up with him again at Capernaum. They are puzzled about how he got there. The reader of the gospel knows that he had crossed the lake by walking on the water. That was even better than Moses, for whom the waters parted! The parallel with Moses continues to run through this passage.

They ask Jesus: 'When did you come here?'

'I tell you most solemnly,' they hear him answer. It is time to take out the note-books. This answer will be weighty. Write it down. The question as to when he crossed the lake was so trivial that he disregards it. It is time for them to move beyond the signs to where the signs were pointing: to ask what the signs meant. There were some really important questions which they should be asking:

Who is this man who mutliplied the loaves and fishes?

Where did he originally come from?

Why did he come?

But they remained rooted on the level of materialistic thinking. More interested in having free bread to satisfy their daily needs than in mentally searching for the meaning of the signs. Jesus challenges them to move forward from today and its physical requirements.

'Do not work for the food that cannot last
but work for the food that endures to eternal life.'

'Work', they ask, 'how do we work for God?' Now comes the punchline of the entire passage: 'This is working for God: you must believe in the one he has sent.'

213

They catch the implications of this: that he is claiming to be the Messiah sent from God. The crowd then voice the popular expectation that the Messiah would work even greater wonders than Moses did in his time.

Jesus takes up the wonder of the manna. One feature of this food was that it lasted no more than a day. The sort of food that Jesus offers is not only for today's needs but for the needs of every day and for all-time.

The eminent psychiatrist K.G. Jung wrote of one factor common to all his patients who were in the second half of life, that is, past the mid-thirties. Without exception, he claimed, whatever their problem, it was in some way rooted in finding a religious outlook on life. None of them was really healed unless they found a religious outlook. We need a comprehensive meaning to hold all the parts together, a lasting direction.

The Roman emperors of old diverted the attention of people from the social injustices of their reign by supplying them with bread and circus. Nowadays the questions which the soul needs to ask are diverted into escape routes which are liberally supplied by the emperors of the ever-increasing entertainment business. But life falls apart from the inside and society rots at the core when the hungers of the soul are not attended to. Is it any wonder that there is such an increase in suicide, instability of relationships, infidelity, dependence on chemical supports? We need to clarify for ourselves the whence and whither of life: and to be committed to a why and how.

The crowd at Capernaum were challenged by Jesus to move beyond the physical hungers of everyday needs to the deeper quests of the human spirit ... to search for the true and lasting bread. 'Sir, give us that bread always.'

Jesus answers: 'I am the bread of life.'

This is the first of the seven great 'I am' statements in John's gospel. The 'I am' part echoes God's identity as revealed to Moses. The words that follow express some aspect of his divine relationship with us.

'I am the bread of life' ... the true and lasting bread for the soul's hunger ... and for the mind's thirst. Eternal bread: all-time food.

'He who comes to me will never be hungry
he who believes in me will never thirst.'

The episode is a call to faith: to believe in Jesus: to enter into an enduring relationship with him which involves leaving behind the old, corrupt ways of thinking.

Faith means dying with Christ to self-centered thinking so as to journey in an exodus with him ... as the people journeyed with Moses from Egypt.

Without the bread that is Jesus our lives would fall apart. As St Augustine put it: 'Our souls are made for thee and find no rest until they rest in thee.'

Second Reflection
Liturgy of the Word
The text for our second week with John Chapter 6 leads us to reflect on the liturgy of the word as the nourishment of our faith. Jesus stressed that the work which God asks of us is to believe in the one he has sent. And the primary source of what we believe is the sacred word of scripture.

In John 6 Jesus speaks of himself as the bread of life. Initially he is referring to himself as God's revealing word. He is the bread to satisfy the deepest hungers of life and the insatiable thirsts of the spirit. Only later will the chapter change to the theme of his presence in the bread of the Eucharist. He feeds our faith with the bread of his word before he nourishes our souls with his own flesh and blood. Hence the two tables in the sanctuary: one for the liturgy of the word; the other for the sacrificial meal.

All Christian liturgy must be traced back to the exhortation of Jesus at the last supper: 'In memory of me, do this.' Our memory of Jesus Christ is rekindled and activated as we listen to the word. Then with our faith refreshed we are ready to re-enact the last supper.

St Justin has left us a written account of the Christian Sunday celebration around the year 150. On that day called after the sun, he says, all who are in the towns and the countryside gathered together for a community celebration. The memoirs of the apostles and the writings of the prophets were read ... 'for as long as time permits,' he adds. Then the president of the assembly addressed the people, exhorting them to practise those beautiful teachings in their lives. That is what the homily is all about, making the connection between the word of faith and the experiences of everyday life: connecting God's story with our story: enabling people to read the book of everyday life in the light of the revealed book.

The Second Vatican Council set the target of restoring the importance of the first part of Mass and to promote that 'sweet and living love for the sacred scripture to which the venerable tradition of Eastern and Western rites gives testimony.'

The post-Conciliar generation find it incomprehensible that

the readings at Mass were for so long in a language which the vast majority did not understand.

The rites of all the sacraments have been revised so as to give an important place to sacred scripture in each celebration. Yet the attitude too often prevails of getting the readings out of the way before we get at the real sacrament. The use of sacred scripture is even omitted from many sacramental celebrations. While there is much to-do in some places about experiments in the use of communal celebrations of Reconciliation, nothing is heard about the absence of scriptural reading in the majority of one-to-one confessions!

With regard to Sunday Eucharist, we are still labouring with the Latin Mass mentality to a great extent. The readings might as well still be in a foreign language for the shabby way they are treated. The sheer effort of listening is often a battle with faulty speaker systems, crying babies, rustling leaflets and goodness knows what other distractions. It is a bit too much to expect the sacred word to nourish one's faith if it is never encountered apart from these distracting conditions. Little wonder if faith remains on the infantile level, gullible to every novelty or sensation like moving statues or private hotlines from Jesus or Mary. 'They have abandoned me, the fountain of living water, only to dig cisterns for themselves, leaky cisterns that hold no water.' (Jer 2:13) The fact that you are reading this book probably indicates a desire to treat the sacred word more seriously. Those who make some effort to study the liturgical texts beforehand testify that the Mass then comes alive for them.

Anybody who is called to be a minister of the word should be aware that this is a call to proclaim the word of God. The reader has responsibility for the word which nourishes faith and activates the memory of Jesus Christ, in whose name the congregation comes together. It is a holy word, living and active, penetrating into the innermost mysteries of life.

It is not enough merely to avoid incorrect pronunciations. Every reader should first pray with the sacred text before proclaiming it to others.

As we gather from town and countryside to celebrate the Eucharist, we first attend to the table of the word. There the story of God's marvellous deeds is retold. Memory is activated. Our faith is nourished with the bread of God's word.

Jesus is the bread which came down from heaven to give life to the world.

'He who comes to me will never be hungry;
he who believes in me will never thirst.'

Nineteenth Sunday

This is our third Sunday with John's deep reflection on the miracle of the loaves and fishes. In today's reading we are drawn up to the level of believing that in the Blessed Eucharist Christ give us his flesh to eat for the life of the world.

John 6:41-51

The Jews were complaining to each other about Jesus, because he had said, 'I am the bread that came down from heaven.' 'Surely this is Jesus son of Joseph,' they said. 'We know his father and mother. How can he now say, 'I have come down from heaven'?'

Jesus said in reply, 'Stop complaining to each other.

No one can come to me
unless he is drawn by the Father who sent me,
and I will raise him up at the last day.
It is written in the prophets:
They will all be taught by God,
and to hear the teaching of the Father,
and learn from it,
is to come to me.
Not that anybody has seen the Father,
except the one who comes from God:
he has seen the Father.
I tell you most solemnly,
everybody who believes has eternal life.
I am the bread of life.
Your fathers ate the manna in the desert and they are dead;
but this is the bread that comes down from heaven,
so that a man may eat it and not die.
I am the living bread which has come down from heaven.
Anyone who eats this bread will live for ever;
and the bread that I shall give
is my flesh, for the life of the world.'

Good News

Jesus, the Word made flesh, has become our bread of life, raising us up to eternal life.

First Reflection
From sign to sacrament

We have called John the skylark because his writing rises like the songbird on a spiral of warm air from the material things of earth to the realms of highest faith.

St Francis, who loved all creatures, regarded the lark as his favourite bird. Not only for its beautiful song, but because its earthy, brown colour and lighter hood behind the head made its plumage resemble the Franciscan habit. John, the lark, keeps linking the things of earth with heavenly thoughts.

He tells how the Jews were complaining and resisting. Note the irony as John records their sureness about the origin of Jesus ... 'son of Joseph!' The reader already knows from John where Jesus came from. He is the Word of the Father, made flesh. Their earthbound knowledge is insufficient. They must rise up in the leap of faith.

Faith goes beyond the material evidence or the range of rational speculation and argument. Nor is it based on whether we feel something to be true or not. Faith is the acceptance of divine truth and it involves three elements combining together.

First, it is an interior gift of God's grace: 'No one can come to me,' says Jesus, 'unless he is drawn by the Father who sent me.'

Secondly, the content of faith is based on the words and signs given by Jesus Christ. The third element is our free cooperation with the Father's gift and the teaching of Jesus. So, Jesus goes on to say that the believer is one who has been taught by the Father, learns from this teaching and freely comes to Jesus. He then goes back to the theme of Moses and the manna. Moses, for all his greatness, could not look on the face of God. And the manna of his time was food for a day and did not give eternal life. By contrast, Jesus, who has come from God, can give a bread from heaven which will raise us up to divine life.

The discourse now takes a critical turn from past history towards what Jesus will bring in the future:

'The bread that I shall give is my flesh, for the life of the world.' His words henceforth point forward to the last supper and to the giving up of his life in sacrificial death. His sacrifice will be the way of releasing the flow of divine life, eternal life, for the world.

Through dying Jesus transcended all bodily limitations. In his glorified state he, the Word made flesh, can share his flesh with us as our bread of eternal life.

The Word was made flesh: and the flesh would be made bread.

218

In this passage John has drawn our thoughts upwards into the mystery of faith. He has moved from bread as a sign to bread as a symbol and now, to bread as a sacrament.

A sign is something perceived which points beyond itself to a greater reality of which it is a part. Smoke is a sign of fire somewhere. The miracle of loaves and fishes was a sign of supernatural power in Jesus.

A symbol is a sign which makes such powerful suggestions that it begins to transfer its own life and meaning to the beholder. Literally, symbol comes from the Greek words for energies moving or flowing together. So, the tranquility of a sunset can flow into my being and fill me with a sense of vastness and peace. Music can take me and transform me to tears or marching, to terror or romance. T.S. Eliot wrote of 'music heard so deeply

That it is not heard at all, but you are the music

While the music lasts.' (The Dry Salvages).

As a symbol, the Eucharist suggests food for our spiritual life: or in the multiplicity of grains it suggests the community of the participants. But the Eucharist is more than a symbol: it is a sacrament. A sacrament is that sort of symbol which transmits a divine energy to the recipient.

In a symbol the transfer of energy depends on the extent of suggestion and feeling. But in a sacrament there is a real connection between the visible sign and the interior effect. It goes beyond feeling or suggestion. It can be accepted only on faith.

Thus, the sacrament of marriage is divinely different from the contract signed in a registry office. Or the Sacrament of Reconciliation has a divine power of forgiveness beyond the effect of confessing one's sins to a friend, agony aunt or psychiatrist. The Sacrament of the Eucharist is essentially different to any other meal, no matter how lovely the hymns or prayers that may accompany it.

John began with the miracle of the loaves and fishes as a sign of the supernatural power of Jesus. Then his song ascended to where Jesus was seen as the bread of life to satisfy the hungers of the human heart and mind. Now he has risen to the highest plane of faith ... to the mystery of faith.

In the Eucharist there is a divine infusion of Christ's life into our souls. There is a mysterious, divine connection with us. Our belief in this dynamic presence of Christ in the Eucharist is not based on feelings or the power of suggestion. It is not subject to scientific analysis. Faith is a gift from the Father enabling us to accept the word of Jesus and to leap beyond all physical evidence. It accepts his words:

'The bread that I shall give
is my flesh for the life of the world.'
It is the mystery of faith.

Second Reflection
The Eucharist as sacrifice
For our third reflection on the Eucharist we move from the table of the word, where our faith is nourished, to the table of sacrifice. This is no ordinary dining-table: it is a table of sacrifice, and that is why we call it the altar. Nowadays there is a great popular emphasis on the Eucharist as a meal of celebration. But it must never be forgotten that it is a meal which recalls and makes present again the sacrifice of Christ on Calvary.

The last supper was no ordinary meal of farewell. It was the fulfilment of the Jewish Passover meal by anticipating the sacrifice of Christ as the new Passover Lamb. 'This is my body which will be given up for you.' (Lk 22:19)

The practice of offering sacrifice to the spirits or invisible powers goes back to primitive times. Sacrifice, *sacrum-facere*, means to make something sacred by offering it to the Sacred One. It is a return of life to the Giver in the hope that the flow of life will be maintained or improved.

Something representing life, usually an animal, was destroyed. Sometimes part of the animal was burnt and the ascending smoke was regarded as going to the god. Indeed it seems likely that the Greek word for god, *theos*, derived from the word for the smoke of incense, *thus*.

An important part of the ceremony involved sprinkling the people with blood to express their participation. Blood was regarded as the official way to ratify a contract or treaty. A sacrificial meal followed in the belief that the god gave back life or a favourable answer to the people through the meal. So, the important elements in sacrifice were the slaying of the victim, sprinkling with the blood and eating the meal.

The great festival of the Jewish calendar was the Passover feast. It recalled the wondrous events of creation and of God's involvement in their history. In a special way it focused on that night when Moses led them out of Egyptian slavery into freedom. Every year they recalled the story of how the destroying angel passed through the land of Egypt but saved the houses which were sprinkled with the blood of a lamb. In their journey to freedom God renewed his covenant with them through Moses. Animals were sacrificed and the people were sprinkled with blood as a mark of their participation in the covenant.

Each year they recalled this covenant. And the most important item of the celebration was the meal with the Passover lamb. It had to be a male lamb without blemish: slaughtered in the Temple and eaten in the precincts of Jerusalem: it was ritually set out on firewood for cooking.

At the last supper, Jesus brought the old covenant to fulfilment. 'This cup is the new covenant in my blood which will be poured out for you.' (Lk 22:20) The following day on Calvary, he, the spotless lamb, gave up his life as the sacrificial victim and shed his blood to ratify the covenant. The veil of the Temple was rent asunder, signifying the end of the old covenant. The new covenant with God was thus begun: a covenant offering eternal life, a sharing in divine life. The sacrifice of Jesus must never be thought of only in terms of his death: it also involves his return to the Father in resurrection and ascension.

At Mass we are asked to proclaim the mystery of faith. Aloud we recall that Christ died and rose. The Eucharistic Prayer then continues in words which remember his death, resurrection and ascension. In biblical and liturgical senses to remember is to make present again.

The Eucharist is the body of Christ given up to the Father for us. And it is the blood of Christ which ratifies the new covenant. It is truly and really the memorial of Christ's dying and rising in sacrifice.

How can anyone understand this? Only by faith ... faith which grows on the words of Jesus:

'The bread that I shall give
is my flesh, for the life of the world.'

Twentieth Sunday

For the fourth week we read from the great discourse of Jesus on the bread of life, developed for us in John Chapter 6. Today's extract invites us up to the heights of faith to accept that in the Eucharistic Bread we share in the divine life of Christ.

John 6:51-58
Jesus said to the crowd:
>'I am the living bread which has come down from heaven.
>Anyone who eats this bread will live for ever;
>and the bread that I shall give
>is my flesh, for the life of the world.'

Then the Jews started arguing with one another:
'How can this man give us his flesh to eat?' they said.
Jesus replied:
>'I tell you most solemnly,
>if you do not eat the flesh of the Son of Man
>and drink his blood,
>you will not have life in you.
>Anyone who does eat my flesh and drink my blood
>has eternal life,
>and I shall raise him up on the last day.
>For my flesh is real food
>and my blood is real drink.
>He who eats my flesh and drinks my blood
>lives in me
>and I live in him.
>As I, who am sent by the living Father,
>myself draw life from the Father,
>so whoever eats me will draw life from me.
>This is the bread come down from heaven;
>not like the bread our ancestors ate:
>they are dead,
>but anyone who eats this bread will live for ever.'

Good News
The Son of God took on our flesh and blood: and in giving us his flesh to eat and his blood to drink, he gives us a sharing in divine life.

First Reflection
To eat his flesh

Today's gospel begins by repeating the final verse of last week's passage. Here the words of Jesus take a decisive turn towards the future. 'The bread that I shall give is my flesh for the life of the world.' He is looking forward to the last supper and to the sacrificial giving of his body for the life of the world.

Throughout the development of this chapter John has raised our thoughts up to different levels. He began on the material level of ordinary bread for physical hunger. The miraculous multiplication of the loaves and fishes was a sign that some higher power was operative here. The sign was a challenge to consider Jesus as supernatural.

As the discourse continued Jesus began to speak of himself as the living bread come down from heaven. Now the bread was no longer just a sign: it had become a symbol: that is, the sort of sign which is so full of life and meaning that it transfers its energy into us. We are changed and charged by a symbol. On the level of symbol Jesus is the bread of life whose teaching satisfies the long term hungers and enduring quests of life. His teaching and moral way offer a deeply satisfying why and wherefore to life.

But the words of Jesus ask us to rise up still higher. We are drawn by the Father beyond physical evidence to the level of pure faith. Jesus speaks of offering himself as something more than a symbol of satisfaction. He is to be a sacrament for us. That is, he offers a real, life-sharing contact between the risen Christ and our lives. His words are so realistic that they shock the audience: 'The bread that I shall give is my flesh.'

Little wonder that the Jews found it very hard to accept. They argued the point. 'How can this man give us his flesh to eat?'

But Jesus did not withdraw his words or try to explain them away. He insisted rather forcibly that this was exactly what he meant. Three times he repeated his message, giving a slightly different angle on it each time.

First of all he insists that eating his flesh and drinking his blood is the only way to share in the fulness of life: 'Unless you eat my flesh and drink my blood you will not have life in you.'

Then he asserts that this meal is the pledge of eternal life, promising to raise up the recipient on the last day ... 'and I will raise him up on the last day.'

Thirdly, he explains that this is his way of sharing intimately with us the life he receives from the Father. 'As I who am sent by the living Father, myself draw life from the Father, so whoever eats me will draw life from me.' As it is expressed in John's opening chapter: 'To all who did accept him he gave power to become children of God.'

Finally, the great discourse comes back to its opening theme of the manna. The manna was a great wonder in its time. But it was only food for perishable life whereas the bread offered in Jesus would be for eternal life.

The doctrine of this discourse can be accepted by faith alone. Through his death and resurrection, the enfleshed life of Jesus Christ moved beyond the limitations of time and space.What Jesus promised is his body as it is 'given up for you': it is his sacrificed flesh which is now in a glorified state. We do not physically eat his earthly flesh as in a cannibalistic sense. In the Sacrament of the Eucharist we receive his body in its eternally glorified condition.

The Word was made flesh ... and this glorified flesh has become bread for us. But in the institution of the sacrament he is the living bread that makes a real contact with us to share divine life with us.

An ancient antiphon beautifully expresses the doctrine:
'This is the holy supper in which Christ is received,
the memory of his passion is recalled,
the soul is filled with grace,
and our future glory is guaranteed.'

Second Reflection
The Eucharist as meal
In our fourth meditation on the Mass we ponder on the Eucharist as the meal in which divine life is shared with us.

'He who eats my flesh and drinks my blood
lives in me and I live in him.'

Even in primitive religions the ritual of sacrifice proceeded to a meal in which the food that had been offered in sacrifice was now eaten. They believed that the spirit of the god had entered the flesh and would share its life-energy and strength with them in this eating.

In last Sunday's liturgy the first reading was a story about Elijah. He was worn out, deflated and praying to die. Lying under a furze bush he fell asleep. An angel came, touched him and led him to a scone baking on hot stones. He ate that food and drank a jug of water. And in the strength of that meal he walked for forty days and nights to encounter God on the sacred mountain. In that sense, the Eucharist is food of the soul for the fulness of days in our life's pilgrimage of returning to God.

'As I, who am sent by the living Father
myself draw life from the Father
so whoever eats me will draw life from me.'

There is a major difference between the Eucharist and our ordinary, everyday meals. Our ordinary food is digested and it becomes part of us. It is absorbed into our blood, bones, muscles, fibre and fat: it is burnt up to supply our heat and energy. That food is changed into us.

But the Eucharist works the other way around. We are changed into it. St Augustine heard these words come to him in prayer: 'I am the food of grown men: grow and you shall eat me. And you shall not change me into yourself as bodily food, but into me you shall be changed.'

As Pope Pius XII put it: 'If you have received worthily, you are what you received.' St Paul could tell the Galatians: 'It is no longer I who live but Christ lives in me.'

Each time we receive with faith and devotion we are being transformed into the likeness of Christ. We gradually grow into his life in mind and will. Our thought pattern will increasingly work according to Christ's light and divine wisdom. As today's first reading expresses it:

'Come and eat my bread, drink the wine I have prepared!
Leave your folly and you will live,
walk in the ways of perception.' (Prov 9:16)

As our wills are strengthened towards union with Christ, then our motivation will gradually become less selfish and more truly Christian. 'It is the kind of food and the way of eating through which you can digest the Father's will into yourself, and become the true person he has created you to be.' (Stephen Verney)

The greatest witness in today's world to the motivating power of the Eucharist is surely Mother Teresa. She and her sisters, after receiving the body of Christ with great devotion each morning then go out to tend the suffering body of Christ in the poor with equal devotion. The Eucharist is their source of Christian energy.

It is important to spend personal time with the Lord prayerfully pondering the wonder of the Eucharist. The public ceremonial of Mass has to proceed at a certain pace but our own mental absorbing of the Lord's gift needs quiet time. It is regrettable that the traditional practice of private thanksgiving has fallen into disuse, by and large.

And yet, Holy Communion is not meant to be only a moment of individual piety, a sort of cosy one-to-one with Jesus. There could be no greater challenge to carry out the works of Christian charity than the Eucharist. The divine energy that we receive from Christ must be expressed in Christian attitudes and behaviour.

In liturgy we remember Jesus Christ so that outside the church we might re-member him. That is, we are to be the living members of his body on earth, continuing his mission of mercy and doing his works of charity. Christ is counting on us. And we are counting on the divine energy that he gives us in the Bread of Life.

'Draw life from me,' the Lord invites.

And like Elijah, in the strength of this food, let us rise from our despondency to journey towards the holy mountain of God.

Twenty-First Sunday

This is our fifth and final Sunday with Chapter 6 of John. It reaches a point of judgment and decision. Those who do not believe no longer walk with Jesus. But Peter speaks on behalf of those who do believe and who will be loyal to him. In today's first reading Joshua, like Peter, calls for a declaration of loyalty to the service of the true God.

John 6:60-69

After hearing his doctrine, many of the followers of Jesus said, 'This is intolerable language. How could anyone accept it?'

Jesus was aware that his followers were complaining about it and said, 'Does this upset you? What if you should see the Son of Man ascend to where he was before?

'It is the spirit that gives life,
the flesh has nothing to offer.
The words I have spoken to you are spirit
and they are life.

'But there are some of you who do not believe.' For Jesus knew from the outset those who did not believe, and who it was that would betray him. He went on, 'This is why I told you that no one could come to me unless the Father allows him.' After this, many of his disciples left him and stopped going with him.

Then Jesus said to the Twelve, 'What about you, do you want to go away too?' Simon Peter answered, 'Lord, whom shall we go to? You have the message of eternal life, and we believe; we know that you are the Holy One of God.'

Good News

By the gift of faith, the believer accepts Jesus as the bread of divine life, come down to raise us up to eternal life.

First Reflection
Time for decision

The long discourse on Jesus as the bread of life leads to a point of decision whether to believe in him or not.

It would be exciting to follow a miracle-worker. And grand to bask in the consolations of religion, hearing about mercy and forgiveness and healing.

But to believe! To believe in Jesus totally as the one, true source of divine satisfaction for the deepest hungers of soul and mind! To believe that he would give us his flesh and blood in some sacrificial way and thereby share divine life with us!

Many of his followers found all this too much to accept. They had come so far but would go no further. Intolerable claims! Sayings too hard to accept.

But we cannot be selective in choosing what we like in the teaching of Jesus and conveniently off-loading what does not please us. Quoting to our own use how he forgave the adulterous woman while overlooking that he told her to sin no more.

Unless we see how lofty are the Christian ideals ... how hard are the demands of total charity ... how his messge is a declaration of death to selfishness ... unless we see how hard his message is, we have not yet come to the point of decision.

He never promised an easy road to his followers. He asked for the courage to take up one's cross. Yet he did say that his load would be easy and his burden light. But load and burden there will be.

Jesus hears the complaints and takes up the point. The nub of the matter is his claim about divine life coming down to our flesh so as to lift us up to eternal life. It is a question of God coming down and humanity being lifted up ... of a bread from above to share divine life with us.

His words look forward to his glorification ... the Son of Man ascending to where he was before. When he is called the Son of Man it brings out how he belongs to our flesh and blood. Now, since one of our flesh and blood has been raised on high, why can't he share this above-life with us here below?

What Jesus promised was that when he was glorified he would give us his flesh to eat and his life-blood to drink. Earth-bound reasoning (the 'flesh')) cannot accept this: for the earthly mind has never been up in the divine life. It is in the realm of the spirit, beyond earthbound, physical reasoning, that faith resides. This recalls the necessity of grace for believing.

'No one can come to me
unless he is drawn by the Father who sent me.'

The crunch has come. It is time for decision. Many of his followers turn away, no longer to walk with him. What a powerful, vivid expression!

We can marvel at the restraint of God as shown in the respect of Jesus for the free decision of these followers. He even turns to the Twelve. The door is open. They can go or stay. The choice is their own.

Peter, to his eternal credit, speaks up. His words form the

prayer of believers ever since. 'Lord, who shall we go to? You have the message of eternal life, and we believe: we know you are the Holy One of God.'

Total loyalty to Jesus. Absolute, single-minded commitment. There can be no other one, only you.

It was a day of confrontation and decision. Like filling a sack of potatoes, they needed a good shaking up. No doubt, a day of pain and soul-searching. But a day that cleared the air as to where people stood.

Were they following Jesus for miracles, for consolations, for God on their own terms? Or, like Peter, were they making an unconditional commitment to follow Jesus on his terms? The true disciples were more settled in their commitment after this decision.

Perhaps our age needs a similar day of clearing the air. Do we take Jesus in the totality of his teaching or not? It is not good enough to remain a luke-warm, pick-'n-choose follower. Either we walk the whole way with him or stop pretending to walk.

Second Reflection
God in his name

Our fifth eucharistic reflection focuses on the solemn dismissal at the end of Mass: 'Go in peace to love and serve the Lord.' The English word *Mass* comes from the Latin term, *missa*, which refers to this sending forth..

The Eucharist is incomplete unless it is brought out beyond the church building: unless it extends beyond Sunday to the rest of the week. The light of faith which is fanned to flame at the table of the word and the energy of divine life which is given to us at the sacred meal must now be translated into Christian thought and behaviour.

The great eucharistic discourse of John 6 concludes at a crossroads of decision. Some do not accept what Jesus has said. They walk no more with him and go their separate ways. But others, like Peter, decide that for them there will be no other way but Christ.

The conclusion of the Eucharist also sets us out on our separate ways. But wherever we go it should be with the light of God's word to guide us and the energy of Christ to strengthen and sustain us.

We recall the two tables at which we were fed. At the table of the word our faith was nourished in the re-telling of the story of God's workings in salvation. Faith is more than a philosophical sort of knowledge which remains in the mind alone. Faith is also a heart-knowledge of God. Peter linked this mental knowing and heart knowing together. 'We believe and we know that you are the Holy One of God.' It is the sort of knowledge which drops into the heart and sets love aflame. The word *creed* comes from *cor-dare*, to give your heart.

If the message is alight in the mind and aflame in the heart, then it will pass out into feet and hands. In other words, it is the sort of knowledge which is translated into action.

But where can we obtain the strength to live and act in a truly Christian manner? From the sacred bread, which is really and truly the body and blood of Christ, given up for the world.

The high ideals of gospel-living would totally overwhelm us unless we knew that our strength would come from the Lord's own body and blood. We remember the explanation of Pius XII: 'If you have received worthily, you are what you received.' We are sent out at the end of Mass so that Christ, who is within us, might reach out to others through us.

How is this teaching of Christ to penetrate the darkness of to-day's world? How is the mercy of Christ to reach out in welcome to the broken sinner? How is the compassion of Christ to touch the lives of the sick and downhearted? Only through the lives of people who have the energy of Christ in them from the Eucharist.

For too long a distorted eucharistic devotion centred all attention on the personal piety of meeting Christ in the secrecy of one's soul but neglected the social responsibilities of bringing Christ's energies into the world. What happens in church cannot be authentic unless it sends people out to work more energetically for the kingdom of God on earth.

The life and love of Christ which we receive in the Eucharist must be the source of all genuine liberation from injustice and oppression. The Eucharist is the greatest powerhouse of Christian energy to transform the world into the kingdom of justice and love where God truly reigns. It is from Christ's meal that we draw the strength to turn the other cheek, or have the sort of love which is so much greater than wrong-doing that we know how to forgive.

Lord, to whom shall we go? You alone have the message of eternal life.

Christ the Word is the message.

Christ the Bread is the energy to live up to the message.

We listen to his word and eat his bread so that we might be strengthened to walk the road with him.

Twenty-Second Sunday

After five Sundays with John's gospel we return to Mark. A relatively trivial issue about washing hands becomes an occasion for Jesus to show what a travesty of religion it is when human regulations take over from God's true commandments. Today's first reading emphasises how the true law of God leads to wisdom and understanding.

Mark 7:1-8, 14-15, 21-23

The Pharisees and some of the scribes who had come from Jerusalem gathered round Jesus, and they noticed that some of his disciples were eating with unclean hands, that is, without washing them. For the Pharisees, and the Jews in general, follow the tradition of the elders and never eat without washing their arms as far as the elbow; and on returning from the market place they never eat without first sprinkling themselves. There are also many other observances which have been handed down to them concerning the washing of cups and pots and bronze dishes.

So these Pharisees and scribes asked him, 'Why do your disciples not respect the tradition of the elders but eat their food with unclean hands?' He answered, 'It was of you hypocrites that Isaiah so rightly prophesied in this passage of scripture:

This people honours me only with lip-service,

while their hearts are far from me.

The worship they offer me is worthless,

the doctrines they teach are only human regulations.

You put aside the commandment of God to cling to human traditions.'

He called the people to him again and said, 'Listen to me, all of you, and understand. Nothing that goes into a man from outside can make him unclean; it is the things that come out of a man that make him unclean. For it is from within, from men's hearts, that evil intentions emerge: fornication, theft, murder, adultery, avarice, malice, deceit, indecency, envy, slander, pride, folly. All these evil things come from within and make a man unclean.'

Good News

God reads the innermost heart and is not deceived by outward show or lip-service.

First Reflection
Dirty hands

The lectionary returns to Mark today. When last we read from Mark we saw Jesus look on the people with pity for they were like sheep without a shepherd. So, he set himself to teach them at some length, for it is the first task of the shepherd to lead the flock. The second task is to feed them: which Jesus did in the miracle of the loaves and fishes. Instead of taking Mark's version of that miracle, the lectionary gave us John's much longer meditation on the event. For five weeks our reflections were enriched with the beautiful doctrine of the bread of life.

Back with Mark today, we are given a different aspect on eating. The issue of washing hands before eating becomes a matter of criticism.

We notice the typical Marcan picture of the crowd gathering around Jesus. But in this instance there were more than the ordinary Galilean folk who were pressing him for favours. Some very important people had come, big wigs from Jerusalem, department officials to run the line over Jesus and all this Galilean excitement.

There were Pharisees who were obsessed with the danger of contamination, whether from outside religious influences, foreign culture or ordinary plain dirt. They had made a negative religion out of dirt.

Also there were scribes. Before the days of printing, copyists were very important. Scribes were more than copyists. They were the experts who knew all the details of the regulations and interpretations which had grown up around the code of cult and behaviour which Moses had set out as their side of the covenant with God. There were 613 man-made regulations, 365 of them negative and 248 positive ... corresponding to the days of the year and the joints of the body. It was impossible for the ordinary person to know where their obligations started or finished. Hence the power of the experts, the scribes.

This particular issue about washing hands might appear trivial to us. But we note how Mark goes to some length to show his readers that this business of washing was very big indeed. Nothing is trivial to the mind that is enmeshed in laws and scruples. It takes but a short memory to recall when Catholic life seemed similarly enmeshed in mortal sins at every hand's turn. People were worried about a crumb between the teeth breaking the eucharistic fast, or a little knitting breaking Sunday observance. Legalism will always be an occupational hazard for religion.

The issue here acts like a trigger to Jesus. It gives him the occasion to speak about the travesty of religion that is spawned by legalism. Up to this point Mark has told us that Jesus taught the people and impressed them. But we were not given any of the teaching until now.

We hear an important pronouncement of Jesus on true religion. Lip-service, without the worship of the heart, is worthless. And human regulations or interpretations must never take over from the genuine commandment of God.

Jesus explains himself in a very simple comparison ... one of those short gems of wisdom which light up the gospel: 'Nothing that goes into a man from the outside can make him unclean; it is the things that come out of a man that make him unclean.'

What Jesus is criticising is that legalism which takes over the heart of true religion. But he is certainly not doing away with the need for religious laws.

An excess of legalism in the past is no excuse to rush to the other extreme of disregarding the need for clear laws. Modern permissiveness does not like laws and is uncomfortable with clear statements. Permissiveness thrives in grey areas. There is nothing unclear in the list of twelve evils here condemned by Jesus.

Some of these would be readily condemned by anybody with a conscience ... murder, theft and malice. But the so-called humanist will wince at the condemnation of sexual evils ... adultery, fornication and indecency. Any Pope or preacher who repeats this gospel teaching is not making up his own morality: it is the teaching of Our Lord himself.

There are two evils associated with what we say or do ... deceit and slander. Another two are internal attitudes of the heart ... avarice and envy. And finally there are two evil attitudes which set out to remove God from life: pride, which makes a god out of oneself; and folly, which is a scriptural expression for that mentality which refuses to accept God's law in moral affairs. 'The fool has said in his heart "there is no God above".'

The clash with the Pharisees and scribes shows how Jesus was sad and angry at the man-made regulations which obscured the heart of true religion and the genuine commandments. 'You put aside the commandment of God to cling to human traditions.'

The true law of God is the basis of wisdom and understanding: wisdom in divine affairs and understanding in human matters. 'Your words are spirit, Lord, and they are life.'

Second Reflection
Religious prudence

Religion is a highly dangerous commodity which should always be handled with care ... and prudence.

Religion is invested with tremendous potential for human growth. Indeed, full human growth is unthinkable without due attention to our religious dimension.

However, any warped version of religion is guaranteed to stunt human development. Jesus was clearly angry at the travesty of religion enmeshed in legalism. 'You put aside the commandment of God to cling to human traditions.' It is a real tragedy when people cling blindly to a version of religion which belittles life and leaves them worse off.

Jesus was eventually done to death in the name of religion under a plot conspired by religious leaders. So-called religion motivates war and all manner of human atrocity to this day. Religious self-righteousness underpins injustice in the forms of political prejudice, housing allotment and promotion prospects. The Bible is quoted to legitimate apartheid.

The dark side of Church history tells the brutal story of inquisition, burning of heretics and sometimes the inhibition of learning. Warped versions of religion have loaded people with morbid guilt, burdened them with sanitary obsessions and driven them to insanity.

Today's unstable world, unable to cope with the rapidity of change, is a fertile picking ground for religious neurotics in search of disciples. One does not have to go to such extreme examples as Pastor Jim Jones who led his People's Temple to their mass suicide. Within the Church one finds religious neurotics who have the best of intentions, but they are leading people down the doubtful paths of fanatical devotion. You will find them highly excited about alleged apparitions, extraordinary phenomena and private revelations. Events of history are interpreted in the light of these private revelations ... heedless of Christ's warning not to interpret catastrophes as a punishment from God. (*cf* Luke 13:1-5)

Invariably, their message is a foreboding of doom and gloom. Their imagery will be apocalyptic with swords of judgment hanging over us, clouds of fire descending and oceans of blood awaiting us.

Is there any way out of this impending doom? The self-appointed prophet has the answer in a neat prescription. It will involve penance and prayer. Obviously this is in line with the gospel. However, the impression is given that it must be in one particular form of devotion, as if any other form of prayer is not of any real value.

Make this novena to save the world! Propagate this picture and ward off the avenging hand of God! God must be very small-minded if the saving of a city from destruction in war depends on the number of holy pictures there.

Many people are afraid to resist their friends who push these devotional prescriptions on them for fear that they might be visited by all manner of bad luck. It's a form of spiritual blackmail.

One hears imbalanced statements like: 'No prayer is any good unless it is offered through the hands of Mary.' Or, 'You should never pray for your own intentions but for Mary's intentions.' No wonder devotion to Mary can get a bad name.

Religious neurotics are not new arrivals. St Paul met them at Colossae. There they contaminated true faith with theories about cosmic powers and apparitions of angels. Paul advised: 'Do not be taken in by people who like grovelling to angels and worshipping them; people like that are always going on about some vision they have had.' (Col 2:18) He goes on to write about 'their self-imposed devotions, their self-abasement, and their severe treatment of the body.' (2:23) Paul called them back to the centrality of Christ and the baptismal rhythm of dying and rising with him.

Prudence is a great virtue. Along with justice, fortitude and temperance, it completes the four pillars of a balanced life. Prudence will quickly detect the self-appointed prophets with their private interpretations and their human regulations. Prudence keeps religion for God ... and for true human growth.

Twenty-Third Sunday

The healing of the man who was deaf and impaired of speech is told in great detail by Mark. It is a story that can be read on many levels: as a commentary on the slow progress of the disciples towards hearing the message and proclaiming it; in connection with the Sacrament of Baptism; or as expressing the power of Christ which is still operative in our lives to open our ears and release the proclamation of goodness.

Mark 7: 31-37

Returning from the district of Tyre, Jesus went by way of Sidon toward the Sea of Galilee, right through the Decapolis region.

And they brought him a deaf man who had an impediment in his speech; and they asked him to lay his hand on him.

He took him aside in private, away from the crowd, put his fingers into the man's ears and touched his tongue with spittle. Then looking up to heaven he sighed; and he said to him, 'Ephphatha,' that is, 'Be opened.'

And his ears were opened, and the ligament of his tongue was loosened and he spoke clearly.

And Jesus ordered them to tell no one about it, but the more he insisted, the more widely they published it.

Their admiration was unbounded. 'He has done all things well,' they said, 'he makes the deaf hear and the dumb speak.'

Good News

God has visited our world in Jesus Christ. He has opened our ears to hear his word and our mouths to proclaim his faith.

First Reflection
Avenging love

The Greek word chosen by Mark to express the man's dumbness has a great ring to it: *Mogilalos*. Even if you haven't a word of Greek, try saying that word aloud ... Mogi-lalos. Isn't it exactly the sound you'd hear from somebody whose hearing is defective and who is struggling with sounds.

The only other place the word occurs in the Bible is Isaiah 35:6, which is part of the first reading of today's liturgy. Isaiah is encouraging the people in exile to look forward to the coming of God. He speaks of the vengeance and retribution of God which are coming. Normally these are words we associate with hatred and terror. But when we read on, we see that the vengeance that God brings is not destructive. God, who is totally loving, has no desire to destroy his own creation. His coming is the movement of love to save and heal.

This is God's idea of coming with vengeance:
'Then the eyes of the blind shall be opened,
the ears of the deaf unsealed,
then the lame shall leap like a deer
and the tongues of the dumb sing for joy.'

Mark could see the hopes of Isaiah realised in the healing work of Jesus. He tells us how Jesus looked up to heaven and sighed. The eyes towards heaven express his intimacy with the Father. And his sigh is part of the vengeful love of God which pains with (compassion) the poor man and is angry with the sinful condition in which the evil spirits have messed up so many peoples' lives. There may even be a hint in the way that the man's speech was released that this was an exorcism. Mark always gives us a great sense of the physical involvement of Jesus with people. This is no healing from a distance. Jesus is asked to lay his hands on the man. That phrase became common in the New Testament but it was never associated with healing in the Old Testament. Jesus feels the need for more concentrated attention to the man so he draws him aside by himself, away from the crowd. Behind a bush maybe. He put his fingers into the closed ears. He touched his tongue with spittle: folk medicine holds that spittle has great curative powers.

From the depth of his being Jesus sighed. The healing word is a command, 'Ephpheta.' The word is precious, so Mark preserves it in Aramaic.

The use of fingers, saliva and words was important for the later development of the sacraments. Christ used physical things, human actions and words as the means of divine power for peoples' lives.

Jesus tells them to tell nobody of the miracle. The plea for secrecy is something we have already met in Mark. Many explanations have been offered for this messianic secret, as it is called. Jesus did not want to be publicised as a curiosity, a worker of the sensational, or a likely political leader. He calls for no publicity of his miracles because the full truth of who he is still escapes them. In the development of Mark we are close to the peak of the recognition of Jesus. In fact, next Sunday's gospel will bring us there in Peter's confession of faith. But for the moment he wants no publicity.

Yet the admiration of the people is unbounded. 'He has done all things well,' they say. Their comment echoes the remark that at the end of each day of creation, God saw what he had made and he said that it was good.

The ministry of Jesus as messiah was to heal and restore. The avenging love of God came down, not to destroy, but to re-create. Rivers of joy course through parched souls and the lame leap in dance before God. The deaf hear and poor, old Mogilalos can sing out his joy for all to wonder.

In prayer, we let our minds and souls bask in the light of God's saving and restoring work. We are moved to take up the words of today's psalm:

My soul, give praise to the Lord.

Second Reflection
A baptismal prayer

The Rite of Baptism recalls the healing of the man who was deaf and had an impediment in his speech. The celebrant touches the ears and mouth of the newly baptised, saying: 'The Lord Jeus made the deaf hear and the dumb speak. May he soon touch your ears to receive his word, and your mouth to proclaim his faith, to the praise and glory of God the Father.'

To receive God's word is obedience. The word, obedience, comes from the Latin word for hearing.

You know how it is when you are talking to somebody but you cannot break through. You might as well be talking to the wall. God must often have that experience with us because no matter how he tries to talk to us we carry on with our own ways.

We go to pray. What happens? Words fly about, pages turn, we knock sparks off the beads. But there's no listening!

We can wrap ourselves around with a cosy, comforting blanket of religion but fail to hear what the teaching Church is saying on social obligations. Or fail to respond to the cries of the poor or the various victims of injustice.

Jesus had a problem with the crowds who would gladly use him for their own ends but would not wait for his message to be given. He tried to control the publicity of his miracles.

The great spiritual directors have constantly warned against placing too much emphasis on any sensational or extraordinary phenomena in religion: and to treat private revelations with extreme caution. As last Sunday's gospel emphasised, it is a recurring temptation of religion to let human traditions take over from the word of God.

The prayer for the newly baptised expressed the wish for 'your mouth to proclaim his faith.' Note that it does not say 'your faith', but 'his faith'. Christian witness is not in boasting about oneself but in telling of the presence and power of Christ's Spirit in us. 'If anyone wants to boast, let him boast about the Lord.' (1 Cor 1:31) And Paul instructed Timothy to proclaim the Christian message and insist on it, whether welcome or not. 'Refute falsehood, correct error, call to obedience.' (2 Tim 4:2)

> Lord Jesus, you first touched our ears and tongues
> on the day of our baptism.
> May we live each day faithful to what you have begun in us.
> Open our ears, Lord,
> to hear your word in the Scriptures,
> to heed your guidance in the commandments,
> and to listen with you in quiet reflection.
> Clear away the deafness of our selfish preoccupation
> so that we might listen to what others need to say,
> draw out what is locked away in their darkness,
> and respect each person's unique history.
> Open up the doors of our hearts
> in sensitivity to pain,
> in concern for injustice,
> in compassion with all suffering.
> Release our tongues of their impediments
> so that we might gladly sing your praises,
> gratefully proclaim your kindness,
> and confidently witness to your presence.
> Remove all vestiges of envy,
> comparison or vindictiveness
> from our speech,
> so that we might be quick to affirm but slow to blame,
> ready to thank and slow to begrudge,
> open to forgive and loathe to condemn.
> Release our tongues from scandal and free them for goodness;
> cleanse them of obscenity and brighten them with joy;
> rid them of vulgarity and prepare them to bless.
> Lord, Jesus, you do all things well.
> You make the deaf hear and the dumb speak.

Twenty-Fourth Sunday

Today's extract spans the ending of the first half of Mark and the beginning of the second half. The first half builds up to Peter's recognition of Jesus as the Christ or Messiah. The second half is about the destiny of Jesus to suffer and to die. It will be in the manner of the Suffering Servant of God in today's first reading. For the followers of Jesus the message is that their way too will be in self-renunciation. This way of discipleship will be considerably developed by Mark over the coming weeks.

Mark 8: 27-35

Jesus and his disciples left for the villages round Caesarea Philippi. On the way he put this question to his disciples, 'Who do people say I am?' And they told him. 'John the Baptist,' they said, 'others Elijah; others again, one of the prophets.'

'But you,' he asked, 'who do you say I am?' Peter spoke up and said to him, 'You are the Christ.' And he gave them strict orders not to tell anyone about him.

And he began to teach them that the Son of Man was destined to suffer grievously, to be rejected by the elders and the chief priests and the scribes, and to be put to death, and after three days to rise again; and he said all this quite openly.

Then, taking him aside, Peter started to remonstrate with him. But, turning and seeing his disciples, he rebuked Peter and said to him, 'Get behind me, Satan! Because the way you think is not God's way but man's.'

He called the people and his disciples to him and said, 'If anyone wants to be a follower of mine, let him renounce himself and take up his cross and follow me. For anyone who wants to save his life will lose it; but anyone who loses his life for my sake, and for the sake of the gospel, will save it.'

Good News

The way to salvation and completeness of life is by following Jesus in dying to self.

First Reflection
The Way of the Messiah

In Mark's gospel the ministry of Jesus falls into two parts. The first builds up to Peter's recognition of Jesus as the Christ or Messiah:

240

the second half is the road to Calvary.

It reminds one of a mountain. In the first half we are climbing higher and the view is clearing all the while. In an exciting moment we reach the top and we can see perfectly in every direction. At last Jesus is known for who he is ... the Christ. Many people had been excited by him: they were ready to believe him to be an Elijah, or John the Baptist, or a prophetic character come as a forerunner of messianic times. But Peter's witness goes the whole way: 'You are the Christ ... you are the promised Messiah.'

The episodes immediately before this witnessing at Caesarea Philippi were part of the build up to it. After the second miracle of the loaves the disciples still had not grasped who Jesus was. 'Are you still without perception?' he asked them. Then follows the curing of the blind man at Bethsaida, a story told in a most unusual way. At first Jesus partially restored his sight. 'I can see people; they look like trees to me, but they are walking about.' So Jesus laid hands on him again: and then he could see plainly and distinctly. It is not as if Jesus was losing his touch, but this gradual healing indicates the slow advance in the perception of the disciples.

Then at last they crest the top of the climb. Peter, spokesman for the disciples, can see.

'You are the Christ,' he said, meaning the Messiah. This climactic moment celebrates the end of the first half of the ministry of Jesus.

But Mark, as ever in a hurry, brings the celebration to a hasty ending. Matthew's account lets the disciples bask for some time in the delight of that blessed recognition as Jesus proclaims the blessedness of Simon Peter and gives him the role of foundation rock. But Mark has Jesus straightaway binding them to strict secrecy about his messiahship. And the climb down from the peak of light to the valley of darkness commences immediately, for he begins to teach them of his destiny with suffering and death. About this there is no mention of secrecy. On the contrary, 'he said this quite openly.'

People had their own preconceptions of what the messiah would do for them. They remembered the promises about power and glory, hoping that it would accrue to their own benefit in political and material ways. They conveniently overlooked the prophetic figures of suffering and martyrdom. Today's first reading is about one such suffering servant who would atone for sins by death.

Peter took Jesus aside and remonstrated with him. All he could see was the human angle and it did not make sense. But Jesus strongly rebuked Peter, rebuked as in the ceremony of exorcism. 'Get behind me, Satan! Because the way you think is not God's way but man's.'

Peter's thinking was worse than merely human misjudgment. It was Satanic, diabolical thinking. We have several times come across Mark's awareness of the great war being waged by Jesus on the evil spirits.

The invitation to get into line behind Jesus is then extended beyond Peter to all the disciples. They must all let go of their narrow, human ways of thinking, which may be diabolically inspired. They must hand over to God's ways. They will be true followers of Jesus Messiah only if they renounce self and take on the cross, a brand-mark of repentance.

Perhaps now we can understand why Jesus constantly had to impose silence on people regarding his power and glory. He never denied his divine power. But he wanted them to understand that the destiny of the Messiah meant being the servant of the people by dying for them. Then, and only then, would the full power and glory of the Messiah be revealed. Only when the disciples believed in the resurrection would they be free to proclaim to all nations that Jesus is the Christ, the Lord. The time for secrecy would be over.

Jesus had a vision of life that transcended death and went beyond the grave. The disciples would have to renounce an earth-bound vision of life which sought success, power and gratification only on this side of the grave. They would have to grow in the mind of Christ, learn his good news, and then live out of that vision.

Holding onto the earthbound life is the recipe for loss of full life: 'but anyone who loses his life for my sake, and for the sake of the gospel, will save it.'

The way of Jesus was in the manner of the Suffering Servant of God. It was the way of the cross. And such too must be the way of anyone who would follow him.

Second Reflection
The Way of Discipleship
We have entered upon the second half of Jesus's ministry. Over the coming weeks we will learn much about the way of Christian discipleship. The way of the follower, like that of the Master, will be costly.

Peter is told by Jesus that his way of thinking is the merely human point of view. Worse again, it is even Satanic. It is certainly not God's way. So Peter is told to step into line behind Jesus. And all the other disciples are told to join Peter if they want their journeys of life to go where Jesus would lead. There are three things the follower must do.

(1) Let him renounce himself.

What is meant here is something deeper than various acts of self-denial. There are many different reasons why people may deny themselves chocolate, tobacco or some entertainment, and these motives have nothing to do with following Christ. The context here suggests that what must be renounced is the narrowly human or earthbound way of thinking, so as to take on God's way in the values of the gospel.

It involves a total self-surrender to the vision of faith. It means giving up the worldly, secularistic vision of life which disregards the reality of God and fails to transcend death. Secularistic thinking generates energy for material possessions, security, power, pleasure and the gratification of our appetites. The Christian vision of life generates energy for values related to love of God and our neighbour. The follower of Jesus must renounce all secularistic, earthbound values so as to grow in the mind of Christ.

(2) Let him take up his cross.

We tend to read this condition with a picture in our minds of Jesus struggling under the burden of the cross on his way to Calvary. But what would the word, cross, have meant to people before the crucifixion of Jesus? The cross was like a brandmark indicating the ownership of animals: a mark in the shape of the capital X, or the plus sign +, or even the capital T, called *Tau* in the Hebrew and Greek alphabets.

Ezechiel wrote of his vision of a time of repentance when the brandmark of *Tau*, the cross, would be a sign or seal of repentance: 'Go all through the city, all through Jerusalem, and mark a cross on the foreheads of all who deplore and disapprove of all the filth practised in it.' (Ez 9:4) At the opening of the Fourth Lateran Council, Pope Innocent III used this text as a symbol of the spiritual renewal of the Church. Francis of Assisi heard the Pope's use of the image and adopted the *Tau* sign as his signature. To take on the cross-sign indicated a repudiation of sinful ways and a commitment to the standards of Jesus Christ.

(3) Let him follow me.

Christian life is not static but one is ready to move. It calls for energy on the Christian way and courage in persevering when the journey is hard.

Mark has written for us that the way of the Master shunned shallow popularity and the use of God for selfish purposes. Jesus is called to be the Servant of God, a sacrificial victim for the rescue of sinners from the hold of evil. The way of the Master is to be the way of the disciple too.

An alcoholic – let's call him Jack – told me of the turning point of his life. Giving up the drink was no problem to him: he had done so hundreds of times. Staying off it was another matter. One night at an AA meeting he was approached by another member, an oldish man who bore the battered signs of long years of abuse. But this man took a little crucifix from his pocket and confronted Jack. 'There's only one problem in your life, Jack,' he said, 'Self-pity. Here take this cross and the next time you're feeling sorry for yourself just look at him there on the cross. And stop all your self-pity.'

Self-pity or any form of self-indulgent living is the way to lose the true meaning of life. It is by renouncing self and taking up the cross of repentance that one follows Jesus to the fulness of life.

No cross, no crown.

Twenty-Fifth Sunday

Here is the second prediction of the passion-resurrection. Again the disciples do not understand. This draws out from Jesus another lesson on discipleship. They must follow his way of service by their loving attention to life's little people.

Mark 9: 30-37

After leaving the mountain Jesus and his disciples made their way through Galilee; and he did not want anyone to know, because he was instructing his disciples; he was telling them, 'The Son of Man will be delivered into the hands of men; they will put him to death; and three days after he has been put to death he will rise again.' But they did not understand what he said and were afraid to ask him.

They came to Capernaum, and when he was in the house he asked them, 'What were you arguing about on the road?' They said nothing because they had been arguing which of them was the greatest.

So he sat down, called the Twelve to him and said, 'If anyone wants to be first, he must make himself last of all and servant of all.' He then took a little child, set him in front of them, put his arms round him, and said to them, 'Anyone who welcomes one of these little children in my name, welcomes me; and anyone who welcomes me welcomes not me but the one who sent me.'

Good News

The warmhearted attention of Jesus to one little child is a model of what constitutes greatness in God's eyes.

First Reflection
The way of God's servant

They were on their way through Galilee. In the second half of Mark – the journey from the height of perception down into the dark valley of death – the evangelist has six references to their being on the way. Scripture experts recognise that Mark's gospel is planned with the architect's attention to the number and placing of details and events. The six references to being on the way correspond to six crossings of the lake in the first part of Mark.

Crossing the lake bridged the difference between the Jewish and Gentile territories. The miracles on one side of the lake deliberately correspond to those on the other side. Crossing the lake was a symbolic way of showing that Jesus was a Messiah for all nations. That was part of the answer to the first question of Mark, Who is Jesus?

Now in the second section of the gospel Mark's question is, Where is Jesus going? The repetition of the phrase 'on the way' is a refrain to make us aware of the journey. The journey of Jesus, as he predicts here for the second time, is towards Jerusalem, where he is to die and rise again. And the journey of true disciples, as he explains to them, is to follow his way by dying to selfish and worldy values so as to grow anew in the mind of Christ.

The mind of Christ is a radical reversal of worldly values. Jesus can see clearly that this clash of values will lead to a violent climax. When he would be 'delivered into the hands of men' he would be mauled to pieces.

Anybody who stands up for an ideal must recognise that this will set off a negative chain of irrational hatred in the consciences of all those who suffer from suppressed guilt. Perhaps Jesus had in mind the observation of human nature which the Book of Wisdom provides for our first reading today. The godless man is annoyed, opposed, reproached and accused by the virtuous man. Instead of being converted, the godless one then turns to violence in an attempt to silence the voice of his guilt.

But for the moment all this was too much for the disciples. This view of the messiah was so contrary to their preconceived notions that 'they did not understand what he said.'

One can be sympathetic with their difficulty in coming to terms with the unpalatable prospect of the crucifixion. 'Human kind cannot bear very much reality.' We have an inbuilt defence mechanism which can turn off our clear thinking if the truth is more than we can bear at any moment. How often do you meet people who simply cannot read the writing on the wall about their drinking or smoking, about the inevitability of death, about failure or a score of other unpleasant facts?

Mark also tells us that the disciples were afraid to ask for an explanation. Was this a sort of holy fear in the face of divine mystery? Or was it the reaction that pupils have when they are afraid to ask teacher for an explanation of what everybody ought to understand after so much repetition?

Their misunderstanding of the destiny of Jesus is shown up in their misunderstanding of what it means to be a disciple. How can they follow his way if mentally they have not yet accepted his values?

They are so far removed from the mind of Jesus that disharmony is still in their ranks. Worse again, they were arguing about which of them was the greatest!

Jesus uses this occasion of disharmony and ugly selfishness as a lead into one of the most beautiful and tender moments of the gospel. His lesson is that the first or greatest, according to his reckoning, would be the one who is most unselfish in the interests of serving others.

'Like this', he says, drawing a little child to himself and putting his arms warmly, protectingly, about the little one.

'As a child rests in its mother's arms
even so my soul.' (Ps 130, Grail)

To let God's motherly care and attention be expressed to others through me! The little ones of life before me represent God. To be lovingly attentive to the least of Christ's brothers or sisters is the way to follow Jesus.

The way of the world will make me keep others at a safe distance, or hold them in suspicion, or use them or manipulate them to my service. But the way of Christian discipleship ... let us repeat it ... is to let God's motherly care and attention be expressed to others through me.

A Christian delights in saying: 'I am here to serve.'

Second Reflection
Welcoming the Lord

Don Bosco, a priest in Turin in the last century, took his inspiration for life from the gospel picture of how Jesus welcomed and caressed the little child. He took to himself the waifs of the street who had no homes, the children of the night already caught up in the cycle of crime, and the uneducated boys who had no prospects.

On one occasion, when his work took him to Paris, he sought a night's lodging of a local priest. His boots were dirty and his cassock travel-dusty so all he was given was a mattress on the floor in the garret between the accumulated boxes, cobwebs and dusty cases. His host of the night lived to see the day when Don Bosco was canonised. 'If I had known that I had a saint in my house for a night,' he admitted, 'I would not have given him such a poor welcome.' But, even then, he was still missing the point of the gospel. The way of the world is to honour the VIP (and someone sure to be a saint is a VIP). But the way of the gospel is to welcome the Very Unimportant Person.

'Anyone who welcomes one of these little children in my name, welcomes me; and anyone who welcomes me welcomes not me but the one who sent me.'

To welcome somebody in Christ's name is to see that person as somebody who is so important to Jesus Christ that he was willing to die for him or her. The way of Christian discipleship is to welcome, to receive, and to listen to Christ in his little ones.

To welcome somebody we must have empty hands and open arms. We have to lay aside what we have in hand. We must have unoccupied time available to others. And the first call on our time comes from the very unimportant people whom we meet every day. It is one thing to make a song and dance about the occasional visitor: but it is more important to welcome the presence of family members and everyday associates.

To receive others we must let them know that we want them, that we love them and care for them. As far a possible we learn a person's name so as to receive each one as a precious individual. Words of affirmation and gratitude show appreciation of their efforts. Their interests, concerns and preoccupations are all part of the person we want to receive.

Then, when we are attentive we listen to the other ... we notice what they are wearing ... what their body-language is saying, beyond what words will ever reach. We anticipate their small needs and discomforts. We try to be so available that we will draw out what they need to say.

In the Eucharist we welcome Jesus into our souls. But our welcome to the head is not complete unless it is extended to the members. It is a lesson which has been totally taken to heart by Mother Teresa of Calcutta. A certain journalist who was observing her work wrote about one of her sisters who arrived back to the convent with an extraordinary light glowing on her face:

'I have just spent three hours with Jesus,' she explained. The journalist discovered later that the Jesus of her ecsatsy was a putrid, maggot-riddled man in the hospice for the dying. 'Anyone who welcomes one of these little children in my name, welcomes me.'

Twenty-Sixth Sunday

The instruction of Jesus on how to follow his way continues in this gospel. Anyone who works in the name of Christ or serves others in his name belongs to Christ. But anyone who leads others astray from Christ is fit only for the rubbish dump of life.

Mark 9: 38-48
John said to Jesus, 'Master, we saw a man who is not one of us casting out devils in your name; and because he was not one of us we tried to stop him.' But Jesus said, 'You must not stop him: no one who works a miracle in my name is likely to speak evil of me. Anyone who is not against us is for us.

'If anyone gives you a cup of water to drink just because you belong to Christ, then I tell you solemnly, he will most certainly not lose his reward.

'But anyone who is an obstacle to bring down one of these little ones who have faith, would be better thrown into the sea with a great millstone round his neck.

'And if your hand should cause you to sin, cut it off; it is better for you to enter into life crippled, than to have two hands and go to hell, into the fire that cannot be put out. And if your foot should cause you to sin, cut it off; it is better for you to enter life lame, than to have two feet and be thrown into hell. And if your eye should cause you to sin, tear it out; it is better for you to enter into the kingdom of God with one eye, than to have two eyes and be thrown into hell where their worm does not die nor their fire go out.'

Good News
Christ promises a reward to all who live and serve in his name.

First Reflection
Belonging to Christ
This gospel passage could be called a question of belonging: belonging to Christ or belonging to the rubbish dump of life.

The disciples had been receiving instruction from Christ about how to belong to his way. We have reflected on his instructions about self-renunciation and attention to the needs of life's little ones. Now John asks a question: 'This man we met, Master, he was casting out devils in your name. He is not one of us so we stopped him. Tell us, were we right or does he belong to your way?'

The reply of Jesus shows how his tolerant heart rejoices in goodness no matter where it is found. 'If he works a miracle in my name, then he is hardly an evil man, is he? Anyone who is not against us is for us.' All goodness belongs to Christ: that is the basis of what is called anonymous Christianity.

Then Jesus returns to the lesson of last week's gospel on Christian service. Repetition is the secret of the teacher's success.

'Remember the little child,' he says. 'Anyone who cares for the little one in my name is doing my work. He belongs to me. Even a cup of water, that's sufficient proof of belonging to me.'

The disciples must have been wondering at this stage. This Christianity business is beginning to sound very uncomplicated. The question was forming in their minds, 'Does he mean that there are no outsiders? Does everybody belong to Christ?'

Certainly it is the desire of Jesus that everybody would avail of his salvation and belong to his way. But the sad fact is that we can cut ourselves off from him. The thought of the little child comes back again. Woebetide that man or woman who would mislead any little one from the way of faith!

True Christian love must have room for anger. Love must have the energy of anger to confront evil. The tone of anger is heard through the recurring imagery of stones in the words of Jesus: stones representing hard hearts.

Anybody who would be a stone to trip others deserves to suffer by the stone, in the fashion of the Romans who would hang a huge stone around the neck of certain wrong-doers and throw them into the sea to show the vehemence of their desire to rid society of this source of evil. Jesus makes it clear that those who mislead any of his little ones do not belong to him.

But now, let us turn the spotlight on ourselves. Do I belong to Christ? To his way? Every single part of my life?

Jesus speaks of cutting off the sinful hand or foot and tearing out the sinful eye. He is not adovcating self-mutilation in a literal sense. Sin does not reside in the poor hand or eye which might be its instrument. Sin is in the will. We must ask what these organs of the body represent. What seat of energy is located in each one of them?

Hands are for welcoming and greeting: for serving and giving: healing and caressing: reconciling and uniting: praising the Lord in toil and in prayer. Such hands belong to Christ.

But hands may be cold and withdrawn: closed and off-putting: thieving and deluding: violent and hurtful: destructive and sinful. Such hands are already cut off from Christ.

Feet are for going and for mission: for standing firm in storm and trial: for bringing the beautiful sound of the good news. Such feet belong to Christ.

But feet may also be used for running away from responsibility: shifting with every passing wind or popular fancy: marching with echoing menace of terror and destruction. Such feet do not belong to Christ.

Eyes are the windows of the soul: windows that let in God's heavenly light and fill the soul with wonder, goodness and praise: windows that shine out with the love of God which is in the heart, through attentiveness, caring and sharing.

But these same eyes may be smudged and darkened. Those who do evil hate the light and avoid it for fear their actions should be exposed. Eyes can be darkly fascinated by lust and violence, as the purveyors of pornography know. And dark, shifty eyes express hatred, prejudice and coldness.

Our hands, feet and eyes are made for God's service. They are consecrated in Baptism to be members of Christ's body on earth to-day. But if we live contrary to Christ's ways, then we do not belong to him. We deserve the rubbish dump. That is the meaning of what is translated as hell.

The word in the Greek text of Mark is *Gehenna*. *Gehenna* was the valley outside Jerusalem which served as the city's rubbish dump. Worse again, it was a valley under curse because, at one time, child sacrifice to the pagan god, Moloch, used to take place there.

The rubbish dump is never without a fire and the maggots and bacteria are ever busily decomposing all matter there. Preachers and artists down the ages have exaggerated the image of fire beyond all proportion and context. Here it means the rubbish dump of wasted life and talent.

Belonging to Christ or to the rubbish dump?

Where does my life, every part of it, stand ?

Second Reflection
In Christ's name

Today's gospel commences with a threefold repetition of the power in Christ's name. Miracles are worked in his name, devils are cast out and a cup of water acquires a new value when it is given to one who bears the name of Christ.

The disrespect shown by many Christians to the sacred name of God or to the name of our Saviour, Jesus Christ, defies understanding. One wonders what an outsider must think if that is the respect we show for God. One would have to question the depth of faith of anybody who habitually disrespects the sacred names.

Sacred scripture reflects the mentality of its time in a deep respect for all names. The writers were keenly aware of the meanings and associations of names. Frequently a new turning in life was marked with a new name. Army generals took on a name associated with a triumph. Simon's new vocation was marked by a change of name to Peter, the rock. The second commandment forbids the invocation of God's name in vain. What is at issue here is not the careless, slip-of-the tongue use of God's name but the solemn invocation of God's power in some evil action. The name of God invoked God's power for good or ill.

It was considered necessary to call upon the name of a spirit in exorcism. To know the adversary's name was thought to give one magical power over the possessing spirit. There are suggestions in the early chapters of Mark that the evil spirits try to gain power over Jesus by calling out his name, 'the Holy One to God.' (Mk 1:24) Mark's gospel reaches its moment of climax when Peter reaches sufficient faith to give Jesus his vocational name, Christ. 'You are the Christ.' (8:29)

It is our privilege as Christians to belong to Christ and to bear his name. Our participation in liturgy depends on our belonging to him. Liturgical prayer is directed to God the Father in the name of Jesus Christ, 'through him, with him and in him.' Such is the power of his name.

'Whatever you ask for in my name I will do
so that the Father may be glorified in the Son.' (Jn 14:13)

The beautiful story of the healing of a crippled man brings out the confidence that Peter had in the sacred name of the risen Lord Jesus. 'I have neither silver nor gold, but I will give you what I have; in the name of Jesus Christ the Nazarene, walk.' (Acts 3:5)

One saint who was deeply devoted to the holy name of Jesus was Bernardine of Siena. He was a great Franciscan preacher in Italy in the fifteenth century. It was a time when towns were deeply divided by faction fighting and family rivalries, as instanced in the tragedy of Romeo and Juliet. Bernardine united people in the name of Jesus and devised his own banner, IHS, the first three letters of the name of Jesus in Greek. Their family ensigns were discarded in favour of the banner of Jesus. We could do with a Bernardine on the football terraces today.

His powerful preaching conveyed his deep belief that the holy name of Jesus brought to people all the healing power and saving merits of our Saviour.

252

Here is an extract from one of Bernardine's sermons:

'Glorious name! Beautiful name! Name that tells of love and excellence. Through you we have forgiveness of our sins, victory over our enemies, healing in sickness, strength and joy as we suffer the trials of life ... In the furnace of your burning love our desires are kindled, our prayers are granted, contemplative souls are entranced. Through you all who are glorified come in triumph to everlasting glory. Most merciful Jesus, grant through your most holy name that we too may be numbered amongst those who share your kingdom.'

All who belong to Jesus Christ are proud of his name, deeply confident in his name, and prayerfully sensitive to it.

Twenty-Seventh Sunday

We continue today with what it means to be a follower of Jesus Christ. He teaches that true marriage is not to be dissolved by human law. Children are a model of total confidence that the Father will provide the necessary support for living up to the ideals of the kingdom.

Mark 10: 2-16

Some Pharisees approached Jesus and asked, 'Is it against the law for a man to divorce his wife?' They were testing him. He answered them, 'What did Moses command you?' 'Moses allowed us,' they said, 'to draw up a writ of dismissal and so to divorce.'

Then Jesus said to them, 'It was because you were so unteachable that he wrote this commandment for you. But from the beginning of creation God made them male and female. This is why a man must leave father and mother, and the two become one body. They are no longer two, therefore, but one body. So then, what God has united, man must not divide.'

Back in the house the disciples questioned him again about this, and he said to them, 'The man who divorces his wife and marries another is guilty of adultery against her. And if a woman divorces her husband and marries another she is guilty of adultery too.'

People were bringing little children to him, for him to touch them. The disciples turned them away, but when Jesus saw this he was indignant and said to them, 'Let the little children come to me; do not stop them; for it is to such as these that the kingdom of God belongs. I tell you solemnly, anyone who does not welcome the kingdom of God like a little child will never enter it.'

Then he put his arms round them, laid his hands on them and gave them his blessing.

Good News

God is the love that unites man and woman in marriage: and as God's children we can trust totally in his support.

First Reflection
Trusting and faithful

This episode begins with a trap set by the Pharisees: then we hear the reply of Jesus: and lastly, the utter need of the children to trust in their parents exemplifies the disciples' need to place their total trust in God.

Mark first introduced the Pharisees to us as dour, silent observers of the ministry of Jesus. By now they had become vocal in their opposition to him. They came up with the ever controversial question of divorce. Divorce is one of these no-win situations where the interviewee is sure to alienate some people no matter which way he answers.

The territory they were in was under the jurisdiction of Herod Antipas whose affair with his sister-in-law had drawn down the condemnation of John the Baptist. As a result, John was arrested and imprisoned. Perhaps now Jesus too might come out with some statement which would lead him to a similar fate as the Baptist.

Jesus, they schemed, was sure to alienate a section of his audience because the Jews at the time were divided into two schools of thought about the grounds for divorce: the school Rabbi Shammai demanded a very serious pretext; but the followers of Rabbi Hillel accepted trivial grounds, such as bad cooking, as sufficient.

Yet another tantalising prospect was attached to their question. They were well aware of how Jesus had debunked the tradition of human laws which had accumulated about fasting and Sabbath observance. Supposing he were to give the appearance of disregarding the sacred teaching about marriage, then they could turn many of the people against him.

Jesus did not fall for the trap. He threw a question back to them to draw their fire. 'What did Moses command you?' They replied that Moses recognised the fact of divorce when he ordered that a writ of dissmissal should be given to the wife. In fact, what Moses had done was to make the best of a bad job by salvaging some protection for a woman out of the wreck of divorce.

In Jewish law women had no rights and were regarded as chattels. A man could initiate divorce proceedings but a woman could not. When a man left his wife she was left without security or property rights and could not remarry without being guilty of adultery: and as an adulteress she should be stoned to death. Moses, by entitling her to a writ of dismissal, enabled the woman to remarry without being regarded as an adulteress.

Jesus now launched into his reply. Moses had not sanctioned the privilege of divorce, he explained, but had made a concession to the hard hearts and sinful situation which existed. But the original plan of God was for marriage as an indissoluble union. Marriage is a divine institution ... 'what God has united'. It is not an affair of merely human arrangement which can be abolished at will.

Later, the disciples questioned Jesus at greater depth about his teaching here. Jesus in reply made it even more clear the he accepted no grounds for divorce. 'The man who divorces his wife and marries another is guilty of adultery.' He allows no exceptions. Then he adds: 'And if a woman divorces her husband and marries another she is guilty of adultery too.'

The teaching of Jesus was new in two aspects. Firstly, he absolutely forbade the breaking up of a partnership which God had united. In this respect his teaching stepped out of line with the written and oral laws of Jewish marriage. And secondly, he regarded women on an equal basis as men with respect to the privileges and responsibilities of marriage.

Then Mark leads us into the beautiful picture of Jesus wanting the little children to come to him. The disciples have not fully entered the mind of Christ yet, for they try to turn the children away. But Jesus wants them to come. Mark paints a picture of warmth and tenderness: Jesus put his arms around them, laid his hands on them and gave them his blessing.

'See the children,' his actions are saying. 'See how vulnerable they are without daddy and mammy to look after them. These children know how much they depend on love. They trust totally on their parents' provision. So must it be with you. The ideals I set before you are high and demanding. Be not afraid. What God has united God will support. Be as trusting and as confident as these little children here. The kingdom is really about trust like this.'

Second Reflection
What God unites
Since our love is the mirror of God's life, then true love must be faithful and unconditional.

Jesus told his disciples that if they wished to follow his way they must renounce self and take on the cross or mark of repentance. This means renouncing secularistic thinking with its earth-bound values, in order to grow in the mind of Christ and sacred values.

The clash between secularistic thinking and Christian values comes to a head in attitudes to sexuality, marriage and divorce. In secularistic thinking, fidelity in marriage is regarded as highly desirable but infidelity is excused: excused sometimes on the most trivial of pretexts. Where secularistic values are allowed to dominate the laws of a country then the mental climate develops in which fidelity seems to be the exception rather than the norm. Each year over one million children become the victims of broken marriages in the USA alone.

Christian teaching regards marriage as a sacred union of love between man and woman. Each is incomplete in their own sexuality but find a fulfilment and fruitfulness in the sacred union of body and mind. It is a mixture of vulnerability and trust, of risk and commitment. Marriage is of God's overall plan. Not only that, but God is the love who unites the couple. What a depth of strength there is in the phrase of Jesus: 'What God has united.'

St Paul compared the bond between husband and wife to the greatest example of loving union he could think of, the love of Christ for his Church.

The Church has no option but to uphold the Christian ideal of absolute fidelity in marriage. The Church does not base its moral principles on statistics, opinion polls or media debates. The basis of our principle is the unequivocal teaching of Jesus Christ: 'What God has united, man must not divide.' God is the love who unites the couple in the sacrament of marriage, and no human institution or individual can dissolve God's bonding.

The sacrament of marriage is the vocation of man and woman to unite in a procreating love which is a mirror on earth of God's love.

God's love is ever faithful.

God's love is not tied to various conditions. It is not a love until further notice ... until the seven-year itch ... until a mid-life reappraisal. God's love is unconditional and forever.

But, admidst life's changing conditions, who can say 'forever'? The earth-bound mind sees the number of broken promises: and is caught up in a morality of permissiveness rather than strength of principle. The people of this secular outlook are afraid. Afraid to say 'forever' and mean it. For if they do not know of God's love and allow the possibility of sacramental grace, then there is not sufficient basis for ultimate trust.

Like the children who trust not in their own provision but in the parents' care, so the Christian soul places all its trust in God's support. On the strength of this the Christian partner promises faithful, enduring love under all conditions ... for better or for worse, for richer or poorer, in sickness or in health.

Love is our origin, our constant calling and our fulfilment in heaven.

'The love of man and woman is made holy in the Sacrament of Marriage, and becomes the mirror of your everlasting love.' (Preface of Marriage, III)

Twenty-Eighth Sunday

In the story of the rich young man we get a further lesson on discipleship. Anything that prevents one from answering the invitation of God must be off-loaded. In the case of this particular man he preferred material wealth to what was offered to him in the loving look and invitation of Jesus. Today's first reading prepares us for the gospel with the message that sharing in God's wisdom is more to be desired than silver or gold.

Mark 10: 17-27

Jesus was setting out on a journey when a man ran up, knelt before him and put this question to him, 'Good master, what must I do to inherit eternal life?'

Jesus said to him, 'Why do you call me good? No one is good but God alone. You know the commandments: You must not kill; You must not commit adultery; You must not steal; You must not bring false witness; You must not defraud; Honour your father and mother.'

And he said to him, 'Master, I have kept all these from my earliest days.' Jesus looked steadily at him and loved him, and he said, 'There is one thing you lack. Go and sell everything you own and give the money to the poor, and you will have treasure in heaven; then come, follow me.'

But his face fell at these words and he went away sad, for he was a man of great wealth.

Jesus looked round and said to his disciples, 'How hard it is for those who have riches to enter the kingdom of God!' The disciples were astounded by these words, but Jesus insisted, 'My children,' he said to them, 'how hard it is to enter the kingdom of God! It is easier for a camel to pass through the eye of a needle than for a rich man to enter the kingdom of God.'

They were more astonished than ever. 'In that case,' they said to one another, 'who can be saved?' Jesus gazed at them. 'For men,' he said, 'it is impossible, but not for God: because everything is possible for God.'

Good News

God, to whom everything is possible, invites us to follow the way of Jesus into the fulness of life.

First Reflection
Treasure in heaven

Jesus was setting out on a journey. It was a road that would lead him ultimately to Calvary as the suffering, serving Messiah.

His encounter with the rich young man raises a question and poses a challenge. Can this man journey with Jesus? Is he free to live out of the same vision as Jesus?

To all who read Mark's account the question is posed: are you free and willing to be a disciple and to journey with Jesus ... that is, to live in a truly Christian way?

Here was a man of great wealth. So we are told. He could have had anything that money might purchase. But he was searching for more, though he could not identify what it was.

'There is one thing you lack', Jesus told him. What he lacked could not be bought by money. On the contrary, money was for him an obstacle on the way. He could only acquire the fuller satisfaction of life by selling what he had, giving the money to the poor and then following Jesus.

There are no grounds for thinking that Jesus meant that particular bit of advice for everybody. But for this one individual in his particular situation in life, riches were such a distraction from inner wealth that Jesus called on him to let go totally of material wealth.

What is meant by this inner wealth? Today's first reading informs us that to share in heavenly wisdom is worth more than silver or gold, more than health or beauty.

The rich young man was so preoccupied with material wealth that he was out of touch with the possibilities of inner life. He was accustomed to the power that wealth brought and to the social status accorded to the rich. His very approach to Jesus suggests an attempt to manipulate him by flattery.

'Good Master', he begins. But Jesus is quick to show that flattery will not impress him one bit. In the language of the time, good was a word applied to God, and Jesus wants to reserve it for God alone.

Together they examine his way of life. He has faithfully observed the commandments , fourth to eight, which regulate our social behaviour. In their written form these are negative commandments and it is possible to observe them exteriorly without making an inner commitment to the positive demands of love and generosity. There is no lacking, therefore, regarding these negative rules. So Jesus throws down the the challenge which will test his inner commitment to God's will. 'Go and sell everything you own and give the money to the poor, and you will have treasure in heaven; then come, follow me.'

The reader already knows that the way of Jesus is towards dying and rising. The young man is challenged to stake everything on faith in a future with Jesus glorified. He cannot make that step. His fulsome piety is shown to be shallow: his holy flattery was hollow.

He turned away sad-faced from the way of Jesus. One hopes for his sake that it was a sadness that led to repentance.

Jesus turned to the disciples and made the observation: 'How hard it is for those who have riches to enter the kingdom of heaven!' The disciples were astounded because Jesus was turning upside-down the popular belief that wealth was a sign of God's favour. Here Jesus is saying that wealth is more of an obstacle to God's will than a blessing from God.

He stressed the point for them: 'It is easier for a camel to pass through the eye of a needle than for a rich man to enter the kingdom of God'. A typical piece of oriental exaggeration is here used to highlight the gap between human efforts and the divine gift of salvation.

Astounded and astonished the disciples ask: 'In that case who can be saved?' We must first be aware of the question before we can understand the answer. Now they are ready to hear.

'Salvation is beyond the range of human efforts,' he answered. 'It is possible only by God's gift. Those who can accept God's gift are those who know their inner poverty, those with empty hands. That is why it is very, very hard for anybody who identifies life with external wealth.'

The whole episode is about discipleship. It asks everybody the question: are you willing to let go of anything which holds you back from Christ's way?

Are you willing and free to journey with him on the road to death and new life?

'Make us know the shortness of our life that we may gain wisdom of heart.' (Responsorial Psalm)

Second Reflection
Jesus looks at you
Mark writes with a powerful sense of close bodily contact. Several times we have noticed the crowds pressing in on Jesus. The miracles of Jesus involve reaching out, touching and the laying on of hands. Remember how he caressed the little children. In this episode we read of three looks of Jesus, of eye-to-eye contact.

Mark is so vivid that it is easy to be caught up personally in the episode. His gospel lends itself to that form of meditation in which I place myself in the middle of a gospel scene and let the incident work on my feelings and reveal my inner life.

The first look of Jesus was towards the rich young man. 'Jesus looked steadily at him and loved him'. This look has all the power of a warm appeal. It is as if he is opening his arms to caress him as he had welcomed the children.

The second look of Jesus made eye contact with the disciples. 'He looked round and spoke to them.' This is the look of Jesus the teacher who must make contact with people before he can impart his message to them.

The third look of Jesus is deeper. 'Jesus gazed at them'. His look at once penetrates deeply into their hearts and yet conveys an immense distance. He is conveying the Father's love to them: offering divine possibilities to our human weakness.

Settle into prayer and let your imagination build on the words of Jesus.

Let Jesus look at you. Why be afraid?

For too long you have avoided his eyes. You felt safe in the crowd, at a distance. Safe, but lacking something. Now he looks at you. He wants you. Your eyes, your heart.

You want to object. Wait until I am worthy, Lord. Wait until I have something to give.

But you do have something to give. Something he wants. He wants your eyes.

Look, and let him look at you. Oh, but I am a sinner. I can't look at him in the eye without feeling stripped bare. Embarrassed.

But his eyes are full of love. Love for you. Personally. His look reaches out steadily to touch you. Don't be afraid of touch. He has always been looking at you.

Why have you run away? Too busy? Too rich in your ways ? Or just afraid of God, afraid of being loved?

Turning away from him now will only leave you sad. So, stay here. Spend time knowing that you are loved. Spend time in the warmth of his look.

His eyes are offering the Father's gift. Your human heart is transformed by God's gift. Feel your courage rising. Your human weakness will no longer hold you back.

Immense possibilities come into view. All you have deeply yearned for. All you have lacked. Even treasure in heaven, eternal life.

For everything is possible to God.

Twenty-Ninth Sunday

Here is a further lesson on the way to follow Jesus Christ. The worldly, pagan attitude is self-seeking and ambitious for promotion, prestige and power. But the way of Jesus is to serve people in humble love. Today's Old Testament reading gives a background to Christ's concept of serving people by suffering on their behalf.

Mark 10: 35-45

James and John, the sons of Zebedee, approached Jesus. 'Master,' they said to him, 'we want you to do us a favour.' He said to them, 'What is it you want me to do for you?' They said to him, 'Allow us to sit one at your right hand and the other at your left in your glory.' 'You do not know what you are asking,' Jesus said to them. 'Can you drink the cup that I must drink, or be baptised with the baptism with which I must be baptised?' They replied, 'We can.'

Jesus said to them, 'The cup that I must drink you shall drink, and with the baptism with which I must be baptised you shall be baptised, but as for seats at my right hand or my left, these are not mine to grant; they belong to those to whom they have been allotted.' When the other ten heard this they began to feel indignant with James and John.

Jesus called the Twelve to him and said to them, 'You know that among the pagans their so-called rulers lord it over them, and their great men make their authority felt. This is not to happen among you. No; anyone who wants to become great among you must be your servant, and anyone who wants to be first among you must be slave to all. For the Son of Man himself did not come to be served but to serve, and to give his life as a ransom for many.'

Good News
Jesus has loved us and served us in life and in death.

First Reflection
Here to serve
The immediate background to this episode about authority is the third prediction of Jesus' passion, death and resurrection. Mark tells us that the disciples were in a daze. Certainly James and John were lost in a cloud of incomprehension. What Jesus had been saying to them in lesson after lesson had not sunk in one iota. They seemed to remember nothing of the outcome of the earlier argument about

which of them was the greatest, and how Jesus set the child in front of them as a model of trust.

They were looking for a favour. They had seen many people come to Jesus looking for favours and getting their requests. But there was something horribly selfish in their approach. For their own prestige they were looking for the two highest places of honour from Jesus. Jesus took their request in the most compassionate way possible and gave them the benefit of ignorance. 'You do not know what you are asking.'

Then he raised the issue to the broader perspective on which they might better understand that the only way to share in his glory would be to take his road to Calvary. Here we meet one of the great concerns of Mark's writing: he wants to move people away from a religion centred on miracles and divine favours to a religion of humble service in Christ's name.

'Can you drink the cup that I must drink, or be baptised with the baptism with which I must be baptised?' We have to put aside our sacramental associations with the cup and baptism and hear the words as the audience of Jesus would have understood them. Drinking the cup was a metaphorical way to describe accepting the will of God, whether sweet or bitter. And baptism meant being bathed in the seas of God's will which sometimes permitted calamity and suffering contrary to one's own wishes.

The only favour Jesus would promise James and John was the privilege of sharing his cross. And as to the glory and the perks they wanted, well, they should happily leave those to the Father!

The other ten apostles were no better in their own way. They were outraged because the brothers had tried to steal a march on them.

It was time for Jesus to call them round him. He used the sorry occasion to give them his unforgettable lesson on the Christian attitude to power and authority. He had just freshly predicted his suffering and death in Jerusalem. He was on his way to Jerusalem. Whoever would follow his way should imitate his attitudes.

He contrasted the secular mind with his own attitude. In the society of that time the Roman attitudes prevailed. These identified the goals to achieve as power, positions of influence and the prestigious trappings of superiority. In a word, they lorded it over others. They made their authority felt.

In the world of today the lust for power is expressed more in competitiveness. The goals are to get on, to advance to be the biggest and the best. Expansion and promotion are ideas which are accepted without question. Sadly, many individuals and companies discover that the pinnacle of their success is precisely where they reach the point of their incompetence. Many feel under such pressure at work that intolerable strains are put on home life and personal health. Consumerism generates the jungle law of survival of the strongest: weakest to the wall.

The attitude of Christ is diametrically opposed to that worldly lust for power. The Christian testing ground for every attitude is life. 'Anyone who wants to become great among you must be your servant, and anyone who wants to be first among you must be slave to all.'

The words of Jesus Christ were backed up by his living example. He served us in three descending steps of humiliation.

His divine glory lay hidden as he put on the human condition of one who had come to serve. But lower than servant, he became our slave. And lower still, the mere price of a slave ... a ransom for many.

'By his sufferings shall my servant justify many,
taking their faults upon himself.' (Is 53:11)

Sadly, the Church has too often forgotten this gospel lesson and aped the trappings of power and prestige. Anybody who wants to follow the way of Christ, to be his disciple, must enter into the mind and attitudes of Christ the Servant.

On a political level, the measure of any Christian society is the way that it treats the poor and lowly.

And on the personal level, the joy of any disciple is to be able to say with Jesus: 'I am here to serve.'

Second Reflection
Let Go, Let God

Psychologists tell us that the task of the first half of life is learning to live to the fullest: and the task of the second half is learning how to let go and die.

In the first half of life we are playing with the wind, down the slope and into the scoring goal. Our task is to put points on the scoreboard. We discover our talents and develop them. We cooperate in teamwork and set ourselves up in career and stable relationships.

It is impossible to put a precise date or age on half-time but we know that the second half is on when we gradually have to admit that the sharpness has gone from some of the areas where we used to be proud of our competence. Memory may not be as sharp, physical fitness more difficult to maintain, much of the old drive gone. We gradually learn that we are playing up the hill and against the wind. Yet, there are some who play much better against the conditions.

The Christian understanding of life's cycle sees it as a journey of return to our creator. And the only door into eternity is death. Long before the final whistle we are prepared by a gradually increasing process of little dyings. Each bereavement takes away part of us. We lose our youthful looks. We must let children go their independent ways. We hand over responsibilities. We have to learn to be less useful, to be no longer indispensible.

Each little dying may be a day of great sadness. Or it can be accepted gracefully on the understanding that we have to let go in order to let God ...

We must leave a blank space on the line for God to fill in.

Our supreme model is Jesus Christ. He accepted full human life. And that meant facing death.

As a young man who knew that he was about to die, he suffered an intense agony in mentally accepting this letting go of life. But his ultimate desire was the Father's will ... to let God. So, he let go of control, of strength, of life itself ... in order to let God. And what God did was the resurrection.

The way of a disciple is to follow Jesus. This is how his lessons on discipleship began: 'if anyone wants to be a follower of mine let him renounce himself, take up his cross and follow me. For anyone who wants to save his life will lose it; but anyone who loses his life for my sake, and for the sake of the gospel, will find it.'

Last Sunday we met the rich man who would not let go of his wealth. Matthew tells us that he was young. Although Mark does not exactly use the word young, he says that the man came running to Jesus. I suppose as long as you can run you must be young. Though it may mean that he was the middle-aged jogger who is resisting the process of nature. (I write out of some experience.) Perhaps his sadness that day lay in his unwillingness to let go of his dream of perpetual youth.

Certainly, Jesus challenged him to let go of his wealth. And that was a sadness to him. Let's wish in retrospect that when he could no longer run he finally let go ... and discovered the joy of God to replace his sadness.

The disciples were astonished at this demand of Jesus to sell off everything and burn his boats. 'Who can be saved?' they asked in panic. 'Let go', repeated Jesus, 'and let God do it'. Learn that everything is possible to God.

James and John were told to let go of their selfish ambition. The other apostles had to let go of their petty resentments, jealousies and rivalries. To let go of their worldly attitudes and to let God's plan of the kingdom grow.

In the second half of life natural happenings around us and within us teach us, little by little, how to let go. It is the rich time of life when we are challenged to develop a contemplative rather than active disposition. The contemplative learns to let things be themselves, with no desire to have power over them, manipulate them, much less destroy them.

If we live in harmony with the God-given, natural process of aging...if we age gracefully, then the final letting go will not really be a letting go, but a reaching out totally, eternally, to God.

A disciple is one who lets go ... in order to let God, who dies ... in order to live.

Thirtieth Sunday

One of the marvels of messianic times would be the restoration of sight to the blind, as today's first reading indicates. Jesus restored sight to the blind beggar, Bartimaeus. As Mark tells the story it is invested with the deeper meaning of seeing with the faith of a disciple.

Mark 10:46-52

As Jesus left Jericho with his disciples and a large crowd, Bartimaeus (that is, the son of Timaeus), a blind beggar, was sitting at the side of the road.

When he heard that it was Jesus of Nazareth, he began to shout and to say, 'Son of David, Jesus, have pity on me.' And many of them scolded him and told him to keep quiet, but he only shouted all the louder, 'Son of David, have pity on me.'

Jesus stopped and said, 'Call him here.' So they called the blind man. 'Courage,' they said, 'get up; he is calling you.' So throwing off his cloak, he jumped up and went to Jesus.

Then Jesus spoke. 'What do you want me to do for you?' 'Rabbuni,' the blind man said to him, 'Master, let me see again.'

Jesus said to him, 'Go; your faith has saved you.' And immediately his sight returned and he followed him along the road.

Good News

The Son of God in pity came down to travel on our road: he gave new sight to human eyes in the light of faith.

First Reflection
A model of discipleship

In Mark's estimation the restoratiron of sight to the blind beggar, Bartimaeus, was a very significant miracle. His deliberate placing of this story and the detailed narrative set up Bartimaeus as a model of all who believe in Jesus Christ and follow his way.

Let us consider firstly Mark's placing of the event. It comes at the very end of the second major section of Mark, just before he enters Jerusalem where the third act of the drama will be placed.

The first part of Mark raised the question: Who is Jesus? That was partially answered when Peter made his profession of faith: 'You are the Christ.'(8:29) Immediately before that climax Jesus had healed a blind man at Bethsaida. Mark told this story in a strange way. The man first received partial sight before Jesus laid hands on him again. Then he saw clearly and distinctly. He represented the disciples who were beginning to see. (8:22-26)

After Peter's profession of faith, Mark began his second part. This addressed the question: Where is Jesus going? The way of Jesus was towards Jerusalem where he would suffer and die but rise again. Peter, representing the other disciples, still had to learn that the destiny of the Christ was to be the humble servant of mankind. His act of faith was only the beginning of seeing.

For seven Sundays we have drawn our gospel reading from the journey of Jesus towards Jerusalem. He constantly taught the disciples that the way to follow him would be in renunciation of self and service of others. Mark does not relate any miracle in this section until the cure of Bartimaeus. The entire section on the way of discipleship is sandwiched between the two miracles of giving sight to the blind. We have already noted that Mark loved sandwiches.

The gradual cure of the first blind man represented the manner in which the disciples were beginning to see. The final miracle sets up Bartimaeus as a model disciple, for he believes, he sees and he follows Jesus on the way.

Now we can consider the significant details of the story. It happened as Jesus was leaving Jericho. Only fifteen miles or so from Jerusalem, this was the last stage of Jesus's journey.

In no other miracle story does Mark tell us the recipient's name. But even here, it is not his own name but his father's: Bartimaeus, the son of Timaeus. Handicapped people are often subjected to the humiliation of not being known as individual persons but as handicapped, or as somebody's relation. Bartimaeus is being presented to us a model of discipleship and the first step is the renunciation of self.

He heard that it was Jesus of Nazareth who was passing. Since faith comes from hearing, this is a loaded term. He began to shout out: 'Son of David, Jesus, have pity on me.' This was a messianic title. So, although physically blind, he is already seeing somewhat in faith.

Normally Jesus called for secrecy at the faintest whiff of a messianic title. Ironically it was the crowd in this instance who tried to silence the title. Jesus did not consider it necessary to preserve messianic secrecy any longer for he was on the threshold of Jerusalem where the nature of his mission would be finally understood.

He asked Bartimaeus: 'What favour do you want of me?' Two of the apostles, James and John had looked for a very selfish favour. Here Jesus offered the favour. The request of Bartimaeus was a pitiful, humble request for sight.

Jesus told him : 'Go, your faith has saved you.' Bartimaeus already had faith! And it saved him, a word suggesting more than the physical healing.

The baptismal signficance of the story is further enhanced by the beggar's action in throwing off his cloak. In actual fact, the usual practice of a beggar was to sit on his cloak which was spread out for people to cast food or money onto it. But the dramatic way Mark describes throwing off his cloak recalls the baptismal practice of laying aside the old clothing before putting on the white garment.

The way of discipleship comes to its climax in this miracle. Bartimaeus is the model for all disciples in the post-Resurrection days when Jesus is no longer seen. Although he does not see Jesus, he hears the word from others and he believes. He casts off the cloak of old ways and follows Jesus along the way.

Second Reflection
The prayer of Bartimaeus
Much has been written over the years about the prayer of Bartimaeus. In a way, it is a model for Christians at prayer, blind as we are before God, and beggars too.

We are all blind in prayer since we do not see God, touch God or hear his answering voice. Our faith is but a dim light. In our times of weakness and fatigue we desire some tangible sign: something to see, something to hold on to. But in the physical absence of Jesus our condition is a blindness.

Bartimaeus had been blind for many years. Every human means has been tried in vain. He has been to every quack and faithhealer: tried every magical potion and holy well. All to no avail. He is the figure of every long-suffering soul. One has reached the depths of despair in debilitating illness: another in a losing battle with addiction or a compulsive humiliation. Not a flicker of light remains.

But somebody had told Bartimaeus about this Galilean, Jesus from Nazareth. Might he be different? Could there be one last chance?

Night and day Bartimaeus thought about this Jesus. But Galilee was a long distance away, an impossible distance for a blind man. The more scraps of information he pieced together about this Jesus, the more his conviction grew. This man is the Messiah the Son of David!

Then one day the road was busy, very busy, because it was the pilgrimage season. But this sounded like no ordinary crowd.

Pilgrims would be subdued, controlled, prayerful. What was

happening, who was causing this excitement? He heard the name cried out: 'Jesus! Jesus!' Could it be? Yes! He filled his lungs and summoned every ounce of strength: 'Son of David! Jesus! Have pity on me!' Sheer desperation reached out from his depths once more. The faceless voices around him scolded him to be quiet.

The voices which weaken our prayer come mostly from within. From our self-doubts, from our guilt, from our past failures. And the devil will use all these black clouds to make our blindness even darker. The devil is never so active as when we are close to a breakthrough in faith.

Bartimaeus persisted ... louder still: 'Son of David! Jesus! Have pity on me!'

This sustained prayer of Bartimaeus is the basis of the Jesus Prayer. This form of prayer has always been popular in the Orthodox Church but forgotten in the West until recent times. The prayer of Bartimaeus is firstly an act of faith in Jesus and then a plea for mercy. Christians change the words of the first part to a higher act of faith: 'Lord Jesus Christ, Son of God.'

The second part, the plea for mercy, remains the same.

The prayer begins on the lips in the preparatory act of calling our faculties together for prayer. Then we cease to formulate the words but let the phrase settle to the rhythm of our breathing. It is not a mechanical, meaningless incantation as if the name were some magical word. The prayer is not about the words but about the person of the risen Lord Jesus Christ.

Nor is the repetition like the hypnotic trance of a TM mantra which induces a mental emptiness. Prayer is an alertness, a constant loving attention to the invisible but present Lord Jesus. For those who persevere with this prayer, the rhythm may go more deeply within to be associated with the heartbeat. 'I live, now no longer I, but Christ lives in me.' (Gal 2:20)

Great masters of the spiritual life testify to the value of the Jesus Prayer in helping the soul to advance from prayer as a series of isolated exercises to prayer as a constant state of loving attention to the risen Jesus with us.

'The Jesus Prayer aims at bringing us to stand in God's presence with no other thought but the miracle of our standing there and God with us, because in the use of the Jesus Prayer there is nothing and no one except God and us.' (Archbishop Anthony Bloom)

Bartimaeus was blind but he prayed, he persevered and he saw. And in that new light, he cast off the old way and walked the road of life in union with Jesus Christ.

Thirty-First Sunday

Today we are brought back to the fundamental commandment of religion: to love God in every part of our being and to love our neighbour as ourselves.

Mark 12:28-34

One of the scribes came up to Jesus and put a question to him, 'Which is the first of all the commandments?'

Jesus replied, 'This is the first: Listen, Israel, the Lord our God is the one Lord, and you must love the Lord your God with all your heart, with all your soul, with all your mind and with all your strength. The second is this: You must love your neighbour as yourself. There is no commandment greater than these.'

The scribe said to him, 'Well spoken, Master; what you have said is true: that he is one and there is no other. To love him with all your heart, with all your understanding and strength, and to love your neighbour as yourself, this is far more important than any holocaust or sacrifice.'

Jesus, seeing how wisely he had spoken, said, 'You are not far from the kingdom of God.' And after that no one dared to question him any more.

Good News

There is one Lord, a God of love. We are to listen and receive his love so that we might pass it on to others.

First Reflection
The greatest commandment

For the past seven Sundays our gospel was taken from Mark's narrative of Jesus on the way to Jerusalem. As he travelled he instructed the disciples on the way of discipleship. Now Jesus has reached Jerusalem. This is the third section of Mark and we will draw from it on the next three Sundays.

The atmosphere in Jerusalem was hostile, as Jesus had predicted. The various leaders of Jewish thought, one after the other, confronted Jesus with questions designed to catch him out. However, one of the scribes was very impressed with the way Jesus answered these contentious questions so he raised the question about the greatest commandment. Mark portrays this man as genuinely searching, though Matthew sees the question as another trap.

271

The greatest commandment was a regular source of debate among the Jews at that time. It was not so much a matter of one rule being more important than the others – and remember, they had 613 prescriptions on their list – but the question was whether one in particular might be regarded as the key to all the others, or a source from which the others flowed.

Jesus did not hesitate for a moment. His answer was ready. But what he quoted first was more a matter of creed than of law. 'Listen, Israel', he began. It was straight from the pious Jew's morning prayer, the Shema.

'Listen, Israel, the Lord our God is the one Lord, and you must love the Lord your God with all your heart, with all your soul, with all your mind and all your strength.' Creed comes before law: it is what you believe about God that makes sense of the laws.

The original context was the Book of Deuteronomy (today's first reading) where Moses is instructing the people on the terms of the covenant between God and his chosen people. Each morning they were to repeat prayerfully their belief in this God who had chosen them in love : and they were to renew their commitment to God in heart, in soul and in strength.

The heart, to the Jew, meant the centre of thought. The soul was the inner souce of energy for outward action. By strength they meant a commitment to justice and upright behaviour.

So far so good. But Jesus did not stop with this quotation. With scarcely a pause for breath he added a quotation from Leviticus: 'The second is this: you must love your neighbour as yourself.'

In so far that the words Jesus used were two well-known texts of old, his answer was not original. But where he was original was in the vital connection between the two. Biblical scholars have searched every relevant document and historical note to see if any other teacher had made this connection. But it appears that Jesus was the first. 'There is no commandment greater than these', he concluded.

The scribe who had put the question was deeply impressed with this answer. We can hear him repeat the answer word for word, obviously savouring it with delight. He appreciated that this answer of Jesus represented a huge advance on the prevailing Jewish attitudes. Any Rabbi would have told him that the world stands on three pillars: the Law, the worship (or sacrifices) and the works of love. There was no doubt in any mind but that the Law came first and it gave the direction to worship and to love.

But here Jesus, in one crisp statement, was challenging the traditional order of priorities. Love comes first, he was saying, because love comes from God. The other two, worship and practical prescriptions, only have meaning if they are a response to God's love.

The scribe appreciated the signficance of Jesus's order of priorities. 'Love', he repeated, 'is more important than any holocaust and sacrifice' and love of God cannot be separated from love of our neighbour.

'You are not far from the kingdom of God', replied Jesus ... the only occasion in this gospel when a member of the Jewish leadership is praised.

In the time after Jesus, it was the former rabbi, Paul, who more than anybody else appreciated the answer of Jesus. Faith in God as a loving God comes first. Laws about worship or morality follow then as an expression of faith. The Jewish regard for the priority of the Law imposed an impossible burden, for it showed up sin but was powerless to remove it. Belief in Jesus Christ changed all that for Paul. He was relieved of the impossible burden and his new belief filled him with a passion for God and for love. 'Freedom is what we have', he tells the Galatians. 'Christ has set us free ... what matters is faith that works through love.' (Gal 5: 1 & 6, TEV)

The greatest commandment is really not so much a commandment as a belief. 'Listen, Israel' is how it begin. Belief in God ... one, true, beautiful and good.

Full living, or true religion, means responding to God ...
with all your heart resting in God's love:
all your mind searching in God's truth:
all your soul thirsting for God's beauty:
and all your strength serving God by loving your neighbour as yourself.

Second Reflection
The wonder of my being

The standard Jesus set was to love your neighbour as you love yourself. He was a sound psychologist. For he knew that anybody who does not love self cannot truly love anybody else.

But didn't Jesus say that the first step in becoming his follower is to renounce self? I know, but what Jesus meant on that occasion was to let go of earth-bound thinking and worldly attitudes which are an obstacle to his way. If we hold onto that false personality we will never discover our true depths of God-given life.

The psalmist had a beautiful phrase to celebrate our life: 'I thank you, Lord, for the wonder of my being.'

Many, many people find it very hard, virtually impossible, to accept their worth. I find them coming on retreat and after a day they are so despondent. The initial relief of getting away from it all does not last long. Because as soon as they begin to reflect, the blanket of guilt comes over them. They want to talk about their sins as if these were the most important things to be talking about.

Somewhere along the line we have learned the necessity to confess but not the need to celebrate. To celebrate God ... God's creation ... God's creation in me. A celebration of me is a celebration of God.

When the blanket of guilt sweeps over, it is advisable to close all the books (even the bible ... and this book!). Instead, go out to Mother Nature and pay attention to life around us. One discovers a tree that tells a story: another finds a wayside flower, so humble and so perfect: a birdsong thrills another heart, glad to be the one there today to hear it. It may be a shell, a leaf, a scent on the breeze or the racing shadows of clouds on the hills. And of course, the ever mysterious sea.

'For whatever we lose (like a you or a me)
it's always ourselves we find in the sea.' (e.e cummings)

When we find the life of some object singing in harmony with life within us, then we have discovered a true symbol ... meaning the flowing together of energies.

The wonder of any object brings us back to God the Creator. Anything that exists is an expression of the Creator's mind. It was first a thought in the mind of the Great Architect. God is incapable of any thought less than beautiful. If only I could discover the beauty of God's thought, of God's love, in myself!

That's why Jesus answered the man's question about the greatest commandment by saying 'Listen, Israel ... listen, Christian soul ... listen, open up, let God in ... think of me, not of your sins ... think of how I have loved you, still love you and always will love you. I know your sins ... but I still love you.'

When the New Testament speaks of love of God it scarcely ever refers to our efforts. Mostly it means God's love for us.

'This is the love I mean', St John explains, 'not our love for God, but God's love for us when he sent his Son.' (1 Jn 4:10)

It is when we find God's love in ourselves that we discover our self-worth. Then, and only then, will we cease from projecting all our self-hatred out onto others. When we begin to know how much God loves us, the news will set us on fire with a passion to pass it on to others. When we find God in ourselves we will find him in others.

And, hopefully, they in turn will find God in their self-worth.

I thank you, Lord for the wonder of my being.
Forgive me for ever despising the work of your hand.
Help me to grow daily in appreciation of the wonders of life,
especially of your life in me.
Make me sensitive to the pulsations of your heart in my heart.
How could I ever have doubted your love,
O God, my Creator,
Redeemer and Sanctifier.
Help me to truly love myself
with something of the love you have for me.
And then, filled with your love,
my life will be charged with a power of divine love for others.

Thirty-Second Sunday

Jesus and his disciples have reached Jerusalem where he will lay down his life for sinners. The widow who gives all she had to live on is an example to the disciples of how to follow his way of self-sacrifice.

Mark 12: 38-44

In his teaching Jesus said: 'Beware of the scribes who like to walk about in long robes, to be greeted obsequiously in the market squares, to take the front seats in the synagogues and the places of honour at banquets; these are the men who swallow the property of widows, while making a show of lengthy prayers. The more severe will be the sentence they receive.'

He sat down opposite the treasury and watched the people putting money into the treasury, and many of the rich put in a great deal. A poor widow came and put in two small coins, the equivalent of a penny.

Then he called his disciples and said to them, 'I tell you solemnly, this poor widow has put more in than all who have contributed to the treasury; for they have all put in money they had over, but she from the little she had has put in everything she possessed, all she had to live on.'

Good News

God sees our innermost heart and the smallest acts of trust and generosity do not escape his attention.

First Reflection
Total self-giving

Jesus had reached Jerusalem with his close band of disciples. They had entered the sacred area of the Temple. The disciples, coming from country villages, were probably a bit over-awed by the confident ways of the city. They felt awkward in the tight confinement of city streets. We can imagine them watching and imitating, cautious not to make mistakes, tipping a cap here and bowing a little there for this was a city full of holy people.

They had never seen so many important people who had to be greeted properly. And such holy men! So dedicated to prayer that they wore their long prayer-shawls even as they walked about. Every step was a prayer! And the men of learning with their impressive scrolls, dealing with the queries of the pilgrims, mostly country folk like themselves.

But Jesus soon put them in the right. He could see behind the outward show and read the inner heart.

'Beware', he warned them, 'don't let them take you for a ride. They are rotten to the core with hyprocrisy. The very worst sort of hypocrisy, religious hypocrisy. All this outward show makes a fat living out of gullible folk.'

They entered the place where donations were given for various causes like Temple upkeep, votive lights, or the poor. There were thirteen great moneychests, shaped like upside-down trumpets. Through the narrow top one dropped in the coins and the trumpet shape of the metal chest ensured a fine resounding echo. This was long before the days of paper money so the idea of a silent collection was unknown. The more noise, the greater the takings! The over-awed Galileans were suitably impressed as wealthy merchants and well-to-do farmers out-rattled one another. Then came the poor, old widow. Her two tiny coins scarcely tinkled. It was almost laughable. But Jesus called their attention. 'I tell you solemnly,' he began ... so they knew that it was to be some important pronouncement. 'This poor widow gave more to God than all the others. They gave of their surplus. But she gave the last penny she had, all she had to live on.'

The amount she put in would not have sustained her very long. It is estimated that it was about 1% of the cost of a full meal. About the cost of a sweet. But in Christ's eyes she had given her all, and that is why her story is of significance.

She is important at this point of Mark's story for two reasons. Her giving is the expression of somebody who loved God with all her heart, all her soul, all her strength and all her mind. And she anticipates the total self-sacrifice of Jesus which would shortly take place. She is a model of discipleship: one who gives all she has just as Jesus, the Servant of God, would totally give up his life. There is such a contrast between the showy, hypocritical religion of some of the scribes and the humble, unobtrusive dedication of the widow. God looks at the inner heart and is not deluded by outward show.

By Jesus's reckoning she put in more than all the others. Obviously not more in terms of quantity. But what counts with God is the quality of our dedication. It's how much we try more than how much we succeed. And the only amount that God counts up is the amount of love. There are no calculators in heaven, only the scales of love. A simple act of love is more valuable than huge efforts without love.

The rich people put in some of their surplus money. It raises the question of how much we need to live on. Our definitions of poverty tend to be relative to our expectations. People are called poor today who are very well off by the standards of some years ago. Our wants are relative to what is available rather than to what is absolutely necessary. The luxuries of one generation are regarded as ordinary needs for the next.

Jesus gave his life for us in total self-surrender. The poor widow who gave everything she possessed is a model for all followers of Jesus.

One meets people like that widow who are so close to God that they too willingly let go of their last penny. Whatever God wants they will give. They know that to give begrudgingly to God is not worthy of him. Or to give stintingly to God is not worthy of him.

She put in everything she possessed, all she had to live on.

Second Reflection
Prayer for generosity

Which box did she so lavishly enrich with her two tokens of love? The Poor Box, the Mission Box, or perhaps a votive candle to burn out in self-immolation as an expression of her prayer?

Was she self-conscious because her poor little coins would sound so trifling and everybody would know what she gave? My guess is that a person of such a relationship with God is far beyond worrying what people think.

She disappears from our story as unobtrusively as she entered it. We are not told what happened to her or where she got the next meal. Perhaps she had a family to support her.

Today's liturgy links her with the widow of Sidon who shared her last handful of meal and last drop of cooking oil with the prophet Elijah. God's provident eye noted her unstinted giving. And God rewarded her. The jar of meal was not spent nor the jug of oil emptied as long as the famine lasted.

God will not be outdone in generosity. That lesson was expressed in his own imagery by a certain farmer when he was being complimented by his parish priest for his generous support to any charitable cause. 'The way it is,' he said, 'whenever I give God a shovelful of anything, he shovels more back in my direction. You see, Father, God has the bigger shovel.'

St Paul said that God loves the cheerful giver. In his eyes the spirit in which we give is of more account than the amount given.

O generous Father, fill us with a sense of your love for all people. Help us to realise that what we have is not really our own but ulti-

278

mately belongs to you. Help us to see that it has been given to us so that we might share it with all your other children on earth.

Help us to be generous with the gift of time
which you have given us.
May we show on our faces that we do have time for others ...
time to listen, time to share the burden,
time to celebrate their joy.
Help us to leave behind the self-centred routine
which has taken us away from family and neighbours.
Help us to be generous in our emotions.
May all our feelings and reactions be warmed by love.
When we feel like reacting in self-importance,
show us how to be humble.
When we are stung and seek revenge,
help us to reach out in forgiveness.
When we are fired to anger, help us to be patient and gentle.
When we are full of prejudice and intolerance,
show us how we might allow the other person to be different.
O God of all giving, overwhelm us with a sense of your love,
so that all we have is for you,
all we do is with you,
and all we are is in you.

Thirty-Third Sunday

The gospel about the coming of the Son of Man at the end of time is very appropriate for November, the month when we traditionally reflect on life after death and pray for our departed ones.

Mark 13:24-32

Jesus said to his disciples: 'In those days, after a time of distress, the sun will be darkened, the moon will lose its brightness, the stars will come falling from heaven and the powers in the heavens will be shaken. And then they will see the Son of Man coming in the clouds with great power and glory; then too he will send the angels to gather his chosen from the four winds, from the ends of the world to the ends of heaven.

'Take the fig tree as a parable: as soon as its twigs grow supple and its leaves come out, you know that summer is near. So with you when you see these things happening: know that he is near, at the very gates. I tell you solemnly, before this generation has passed away all these things will have taken place. Heaven and earth will pass away, but my words will not pass away.

'But as for that day or hour, nobody knows it, neither the angels of heaven, nor the Son; no one but the Father.'

Good News

After the pains and distress of life, the Lord Jesus will come in glory, brighter than sun or moon, and call his people home.

First Reflection
Christ will come again

What strikes one first about this passage is its difficulty. It was difficult reading for the Christians of the first century and even more difficult for us, so removed in time from that sort of writing.

This passage in Mark belongs to a style of literature called apocalyptic, the best known example of which is the Book of Revelation. Apocalyptic literature was the product of a time of persecution and mental anguish, attempting to restore the belief that God was still in charge of the world and that there was reason for hope. In times of distress our imaginations can be very active, creating fantastic pictures of doom but also of escape. The creative arts generally flourish in conditions of personal and social distress, whereas times of affluence produce decadent art.

The apocalyptic literature of the Bible is a dramatic expression, in fantastic imagery, of belief in God and of hope in his ultimate victory. The details are not to be taken as a literal foretelling of specific happenings. They are deliberately vague and indeterminate. The most important message conveyed is the hope that God would intervene in history and change everything to good.

Many of us tend to react negatively at the mention of these apocalyptic passages. Perhaps we have been conditioned by preachers and artists to associate them with a doom-'n-gloom message. But a careful reading reveals a message of hope for people who are presently in a gloomy situation.

Hope's message is the assurance of victory because of Christ. Furthermore this victory is very near. That point is brought out in the reference to the fig tree. It is one of the last trees to form its buds, so when it does, summer is very near.

The last point in this gospel is that, although his victory is very near, we do not know when precisely the end will come.

The passage needs to be read on three levels: what it says of Jesus Christ, what it meant to Mark's first readers and what it holds for us today.

Throughout Mark we have seen Jesus emphasising his mission as the Suffering Servant of God who would sacrifice his life in Jerusalem on behalf of sinners. At this point of the gospel they were in Jerusalem. His death was imminent. But death was not to be the end. The Servant of God would receive a great justification from God: a glorification.

The glorified Christ would come again to call unto himself all who are justified in his name. 'After the time of distress'... his glory will be so wonderful that even the sun and lights of the skies will be dark by comparison. The picture is not of darkness but of fantastic light. 'It will never be night again and they will not need lamplight or sunlight, because the Lord God will be shining on them.' (Rev 22:5)

The community for whom Mark was writing knew from experience what darkness and distress meant. Many of their leaders had been arrested and put to death. Each of them lived in danger of a similar fate. They needed this reassurance of their hope. And for our own time too the message is relevant. Many Christians live under constant distress because of health problems, financial pressures or family anxieties.

The social situation is distressing in the extent of vandalism and violence, the abuse of drugs and sexual irresponsibility. Political distress affects those who are deprived of basic rights because of nationality, religion, colour or social background.

For all who are in distress this gospel holds out the message of hope. Pain, anguish and injustice are conditions embraced by Jesus Christ, the Servant of God, on our behalf. He did not remove these conditions but by plunging into the sea of distress he has assured us that God can be found there.

Each winter the message of death is written clearly all around us. But if we look closely at the tips of branches, already the hope of new life is there. Winter reminds us that the only way into Christ's newness of life is by sharing in the pattern of his death. Christ, now glorified, will come again to his beloved ones at the hour of death to call them home.

The gospel of today adds two footnotes. The first is a reassurance: 'My words will not pass away'. Even if the physical universe and blue sky above ('heaven') should pass away, the words of Christ will endure for ever.

The second footnote raises the question, when? When will it happen for us? Wouldn't we love to know! But it is not ours to know precisely when. Ours only to believe and to wait in hope. For Christ will come again.

Second Reflection
The Judgment
There is only one thing you can be absolutely sure of regarding your future: you will one day die. No matter how healthy you think you are, you are suffering from an incurable condition ... called human mortality.

A wise master of the East was once asked by a pupil what did enightenment mean to him.

'It means that I know I shall die some day.'

'But everybody knows that,' said the pupil.

'Yes, but not everybody lives with the knowledge.'

When will it happen to me? What will it mean? When the lights finally go out in my world, will it then be darkness and no more? The Christian belief is that there is more than darkness. 'Then they will see the Son of Man coming in glory.' Coming to call and gather his chosen from the four winds.

When we awaken in the light of God there will be no more hiding from the light of truth. Before us will stretch two options. Today's first reading, from the Book of Daniel which was written a century and a half before Christ, depicts the two options thus: 'Of those who lie sleeping in the dust of the earth, many will awake, some to everlasting life, some to shame and everlasting disgrace.' The after-life will be an awakening either to everlasting life or to shame and disgrace.

The judgment will not be some dread day of reckoning in the dim future when everybody who ever lived will be gathered together to hear an all-seeing prosecutor reading out our debits and credits for all to hear.

The day of judgment is each today. What takes place at death will be the continuation of how I behave each day. The final 'Yes' or 'No,' God is worked out in the little situations of today. 'In so far as you did this to one of the least of these brothers of mine you did it to me.' (Mt 25:40)

'Well done, good and faithful servant, you have shown that you can be faithful in small things, I will trust you with greater.' (Mt 25:21)

What about purgatory? Where does it fit into the scheme of things? Purgatory means the purgation or purification of love. Many souls, I'm sure, are fundamentally saying 'yes' to God and to the ways of goodness and love. Yet they would be the first to admit that self-ishness holds them back from a total commitment to love. They do not love with the whole heart, all our mind and all our strength. Who has not experienced the pain of regret in the realisation that we have hurt or betrayed somebody who loves us very much? So, love needs to be purged of all selfish traces so that the soul is totally open to receive from God.

Forget about purgatory as a place of punishment. God has no interest in punishing people. That is not his way. His forgiveness is total. Purgatory is beautiful. It is God's love overwhelming us. The pain of purgatory comes in so far that we are not ready for this pure fire of love. We have to be purified of our years of selfish living. We have to be cleansed of the residue of sinful ways. Purgatory is a state of happy pain. It has the happiness of knowing the love of God and the pain of knowing our selfish response to that love for so long.

Because of the limitations of our experience, our language about this purgation tends to be in materialistic terms and to be measured in our concepts of time. However we understand the pro-cess, we must regard these souls as being absolutely sure of their final salvation in God's love. Not one of the souls in purgatory would come back here if given the option.

What's the point of praying for the dead? We believe in the principle of the Mystical Body of Christ: that we are all united as parts of the one body. And just as the hand can relieve the irritation of the eye, so the prayers or sacrifices of one person are to the benefit of all members of the body. Our prayers and sacrifices can be intended specifically for certain people, just as we can direct one member of the body to help another part. Praying for the dead is the extension of that principle beyond the grave. 'It is a holy and wholesome thought to pray for the dead that they might be loosed from their sins.' (2 Mic 12:45)

November's dying reminds us that each of us will surely die. But do we live each day with that knowledge?

Our Lord Jesus Christ, Universal King

The final Sunday of the liturgical year is dedicated to Christ as Universal King. Since the gospel reverses the worldly order of values, his kingship is an expression, not of power over people, but of humble service. As he told Pilate, he came to bear witness to the truth.

John 18:33-37

'Are you the king of the Jews?' Pilate asked. Jesus replied, 'Do you ask this of your own accord, or have others spoken to you about me?'

Pilate answered, 'Am I a Jew? It is your own people and the chief priests who have handed you over to me: what have you done?'

Jesus replied, 'Mine is not a kingdom of this world; if my kingdom were of this world, my men would have fought to prevent my being surrendered to the Jews. By my kingdom is not of this kind.' 'So you are a king then?' said Pilate.

'It is you who say it,' answered Jesus. 'Yes, I am a king. I was born for this, I came into the world for this: to bear witness to the truth; and all who are on the side of truth listen to my voice.'

Good News

Jesus Christ is king in the land of truth and justice: all who are on the side of truth belong to him.

First Reflection
What sort of king?

In the course of the Year of Mark the lectionary occasionally borrowed from John where he offers a more intensive reflection on a theme.

We have noted throughout the year that Mark greatly developed the theme of Jesus as the Servant Messiah. Mark portrayed Jesus as avoiding publicity regarding his miracles. At the first whiff of adulation he called for secrecy. But when it was a matter of suffering for the people he spoke quite openly. Furthermore, he repeatedly emphasised that the only true way to follow him is in a life of humble service.

On the last Sunday of the year we again go to John for the final statement of this kingdom of service. The trial of Jesus before Pilate clarifies what the kingship of Jesus is not and describes it as a service to the truth.

Pilate was a soldier turned politician. He homed in straightaway on the question that concerned him.

'Are you the king of the Jews?'

Jesus needed to know where the question came from. 'Is this your own question, Pilate ...,' in other words, a political question about sedition ... 'or is this a Jewish question about a messianic king?'

Pilate disclaimed any interest in the Jewish question. 'These chief priests have landed you here on my doorstep.' But he still wanted reassurance on the political threat.

Jesus set him at ease on the matter. 'My kingdom is not of this world. You have nothing to fear. I have no armies training in the hills.'

'So you are a king then,' Pilate picked him up, although the anxiety had gone from his voice. Whatever else Jesus was, he was no threat to the peace.

Jesus then admitted to being a king of another kind. Was he reaching out to Pilate in any invitation to reconsider the values of his Roman career and way of life? He explained himself: 'I was born for this: I came into the world for this: to bear witness to the truth. That's the sort of king I am. One who frees people from falsehood, pretence, sham ... from hollow values and empty glories. One who has no weapon other than the truth to set people free. The people who have heard my word, who know what I stand for and follow me, they are my kingdom.'

What a contrast between these two men facing one another! Picture Pilate with all the external trappings of power, richly dressed, soldiers armed to the hilt to guard him, a powerful army in the barrack square awaiting his commnad. The soldier he had always been respected the might of weaponry. The politician he was trying to be aspired awkwardly to the art of compromise and the subtleties of wheeling and dealing.

Now picture the itinerant preacher from Galilee, so simply clad, haggard and drawn after a sleepless night in the cold cellar of Caiphas's house, hands cuffed with ropes. But which of them is free? And who has the real power? Jesus, as a king 'not of this world' represented a system of values alien to Pilate's world.

The crown he wanted had nothing to do with personal honour but that the Father be glorified through obedience to the commandments.

The throne he sought did not set him apart from or above the ordinary people. His delight was to be among them and his desire was to have his teaching accepted in their hearts.

He fled from all traces of personal adulation and directed all praise to the Father.

His army was not forcibly conscripted but he lovingly drew together the people who accepted his word.

From Roman governor to colonial master to communist dictator, the kingdoms of this world were established by the unjust use of power and maintained by tyranny, corruption and exploitation. Jesus came with no weapon other than the truth:

the truth of God the Father, loving and merciful;
the truth of our brotherhood and sisterhood in the world;
the truth which like a sword cuts through all vain glory, injustice and falsehood;
the truth that sets people free.

'I came into the world for this: to bear witness to the truth; and all who are on the side of truth listen to my voice.'

Second Reflection
A kingdom of truth

'Truth? What is that?' asked Pilate. But he did not wait for an answer. Truth was standing before him and perhaps Pilate felt the light of that prisoner already challenging the foundations of his life.

The kingdom of Jesus had no ambitions on the acquisition of land. The only territory that concerned him was the human heart. The kingdom is established in the heart of anybody who lives a life of truth. God reigns there when one is true to self, true to others and true to God.

Without truth there can be no justice: and without justice there can be no peace. If you wish to see peace established throughout the world, then start working for justice through the process of truth. It may be a lonely struggle for it involves very uncomfortable tasks like refuting falsehood, showing up the untruth that is masked in the half-truth, and challenging the systems that exploit people and rip them off. But for each of us the most uncomfortable task of all is that the work begins with me.

Truth is a scarce commodity today. Our so-called system of justice serves the law but not necessarily the truth. Very often the truth of a case is disregarded and an injustice is perpetrated on the basis of some small legal technicality. Truth has so departed from the courts of justice that perjury is virtually taken for granted as a means to the end.

We live in a society conditioned by the ethics of consumerism. Most multi-national corporations exist primarily for the motive of profit. Expansion is the law of survival. Marketing and advertising are obviously guided by success rather than the truthful guidance of the potential customer. In some countries government agencies employ experts to supply not the truth but disinformation in the interests of expediency.

At the end of the day, people find it hard to believe anybody. Is it any wonder then that so many people suffer from an identity crisis? They do not know who they are or what their life is for. They experience a major difficulty in establishing a true realtionship between the mind and reality. Many people have become so obsessed with their search for identity that the major goal of life is their self-fulfilment. This is a goal which falls far short of what Jesus called for: self-effacement in the humble service of others. The eminent psychoanalyst, Jung, arrived at this conclusion: 'Our world is so exceedingly rich in delusions that a truth is priceless.'

Jesus came into this world to bear witness to the truth One of his great divine claims was, 'I am the truth.' In John's gospel and his letters the clash between truth and falsehood is one of the major, ongoing struggles of humanity.

The follower of Jesus must be committed to the truth. It is helpful if we consider ourselves to be always before the light of God's eye.'Walk before me and be perfect.' (Gen 17:1) In God's light our pretences are unmasked, the games we play are shown up and our sham behaviour is exposed. But the kingdom person is someone who 'lives by the truth and comes out into the light, so that it may be plainly seen that what he does is done in God.'

The ideal was well expressed by Shakespeare in the advice given by Polonius to his son:

'To thine own self be true
And it must follow as the night the day,
Thou canst not then be false to any man.'

Truth is the backbone of the kingdom of God. It is the only foundation for justice and peace.